Overview of Buddhist Tantra

General Presentation of the Classes of Tantra, Captivating the Minds of the Fortunate Ones

Overview of Buddhist Tantra

General Presentation of the Classes of Tantra, Captivating the Minds of the Fortunate Ones

rgyud sde spyi'i rnam par bzhag pa
skal bzang gi yid 'phrog ces bya ba bzhugs so

BY

Panchen Sonam Dragpa
(Paṇ-chen bSod-nams grags-pa, 1478-1554)

English translation by

Martin J. Boord & Losang Norbu Tsonawa

LIBRARY OF TIBETAN WORKS AND ARCHIVES

First published in 1996
Reprint 2003

ISBN: 81-85102-99-6

Published by the Library of Tibetan Works and Archives, Dharamsala, H.P. (India) and printed at Indraprastha Press (CBT), 4 Bahadurshah Zafar Marg, New Delhi 110002.

Contents

Foreword

O Chos-rje bSod-nams grags-pa-dpal!
In the vast expanse of Your bodhi-mind,
The mind that the Buddhas have lauded for as many as
one hundred times,
You have developed "merit" shining like the sun.
Through Your skill in learning, debate and writing,
As illuminating as one hundred thousand sun rays,
You have developed in You a complete knowledge of
the entire sutras and tantras,
Resembling a garden of flowers in full bloom.
The power of Your speech is like the sun;
The fame of your name has reached the three realms of
this world.
O Sonam Dragpa, the teacher of teachers!
I bow down at your feet.

In the vast garden of Your great teachings,
The intelligent young people gather for
TThe 'six ultimates' and the 'four modes of transmission,'
Just as they are attracted to
The one hundred thousand types of nectar
Dripping from a flower of one hundred petals.
May I be able to experience
The taste of the secret tantra!

Panchen Chos-rje bSod-nams grags-pa-dpal, the holder of sutra and Vajrayana teachings, was a master whose outstanding learning and spiritual accomplishments are well known by all the learned ones in Tibet. His first incarnation came in the form of one of the five prestigious disciples of Lord Tsong-kha-pa and became known as Vinaya Holder Grags-pa rgyal-mtshan. Then came Panchen bSod-nams grags-pa-dpal, the author of the present text. The next was mNga'-ris sPrul-sku Grags-pa rgyal-mtshan. In this way, a line of his incarnations, each with the grags-pa surname, followed successively.

Panchen bSod-nams grags-pa-dpal was born in the 14th century in rTsed-thang in the Lho-kha region of Central Tibet. He entered the great seat of learning, Se-ra theg-chen-gling monastic university, where he became the personal disciple of spiritual master Dhon-yod dang-ldan and His Holiness the Second Dalai Lama dGe-'dun rgya-mtsho. Under them, he studied the entire teachings of sutra, tantra and their commentaries, and became known for his outstanding learning. He also received from them the empowerments, reading transmissions, guides and instructions of the entire body of spiritual training. On becoming the fully blessed one, the Dalai Lama appointed him the abbot of the Blo-gsal-gling college, one of the four colleges of 'Bras-dpung — the most prestigious monastic university in Tibet before 1959, with over 10,000 monks on its register. He continued to be the abbot of this college for the next six years; and after him the tenure for each of his successors in this position was fixed for a period of six years, a rule that is followed even today.

He was then appointed the head of the dGe-lugs-pa order, the throne holder of dGa'-ldan, thus becoming the 15th regent of Lord Tsong-kha-pa, the second Buddha. In his eulogy to him, mKhas-grub dGe-legs dpal-bzang says:

> O Lama, the second successor of the Unsubduable One,
> The regent of the Lord of Dharma,
> You are the one who made the virtuous qualities thrive;
> You are the one who ascended to the golden throne uplifted by the fearless lions.
> May Your success thrive forever!

He continued to be the throne holder for the next seven years, during which time he promoted the spread of Lord Tsong-kha-pa's precious teachings, the dGe-lugs tradition, across the land in all directions. He also paid special attention to the practice of monastic rules and the learning and meditation of Buddhism in the monasteries such as Se-ra, 'Bras-spungs, sKyo-mo-lung, Phag-mo chos-sde, Nye-sdings, 'Od-sna and Chos-sde rin-chen etc. and improved them to a great extent. He taught the Third Dalai Lama bSod-nams rGya-mtsho as the latter's spiritual master. It was from him that the Dalai Lama received the name bSod-nams.

His contributions in the literary field are enormous; and, indeed, they are the most valuable of all his contributions. Tsong-kha-pa has rightly said:

> Of all one's deeds,
> The 'deeds of speech' are the most valuable.

Panchen bSod-nams grags-pa-dpal was a person with an extraordinary talent for teaching, debate and writing. In his colophon to *dBu ma'i spyi don zab don gsal ba'i sgron me*, he wrote:

> In the field of teaching, I am [next to none!] Knowing that

I would outdo them in this field, Arya Asanga and his brother transmigrated into another realm.
In the field of debate, I am [next to none!] Knowing that I would find out the areas they had contradicted and that I would examine them and put forth my arguments, the logician Digh-naga and Dharmakirti tactfully bypassed me.
In the field of writing, I am [next to none!] [In my eyes,] Arya-sura was just good at spreading the works, which are like 'disputes between an insect and a field.'
I am the learned man. Peerless in the field of teaching, debate and writing!

For some this passage might sound utterly nonsensical, but the most learned master of our age, the talented teacher, logician and writer, the late tutor to His Holiness the Dalai Lama, Yongs-'dzin Khri-byang rDo-rje-'Chang, said: "Now, some people of our time, who consider themselves learned scholars, think that this is utter nonsense; but they are wrong."

Panchen bSod-nams grags-pa-dpal wrote over 45 volumes of books dealing with many different subjects, such as the commentaries on the sutras and tantras, the saddhana manuals of the tutelary deities, history, religious history and so forth. Among these, one that is very important for all who wish to learn and meditate on the path of the practical aspect of Buddhism in general and that of Vajrayana in particular is the *Legs bshad rgyud sde spyi'i rnam par bzhag pa skal bzang gi yid 'phrod*. In this book, he has explained precisely how the four tantras differ from one another. He has also fully described the stages of the two spontaneous path practices of the Vajrayana tradition, dealing with the `six ultimates' and the `four modes of transmission', thus interpreting without mistake the intention of Adhi-Buddha Vajradhara.

May the reprint of this text, which the Library of Tibetan Works and Archives is publishing herewith, bring peace and happiness in this world!

Prof. Nawang Jinpa
St. Joseph's College
Darjeeling

January 24 1996

Publisher's Note

The Library of Tibetan Works and Archives is pleased to publish *Overview of Buddhist Tantra: General Presentation of the Classes of Tantra, Captivating the Minds of the Fortunate Ones,* as a contribution to the corpus of works which already exist on the subject of Buddhist Tantra.

This complex and detailed work was written by the outstanding master Panchen bSod-nams grags-pa (1478-1554) and provides an exxcellent framework for the understanding of Tantric practice. The translators, Martin J. Boord and Losang Norbu Tsonawa, are to be congratulated for their sterling efforts in rendering this work into English.

We are sure that this book will be of immense benefit to all serious practitioners of Tantric Buddhism.

Gyatsho Tshering
Director

March 1996.

Author's Introduction

[1] Herein is contained a general overview of Buddhist *tantra* called *Captivating the Minds of the Fortunate Ones.* With respectful salutations I go for refuge to the omniscient rJe Rin-po-che,[1] who has the nature of all the Buddhas of the three times, and to the lineage of his sons, the disciples. Now here I will explain the tantric teachings in two parts: first the general teachings will be explained, and then the Secret Assembly Tantra will be shown separately.

The first section (explanation of the general teachings) has four divisions:

1. The manner in which the Teacher gained completely pure enlightenment.
2. Having attained enlightenment, the manner in which he turned the wheel of the Dharma.
3. In accordance with the above, I will show that all those who wish for liberation must follow only the teachings of the Buddha.
4. And, following that, I will reveal the different doors of the stages of the path.

How the Teacher Attained Completely Pure Enlightenment

The first of these four divisions has two parts: [3] the tradition of the Śrāvakas[2] and the Mahāyāna[3] tradition.

THE ŚRĀVAKA TRADITION

The Śrāvaka tradition is given in the *Treasury of Higher Knowledge*[4] (in which it is stated that) the bodhisattva Vipaśyin[5] arose as a Buddha at the end of three immeasurable aeons, having first generated *bodhicitta*[6] under the Buddha Mahāśākyamuni.[7] As it is said; "Our teacher first aroused the thought of enlightenment in the presence of Mahāśākyamuni. From then until the Buddha Ratnaśikhin[8] appeared in the world, the first immeasurable aeon passed. The second aeon extended until the Buddha Dīpaṅkara[9] appeared in the world, and throughout the third aeon Vipaśyin accumulated the collections of merit [and wisdom], until he himself arose in the world as a perfect Buddha. At the end of this time he was born as Sarvārthasiddha, the son of King Śuddhodana [4] and, at the age of 35, in the month of Vaiśākha, the last month of spring, during the evening of the full moon he destroyed the hosts of Māra. During the middle of the night he entered a state of deep meditation (*samādhi*) and completely traversed the paths of preparation, seeing and meditation.[10] Before dawn he attained complete and perfect enlightenment." In that tradition it is held that, up until the overthrow of Māra, he performed the deeds of an ordinary bodhisattva.[11] Later, at the age of 80 years, the Buddha passed into *parinirvāṇa*. In this tradition it is held that, at that time, the continuum of his mind was cut off, just like the light of a lamp that has run out of oil.

THE MAHĀYĀNA TRADITION

Within the Mahāyāna school, there are two traditions: the Vehicle of the Perfections (*pāramitāyāna*), and the Tantric Vehicle (*mantrayāna*). First I will discuss the view of the Vehicle of Perfections.

THE PĀRAMITĀYĀNA TRADITION

Here it is held that the bodhisattva completed the paths of accumulation and preparation and attained the first level (*bhūmi*)[12] during the first immeasurable aeon. During the second aeon he ascended through the remaining six impure levels, and completed the stages of the three pure levels during the third aeon.[13] The cycle of becoming was ended for him when all the Buddhas of the ten directions bestowed empowerment upon him in the Peerless pure land[14] by means of their great rays of light. In the next moment he attained the *vajra*-like *samādhi* and, gaining the *dharmakāya* and *saṁbhogakāya*, he became a complete and perfect Buddha. That Enjoyment Body (*saṁbhogakāya*) which possesses the five certainties[15] is the ultimate body of form and, while that resided in the Peerless pure land, the *nirmāṇakāya* demonstrated the 12 deeds of a Buddha[16] in [our own world of] Jambudvīpa.[17]

As it is said in [Maitreya's *Analysis of the Jewel Matrix, Great Vehicle Treatise on*] the *Peerless Tantra:*

> The great compassionate Knower of the World,
> Seeing the condition of the world,
> Without stirring from the Body of Truth
> Manifested various natural appearances
> [5] Such as his previous and final births.
>
> He transferred his consciousness from Tuṣita and
> Entered the womb and was born.
> Excelling in all arts
> He experienced the pleasure of his retinue of queens.
> Demonstrating renunciation and ascetic practices
> He went to the heart of *bodhicitta.*
> Conquering Māra, he attained complete Buddhahood
> And turned the wheel of the Dharma of awakening.
>
> Finally he passed beyond all suffering
> And yet in all the impure realms
> He continues to teach, so long as *saṁsāra* remains.

THE MANTRAYĀNA TRADITION

Secondly, I will discuss the tradition of tantra. The way in which Buddhahood was attained is described in *kriyātantra* (Action tantra) and *caryātantra* (Performance tantra) in a manner no different from that of the Perfection Vehicle [discussed above].

The Yogatantra Tradition

Yogatantra and *anuttarayogatantra* (unexcelled *yogatantra*) have separate traditions. The first of these is explained in the root tantra *Compendium of the Reality* [*of All Tathagatas*] and in the explanatory tantra *Vajra Peak.* Regarding these texts, it is said that the commentator skilled in words is Śākyamitra,[18] the commentator skilled in meanings is Buddhaguhya[19] and he who is skilled in both words and meanings is Ānandagarbha.[20] According to the first two of these scholars, all three of whom were proficient in tantric practice, our Teacher for this age was born as Śuddhodana's son and practised ascetism on the banks of the Nairañjanā river as an ordinary bodhisattva. Practising the path of austerity in that place for six years, he attained the fourth concentration[21] known variously as the greatest of the great, as the final concentration, as the unshakeable and as the meditative stabilization that pervades the whole of space. [6] While he sat rapt in this meditative absorption, the Buddhas of the ten directions aroused him by snapping their fingers and said, "You will not reach enlightenment by this *samādhi* alone."

"Well then, how do I go on?" he asked. In reply, they led him away to the peerless pure land. Thus, while his body of karmic maturation remained on the bank of the Nairañjanā river, the Wisdom Body of the bodhisattva who fulfils all wishes went to the highest pure land where the Buddhas of the ten directions bestowed empowerment upon him [in the form of] the crown consecration. Then they left him to meditate on the stages of the five clear realizations (*abhisaṁbodhi*).[22] Completely mastering these five *abhisaṁbodhi* realizations, he achieved Buddhahood in the *saṁbhogakāya* as Mahāvairocana and demonstrated the four miraculous means of a Buddha.[23] Going then to the summit of Mount Meru, he taught the way of *yogatantra*.

Following this, he returned to the human realm and, upon re-entering his karmically matured body of fruition on the bank of the Nairañjanā river, he subdued the hosts of Māra and demonstrated the way of enlightenment and the remaining [deeds of a Buddha].

According to the tradition of the *ācārya* Ānandagarbha, the bodhisattva gathered the accumulations of merit and wisdom for three immeasurable aeons, and at the end of this time reached the stage of the tenth *bhūmi*, which is the limit of cyclic existence. At this time he resided in the peerless pure land, in the equipoise of the space-pervading meditative absorption. Then all the Buddhas of the ten directions gathered together and aroused him by the sounds of their snapping fingers. "It is not possible for you to attain enlightenment merely on the basis of this *samādhi*" they told him.

"Well then, how should I proceed?" he asked. The assembled multitude of Buddhas then bestowed upon him the crown consecration [7] and left him to meditate upon the five clear realizations in their proper order. Upon the completion of this meditation he arose as the Buddha Mahāvairocana in the Body of Enjoyment.

Having thus attained Buddhahood he demonstrated the four miraculous means [of ripening beings] and, going to the peak of Mount Meru, he taught *yogatantra*. Following this, he was born in the human realm as the son of King Śuddhodana and enacted the 12 deeds of a Buddha. Thus it is believed in this tradition.

Now what, it may be asked, is the series of clear realizations? These consist of a prior five clear realizations, arising through the miraculous power of the Teacher, and a subsequent five clear realizations, arising through the practice of a disciple. When the Buddhas of the ten directions conferred the crown consecration upon the bodhisattva Sarvārthasiddha, they left him to meditate on the meaning of the *mantra* OṀ CITTA-PRATIVEDHAṀ KAROMI (*Oṁ* I analyse the mind). As he sat meditating on this *mantra* he clearly realized the natural purity of the *dharmatā* nature of his own mind in terms of 16 voidnesses.[24] As he arose from that meditation he clearly perceived the natural purity of the *dharmatā* nature of his own mind as a moon disc in his heart, and he achieved the mirror-like wisdom (*ādarśanajñāna*) of the *tathāgata* Akṣobhya. The name of this clear realization is 'the wisdom clarity arising from a specific understanding [of the 16 emptinesses]'.

In order to apply this to the stages of a disciple's practice, one recites the *mantra* OṀ CITTAPRATIVEDHAṀ KAROMI and meditates on the 16 vowels [of the Sanskrit alphabet] as symbols of the 16 emptinesses of *dharmatā* which is the nature of the natural purity of the mind, [8] on top of a moon disc in one's heart.

After that, the Buddhas of the ten directions bestowed the *mantra* OṀ BODHICITTAM UTPĀDAYĀMI (*Oṁ* I arouse the mind of enlightenment) upon the bodhisattva Sarvārthasiddha, and left him to contemplate its meaning. As he sat in that meditation he clearly realized the *dharmatā* nature of his own mind, completely free of adventitious stains. During the post-meditation period he clearly saw the disc of the full moon in his heart as the genuine natural purity of the *dharmatā* nature of his mind, free from all adventitious stains. Thus he achieved the realization of the *tathāgata* Ratnasambhava and the wisdom of great equality (*samatājñāna*). The name of this clear realization is 'the clear realization arisen from *bodhicitta*'.

In applying this to the stages of a disciple's practice, one recites the *mantra* OṀ BODHICITTAM UTPĀDAYĀMI and meditates upon the 30 [Sanskrit] consonants as symbols of the stainless purity of the *dharmatā* nature of one's own mind, free of adventitious defilement, upon the full moon disc at one's heart.

After that, the Buddhas left Sarvārthasiddha to meditate on the meaning of the *mantra* TIṢṬHA VAJRA (Stand firm, oh *vajra*), and he clearly saw a white five-pronged *vajra* standing upright on the moon disc at his heart as the completely auspicious fundamental nature of his previously-generated *bodhicitta*. In that way he achieved the nature of the *tathāgata* Amitābha, which is discriminating wisdom (*pratyavekṣaṇajñāna*). The name of this clear realization is 'the clear realization achieved by *vajra* stability'.

In order to apply this to the stages of a disciple's practice, [9] one recites the *mantra* TIṢṬHA VAJRA and meditates on a white five-pronged *vajra* at one's heart as the primordial *vajra*.

After that, all the Buddhas of the ten directions bestowed the name empowerment upon the bodhisatva Sarvārthasiddha, and Sarvārthasiddha thereafter became known by the name Bodhisattva Vajra Realm (Vajradhātu). Then they left him to meditate on the meaning of the *mantra* VAJRĀTMAKO 'HAM (I am of the nature of *vajra*), and by this meditation he achieved the *vajra*-realm body of all the Buddhas of the ten directions, with their *vajra*-realm speech and *vajra*-realm mind, clearly established within the white five-pronged *vajra* at his heart. He clearly saw that that very *vajra* was composed of *vajra* particles which were the actual nature of all the countless Buddhas [of the *vajradhātu*]. In this way he attained the state of the *tathāgata* Amoghasiddhi and the all-accomplishing wisdom (*kṛtyānu-ṣṭhānajñāna*). The name of this clear realization is 'the clear realization arisen from the *vajra* nature'.

When applying this to the stages of a disciple's practice, one recites the *mantra* VAJRĀTMAKO 'HAM and, by means of light rays emanating into the ten directions from the white five-pronged *vajra* in one's heart, one draws the Vajra Realm body, speech and mind of all the Buddhas into one's heart, and establishes them firmly within the white five-pronged *vajra*. This is the meditation.

After that, all the Buddhas of the ten directions left the Bodhisattva Vajra Realm to meditate on the meaning of the *mantra* OṀ YATHĀ SARVATATHĀGATĀS TATHĀ 'HAM (*Oṁ* As are all the Buddhas, so am I). As he sat absorbed in this meditation, the *vajra* and moon disc at his heart completely transformed and he gained a clear realization of himself as the [10] *saṁbhogakāya* Mahāvairocana, fully adorned with all the major marks and minor signs of Buddhahood. Thus he attained manifest Buddhahood. Achieving the nature of Vairocana, he realized the wisdom of the Utterly Pure Realm of Truth (*suviśuddha-dharmadhātujñāna*). The name of this clear realization is 'the clear realization arisen from total equality with all Tathāgatas'.

In order to incorporate that within the stages of a disciple's practice, one recites the *mantra* OṀ YATHĀ SARVATATHĀGATĀS TATHĀ 'HAM and meditates upon oneself arising as the *tathāgata* Mahāvairocana through the complete transformation of the *vajra* and moon within one's heart.

Upon his attaininment of complete enlightenment, the Buddha bestowed blessings and empowerments and demonstrated meditative stabilization and miraculous emanations. After performing these four kinds of activity, without his Enjoyment Body stirring from its place in the peerless pure land, the Blessed One assumed the form of an Emanation Body with four faces and taught such *yogatantra* as the *Compendium of the Reality* [*of All Tathāgatas*] on the peak of Mount Meru. Travelling to the human realm, he conquered the hordes of Māra and showed the manner of attaining enlightenment and the rest [of the 12 deeds].

The Anuttarayogatantra Tradition

Secondly, according to the tradition of Highest Yoga *tantra*, the way in which our Teacher attained Buddhahood is as follows: texts such as the *Wheel of Time Tantra*, the *Supreme Bliss Tantra*, the *Hevajra Tantra* and so forth do not give any explanation, but it is taught in the cycle of the *Secret Assembly Tantra*. With respect to this topic, we find the view and teachings of Āryadeva,[25] as expressed in his *Lamp Compendium of Practice*, to be the same as that put forward by Jñānapāda [Buddha-jñāna],[26] in his *Greater Exposition*. The explanation of these two masters is that bodhisattvas who have achieved the tenth level are of two kinds; there are those for whom cyclic existence has ended and who are certain to attain Buddhahood in their next birth, and there are those for whom cyclic existence has ended and who are certain to attain Buddhahood in this very life.

Now, our Teacher, having accumulated merit throughout three immeasurable aeons by holding to the Perfection Vehicle, [11] had at last become a tenth level bodhisattva and had reached the limit of cyclic existence. At that time he dwelt in the peerless pure land, absorbed in the meditative stabilization that pervades the whole of space. All the Buddhas of the ten directions then gathered around him and roused him by the sounds of their snapping fingers. "You will not be able to attain complete and perfect Buddhahood merely on the basis of this *samādhi*," they told him. "Well then, how should I proceed?" he asked. In reply, all those Buddhas of the ten directions called forth Tilottamā, the supremely beautiful daughter of the gods, and bestowed upon him the genuine third empowerment. Then, having shown him the stages of the clear realizations, they left him to meditate upon those. In the first half of the night, through the successive dissolution of the three emptinesses,[27] he realized the ultimate meaning of the 'clear light' emptiness. Then, in order that that he may gain the stage of union on the path of learning, the Buddhas bestowed the fourth empowerment upon him and left him to engage in that practice. As the sky cleared at the break of day, the bodhisattva purified the most subtle traces of the subtle obscurations to omniscience through his *vajra*-like *samādhi* and attained the stage of union on the path of no more learning. In this way he became a manifest realized Buddha.

In that situation, we find that giving only the two higher empowerments and omitting the vase and secret empowerments is permitted. It is also taught that it is permitted in this special circumstance to meditate on the completion stage (*niṣpannakrama*) without meditating on the generation stage (*utpattikrama*).

Then, while his Enjoyment Body remained in the peerless pure land, his Emanation Body showed the manner of the 12 deeds in the human realm. Thus, having been born as Śuddhodana's son, he practised austerities for six years on the bank of the Nairañjanā river, taking no coarse food other than one seed of the jujube fruit, one grain of sesame and one grain of rice each day. [12] As he sat absorbed in the space-pervading meditative stabilization, the Buddhas of the ten directions came to him and aroused him by the sound of their snapping fingers. "You will not be able to overcome Māra and his host by means of such physically painful austerities, and by this meditative stabilization you will not be able to gain liberation from the obscurations to omniscience," they told him. Then, having eaten substantial food, he approached the Bodhi tree and all the Buddhas called forth

Tilottamā, the most beautiful daughter of heaven, and showed the way of consecrating him with the third empowerment. Then, having shown him the stages of the clear realizations, they left him to meditate. In the first half of the night, through the successive dissolution of the three emptinesses, he clearly realized the ultimate meaning of the 'clear light' emptiness. Then, in order that he should arise in the body of union on the stage of learning, the Buddhas bestowed upon him the fourth empowerment and left him to practise accordingly.

As the sky brightened with the dawn, he cleared away the most subtle of the subtle obscurations to omniscience through his *vajra*-like meditative stabilization and attained union on the path of no more learning. Thus he demonstrated the attainment of complete and perfect Buddhahood.

Well, if someone should propose the argument that the demonstration of enlightenment was sufficient in itself, and questions the need for the third and fourth empowerments and so forth, we answer that, although by relying on the Perfection Vehicle one is able to reach the tenth bodhisattva *bhūmi*, yet, in order to achieve complete Buddhahood, one definitely has to rely on the path of the unexcelled *mantra* tradition.

The Lord of Sages (*munīndra*), demonstrating manifest
Buddhahood,
Showed a vehicle for every being.
This attempt to set out clearly just what was taught
I offer to please the Conquerors and their Children.

(This is a verse [13] inserted between chapters)

How the Buddha Turned the Wheel of Dharma

The manner in which the Buddha turned the wheel of Dharma after attaining enlightenment has two parts: Turning the wheel of *sūtra* and turning the wheel of *mantra*.

HOW THE BUDDHA TURNED THE WHEEL OF THE SŪTRAS

Regarding the first of these, the *bhagavat*, having demonstrated the attainment of complete and perfect enlightenment, rested for seven weeks. Following that he went to Ṛṣipatana in the district of Vārāṇasī, and there in the Deer Park he met his retinue of companions—the all-knowing Ājñātakauṇḍinya, Aśvajit, Bāṣpa, Mahānāma and Bhadrika [28]—and for them he turned the Dharma wheel of the Four Noble Truths:

"Oh *bhikṣus*! This is the noble truth of suffering. This is the noble truth of the origin of suffering. This is the noble truth of the cessation of suffering. This is the noble truth of the path. Suffering must be understood. The origin of suffering must be abandoned. The cessation of suffering must be obtained. The path must be relied upon. Suffering must be understood for, until now, we have not understood it. The origin of suffering must be abandoned for, until now, it has not been abandoned. The cessation of suffering must be obtained for, until now, it has not been obtained. One must meditate on the path for, until now, we have not meditated upon it."

Thus he taught these Four Noble Truths three times. That teaching of the Four Noble Truths is the actual [first] turning of the wheel of Dharma.[29]

Apart from the above, such similar teachings as the *Discrimination of Discipline Sūtra*, the *Four Close Placements in Mindfulness*, the *Hundred Verses on Karma*, the *Hundred Stories of Realization* and so on are all included in the first wheel of teachings.

The Blessed One then sojourned on the Vulture's Peak, and to a retinue of 5,000 *bhikṣus* and others, to a great assembly of Hearers engaged in the practices of calm abiding (*śamatha*) and special insight (*vipaśyanā*), [14] and especially to countless numbers of Mahāyāna disciples, he taught the Dharma without signs, and turned the second wheel of Dharma.

The actual teachings given at this time were the three great sūtras of the Perfection of Wisdom: the extensive *Mother Sūtra*, the medium and the abbreviated sūtras.[30] Also included in this middle wheel of the teachings are the *King of Meditative Stabilizations Sūtra*, the *Very Extensive Garland of Buddhas Sūtra*, the *Descent Into Laṅkā Sūtra*, most of the *Stack of Jewels Sūtra*, and such similar texts.

Then, at Vaiśālī and other places, the Blessed One taught the disciples of all vehicles that each of the elements of existence (*dharma*), from form to omniscient mind,[31] which were taught by him in the first turning of the wheel, exists merely by imputation upon its characteristics.

During the second turning he taught that phenomena do not exist [even] by imputation on their characteristics. And so, for all those who are to be included within the Mahāyāna fold but who have developed doubts, he taught this final series of teachings which fully clarified his intended meaning.

The actual teachings given at that time were those such as the Chapter [of the *Sūtra Unravelling the Thought*] 'Requested by the the Noble One, Arising of Ultimate Truth'.[32] Also included within this final turning of the wheel is the [entire text of the] *Sūtra Unravelling the Thought.*

Now, according to the *prāsaṅgika*[33] view, the sūtras of the first two turnings of the wheel that show the subtle emptiness are sūtras of definitive meaning. The sūtras of the final wheel are the sūtras of interpretive meaning.

According to the *svātantrika* view, held by Śāntarakṣita[34] and his disciples, the first wheel is [made up of] sūtras of interpretive meaning, the second wheel contains sūtras of both interpretive and definitive meaning, and the final wheel is composed of sūtras which are to be understood as definitive.

The school of Siṁhabhadra[35] is not particularly clear on this point, but it seems that they hold the same belief as Śāntarakṣita and his followers.

As for followers of the *cittamātra* school: they believe that the first two wheels [15] reveal teachings, the meaning of which needs to be interpreted, whereas sūtras of the final wheel have a definitive meaning.

Most of the followers of the *bāhyārtha* schools[36] accept only the Dharma wheel of the Four Noble Truths and do not believe that the Mahāyāna sūtras are the word of the Buddha. A few of them, however, accept the *Essence of the Tathāgata Sūtra,* the *Dhāraṇī Requested by Indra,* the *Great Ultimate Nirvāṇa Sūtra* and so forth as the final turning of the wheel. According to our [*prāsaṅgika*] tradition, the subject matter of these texts is similar to the second wheel of teachings.

If we were to analyse extensively all the teachings given in that way by the Buddha, we would find that the 84,000 teachings act as opponent forces to the 84,000 delusions. Summarizing these teachings, we find that all the scriptures can be contained within 12 categories. In the *Supreme Essence,* [*Commentary on the Difficult Points of the Eight Thousand Verse Perfection of Wisdom*] by Śāntipa [Ratnākaraśānti],[37] the 12 divisions of scripture are said to consist of: sūtras, verses of intermediate [length], prophetic teachings, verses, uplifting teachings, legends, rebirth stories, marvellous teachings, expansive teachings, introductory teachings, parables and finalized teachings,[38] and it is just as he says. If we wish further to summarize these teachings, we can reduce them to nine categories,[39] and they can also be said to be contained within the three baskets.[40]

An alternative way of categorizing the teachings of the Buddha is to distinguish between those teachings which were uttered from his own lips, those teachings which were given [in his presence by others] through his blessings, and those teachings which were given [in his absence by others] with his permission. We can also distinguish three classes within the category of teachings given through his blessings: those blessed by his body, those blessed by his speech and those blessed by his mind. Those teachings given through the blessings of his mind are also threefold: there are those blessed by the *samādhi* of his mind, those blessed by the compassion of his mind, [16] and those blessed by the power of truth of his mind.

Finally, having turned the wheel of Dharma [for 45 years], the Lord of Sages showed the manner of passing beyond suffering [at the age of 80] on the night of the full moon in the final month of spring, beneath the constellation Vaiśākā.

After that there were three great councils. The first council took place in the summer of the year of the Buddha's ultimate *nirvāṇa*, in the Cave of Great Happiness in Rājagṛha. King Ajātaśatru was the sponsor and it was agreed that the Elder Mahākāśyapa should lead the monastic community of 500 *arhats* for the summer retreat.

At that time, all the 500 *arhats,* with the exception of Ānanda, made a tall pile of their upper ceremonial robes and Ānanda seated himself upon the top of this. Turning his face toward Śrāvastī[41] and folding his hands in prayer, he began to recite in a melodious voice, *evaṁ mayā śrutam ekasmin samaye ...* ("Thus have I heard. At one time...") and so on. In this way he collected together the entire basket of sūtras, reciting from memory all the sūtras the Buddha had taught, without the omission or addition of even a single word.

Then, in the same way, the noble Upāli[42] collected together the entire basket of *vinaya* (rules of ethical conduct) and the great Kāśyapa collected together the entire basket of *abhidharma* (elements of higher knowledge).

Following the clear explanations of Śākyamuni himself, the teachings of the Buddha had seven great patriarchs: Kāśyapa, Ānanda, Śāṇakavāsin, Upagupta, Dhītika, Kṛṣṇa and Sudarśana. These are the seven [17] patriarchs of the teachings and they are said to have succeeded one another in that order.

The second council took place 110 years after the *parinirvāṇa* of the Teacher. At that time the *arhat* Yaśas and 700 other *arhats,* all of whom had eliminated [from themselves] the ten fundamental transgressions, expelled from their council all those monks of Vaiśālī who had wilfully committed the ten transgressions. Those monks having been cast out, the remainder held an auspicious confessional assembly. The patron on that occasion was the Dharma King Aśoka.

As for the third council, this gathering occurred just as has been explained by the *ācārya* Bhāvaviveka[43] in his *Blaze of Reasoning*, by Vinītadeva[44] in his *Wheel of Proclaiming the Distinctions of the Classes of Scripture* and by the *ācārya* Padmākara[45] in his *Questions for the Novice Monk's Year*.

There is, however, another tradition that tells of how Māra the evil one manifested as a monk named Bhadra in the city of Pāṭaliputra, 137 years after the *parinirvāṇa* of the Buddha. This demonic monk caused divisions in the views of the *saṅgha* so that conflicts and dissension arose [within its ranks]. These conflicts were resolved in accordance with the true Dharma by the teachings of a *bhikṣu* named Vātsīputra. This council was under the joint patronage of both King Nanda and King Mahāpadma.

There is yet another tradition in which it is said that this council took place in the city of Kusumapura[46] 160 years after the Teacher's ultimate *nirvāṇa*. It is believed that the four schools arose at that time, due to the teachings being recited by four elder monks in four different languages.[47] Within these four sects we also find 18 minor schools as subdivisions.[48] [18] "Only this is the teaching of the Buddha, and all those who practise otherwise are not his true followers," they argued among themselves. Some time later, references to all 18 of those schools were found in *King Kṛkin's Prophetic Dream Sūtra*,[49] and it was explained that all of these traditions are to be included among the followers of the Buddha's teaching. The patron on that occasion was the Dharma King Aśoka.

Of the texts which comment on the three turnings of the wheel of Dharma, the *Great Ocean of Specific Explanation*, the [?*Auto-*] *Commentary* on the root text of *abhidharma* [the *Treasury of Higher Knowledge* by Vasubandhu[50]], and the 'Seven Treatises on Higher Knowledge'[51] all deal mainly with the viewpoint of the first turning. Among these, the commentary on the root text and [Viśākadeva's[52]] *Flower Garland* [*of Ethics*] and others explain mainly the aspect of practice.

The group of six Middle Way[53] treatises and other [texts by Nāgārjuna[54]] deal mainly with the viewpoint of the second turning of the wheel. Texts such as the ritual of generating *bodhicitta* composed by Āryadeva [*Oral Instructions on the Stages of Realizing Bodhicitta*] and the *Seventy Verses of* [*Going for*] *Refuge* written by Candrakīrti[55] give explanations of practice, whereas Āryadeva's *Compendium of Sūtras* and Śāntideva's[56] *Compendium of Trainings* and *Entering the Bodhisattva's Deeds* comment on both practice and view. The *ārya* Asaṅga's[57] *Five Levels of Yogic Practice* and his two anthologies (*Compendium of Mahāyāna* and *Compendium of Higher Knowledge*), as well as Vasubandhu's *Eight Collections of Logic* and [Maitreya's[58]] two *Discriminations*, all, for the most part, expound the view of the third and final turning. Except for the Suchness (*tathatā*) chapter of the *Bodhisattva Grounds* [which explains the view], the remaining [chapters] of the *Stages of Yogic Practice* explicate the aspect of practice. [Maitreya's] *Ornament of* [*Mahāyāna*] *Sūtras* explains both view and practice in equal measure.

Other than this, the view of the Sautrāntika school, as set forth in [Dharmakīrti's[59]] *Seven Logical Treatises* is in accordance with the explained meaning of the first wheel, while the works of the Cittamātrin proponents show that their view is in accordance with the meaning of the final wheel.

HOW THE BUDDHA TURNED THE WHEEL OF SECRET MANTRA

The second subdivision here is the manner in which the wheel of the *mantra* Dharma was turned. There are four classes of tantra, in accordance with the four different types of disciple and with the way that each takes desire into the path. [19] This will be explained later.

[Our author bSod-nams grags-pa deals with this topic under the heading 'The Secret Mantra Vehicle'.]

How all Those who Seek Liberation Must Follow the Teachings of the Buddha

It is inappropriate on the part of anyone interested in gaining freedom and omniscience to follow the path of those whose minds remain unmoved by philosophical tenets. It is also inappropriate to follow those who claim worldly existence to be entirely meaninglessness (the *lokāyata* school), or others such as those who deny all previous and future births, or to follow schools such as the Vedic ritualists (*mīmāṁsaka*) and so on, who accept the doctrine of rebirth but deny the possibility of attaining liberation or omniscience.

It is only by accepting the possibility of attaining liberation and omniscience, and then by taking refuge in the Three Jewels and by following the inner teachings of the Buddha, that one can enter the true Dharma.

The Different Doors to the Stages of the Path

The fourth division of this general teaching is the indication of the different doors to the stages of the path. This has two parts: (1) differentiation in terms of tenets and (2) differentiation in terms of vehicles.

DIFFERENTIATION IN TERMS OF TENETS

When distinguished in accordance with their philosophical tenets, there are the four groups: Vaibhāṣika ('Detailed Exposition'), Sautrāntika ('Sūtra School'), Cittamātrin ('Mind-only') and Mādhyamika ('Middle Way').

According to [Bhāvaviveka's] *Wheel of Proclaiming the Distinctions of the Classes of Scripture*, the Vaibhāṣika group contains four sects. The first of these is the Mahāsaṅghika ('Great Monastic Community'), within which are contained the five schools known as Pūrvaśaila ('Eastern Mountain'), Aparaśaila ('Western Mountain'), Haimavata ('Snow Mountain'), Lokottaravādin ('Transcendental Exposition') and Prajñaptivādin ('Determinate Exposition'). The second sect is the Āryasarvāstivādin ('Noble Ones Who Believe in the True Existence of Phenomena') and this sect contains seven schools: Mūlasarvāstivādin ('Fundamentalists Who Believe in the True Existence of Phenomena'), Kāśyapīya ('Followers of Kāśyapa'), Mahīśāsaka ('Instructors of the Earth'), Dharmaguptaka ('Protectors of Dharma'), Bahuśrutīya ('Having Heard Much'), Tāmraśāṭīya ('Red-clothed Ones') and the Vibhajyavādin ('Discriminating Exposition'). The third sect is the Āryasthavira ('Higher Elders') which contains three schools: the Jetavanīya ('Abiders in the Jeta Grove')[60], Abhayagirivāsin ('Fearless Mountain Abiders') and Mahāvihāravāsin ('Abiders in the Great Monastery'). The fourth sect, Āryasaṁmitīya ('Consensus of the Superiors'), also contains three schools: the Kaurukullaka ('Proclaimed Over the Earth'), Avantaka ('Those from the Avanti District'), and Vātsīputrīya ('Followers of Vātsīputra'). Thus there are 18 schools within the four main sects, [20] all of which are included within the Vaibhāṣika group. These arose due to various teachers explaining the meaning [of the teachings] differently on separate occasions.

Some of the schools listed here, for example the Vātsīputrīya and others, accept the existence of an independent person which is neither impermanent nor permanent. However, most of the Vaibhāṣika schools, together with followers of the Sautrāntika, Cittamātrin and Mādhyamika-svātantrika schools, refute the existence of an independent person and accept the view of subtle selflessness. They assert that holding to the idea of an independent person is the delusion of ego-grasping. The Vaibhāṣika and Sautrāntaka schools in particular assert only the selflessness of the person, not the selflessness of phenomena. They assert that by meditating on that selflessness it is possible for a practitioner to eliminate all of the obscurations of defilement (*kleśāvaraṇa*) and attain liberation. Over and above that, they assert that by generating supreme *bodhicitta* and practising for three immeasurable aeons, it is possible to attain complete enlightenment.

For proponents of the Cittamātrin school, the method of attaining liberation is similar to the above, for they also assert the selflessness of all phenomena. For them, the perceiver and the object of perception are devoid of being substantially different, and this is how they define the selflessness of all phenomena. In particular, the nature of all phenomena together with their imputed characteristics is that they are all devoid of any self-existence from their own side. By practising meditation on this selflessness of phenomena and generating the Mahāyāna motivation of *bodhicitta*, they say, one will attain complete and perfect enlightenment at the end of three immeasurable aeons.

Followers of the Mādhyamika-svātantrika school hold that, in addition to the above, in order to attain Buddhahood one must meditate on an emptiness which entirely refutes the existence of all phenomena, as these cannot be established merely on the basis of their appearance to an unmistaken consciousness.

Although all Mādhyamika-svātantrika followers [21] accept the view of the emptiness that refutes true existence, such masters as Jñānagarbha,[61] Bhāvaviveka and others assert external existence but not a self-knowing [consciousness].[62] Therefore their school is called Sautrāntika-mādhyamika-svātantrika ('Middle Way Autonomists Following Scripture'). Śāntarakṣita and his followers, on the other hand, together with Haribhadra[63] and Buddhajñāna[64] and their followers, all accept the reality of internal (i.e. mental) existence while refuting the idea of the true existence of external phenomena. That is, they assert truly existent particles within physical matter and, because of this assertion, their school is called Yogācāra-mādhyamika-svātantrika ('Middle Way Autonomist Practitioners of Yoga').

Adherents of [our own] Prāsaṅgika school do not believe that liberation is possible merely on the basis of meditating on the view that refutes the substantial independence of the person. We believe that one attains liberation by meditating on the two levels of truth as well as by eliminating the obscurations of delusion through meditation upon the view that refutes the inherent existence of both the person and all phenomena. In addition to that, however, in order to gain complete and perfect enlightenment, one must generate the Mahāyāna mind of *bodhicitta* and practise for three immeasurable aeons.

DIFFERENTIATION IN TERMS OF VEHICLES

Secondly, I will explain the differentiation in terms of vehicles. There are two vehicles, known as the Hīnayāna ('Lesser Vehicle') and Mahāyāna ('Greater Vehicle').

The name 'lesser' refers both to the path that leads one to the attainment of liberation from the sufferings of cyclic existence for one's own benefit, and to the actual result itself. The two vehicles of Hīnayāna and Mahāyāna are not differentiated in terms of view, because even the Lesser Vehicle has the wisdom that realizes the non-inherent existence of a self with regard to both the personality and phenomena. Therefore, if we ask in what respect they differ, they differ in terms of the possession of the special 'Body of the Path' of the Mahāyāna: that is, *bodhicitta*.

[22] It is by means of this special *bodhicitta* that one develops a mind of equanimity toward all beings, seeing them all as having been one's own mother. Further, remembering the kindness of mothers, one develops the wish to repay the debt of kindness that is owed to all beings. From this, love arises toward them all, wishing for their complete happiness. Compassion arises, wishing for them to be free of all suffering, and then one develops the supreme thought of taking upon oneself the responsibility for actually achieving this. This supreme thought is the actual *bodhicitta;* which includes both the mind of aspiration toward Buddhahood for the sake of all sentient beings, and the mind which then actually engages in the practice. It is with this attitude that one takes the bodhisattva vows [and makes a promise] to abandon the 18 root downfalls and to protect oneself from the 46 auxiliary downfalls.[65]

In addition to this, one practises the six perfections[66] and the four ways of gathering disciples[67] and, since these practices are found only within the Mahāyāna tradition and not in the Hīnayāna, it is on these points of difference that one can discriminate between the two as distinct vehicles.

THE HĪNAYĀNA

The Hīnayāna can be divided into two: the Śrāvakayāna ('Hearers' Vehicle') and Pratyekabuddhayāna ('Solitary Realizer Buddhas' Vehicle'). These two are not differentiated in terms of either view or practice, because both have the wisdom of the realization of the non-inherent existence of all phenomena, and neither of them include the development of the Mahāyāna mind of enlightenment.

Well then, if we ask how these two differ, the reply is that their difference is based upon whether or not the practitioner has to rely upon another as his teacher at the time of leaving cyclic existence. There is also a difference in their resultant attainments, which are classified as inferior and superior [respectively], and a difference based on whether or not one gives verbal or physical teachings and so on, once the result has been attained.

THE MAHĀYĀNA

The term Mahāyāna refers both to the path that leads to the attainment of complete and perfect Buddhahood for the benefit of all sentient beings, and to the actual result itself. This vehicle can also be divided into two: the

Pāramitāyāna ('Vehicle of the [six] Perfections') and Guhyamantrayāna ('Vehicle of Secret Mantra'). [23] As is said in [Buddhaguhya's] *Introduction to the Meanings of Highest Yoga Tantra:*

> The bodhisattva vehicle is of two kinds: there is the vehicle of the levels (*bhūmi*) and perfections, and there is the resultant vehicle of tantra.

The Perfection Vehicle is also known as the 'vehicle with signs', the 'causal vehicle' and the 'vehicle of attaining enlightenment through the path of parting from attachment'. Why is this path called the 'vehicle of the perfections' and so on? It is called the 'vehicle of the perfections' because it is a path toward Buddhahood which relies on the way of the [six] perfections, and does not involve meditation on the body of a deity. It is called 'causal vehicle' because on this path one only realizes the causes of enlightenment, without meditating on the four complete purities which are gained at the time of the result, nor on their similitudes being taken as the path.

The Vehicle of Secret Mantra is also known as the '*vajra* vehicle', the 'resultant vehicle', the 'method vehicle' and as the 'vehicle of attaining Buddhahood by means of the path of desire'. If we ask, "Why is it called the 'secret mantra vehicle' and the rest?", it is called 'secret' because it is not suitable to be brought within the scope of inappropriate vessels [immature disciples]. It is called '*mantra*' because it protects one's mind[68] from the sufferings of cyclic existence. It is called '*vajra*' because, on the side of wisdom there is the understanding of emptiness, and, on the side of method, there is reliance on the maṇḍala of deities, both arising clearly in one's mind. It is called 'resultant vehicle' because one meditates on the four complete purities which are attained at the time of enlightenment, and takes their simili-tudes as the path. It is called 'method vehicle' because the methods employed within it are far superior to those employed within the perfection vehicle. [24] It is called 'desire vehicle' because, on this path, Buddhahood is attained through utilization of the objects of desire.

This vehicle contains various tantras dealing with the tenets and basic practices of [those realized beings known as] Vidyādhara ('Knowledge Holders') and therefore [the canon of this vehicle] is known as the *vidyādharapiṭaka* ('basket of teachings of the Knowledge Holders').

If we now ask, "To which of the three baskets does this basket belong?", the answer is found in the *Sūtra Requested by Subāhu.* "Listen and I will explain," it says. "Secret mantra is taught in the manner of the basket of sūtras." Also, Śāntipa [Ratnākaraśānti][69] has said, "It is the basket of sūtras which shows the condensed profound meaning."

It is also said that if we analyze the *sūtrapiṭaka* itself, we find within it the *vinayapiṭaka* and the *abhidharmapiṭaka*, and so all three baskets are contained within one.

The Perfection Vehicle

With regard to the Pāramitāyāna; five divisions are recognized, relating to five speeds of travelling along the path. These five are taught in the *Introduction to the Signs of Definite and Indefinite Progress Sūtra* as travelling: (1) as if in an oxcart, (2) as if in a wagon drawn by an elephant, (3) like the sun or moon, (4) like the miracles of a Śrāvaka, or, (5) like the miracles of a Pratyekabuddha.

If we ask how these two Mahāyāna vehicles are differentiated, we can say that they are not differentiated by the superiority or inferiority of their resultant attainments, because the result in both cases is entirely free of faults and replete with all good qualities. Similarly, we cannot differentiate them with respect to their practices, because in both cases the six perfections and the development of *bodhicitta* are practised equally. Nor can they be differentiated by their view, because both of these vehicles have the wisdom that understands the lack of inherent existence. Also, they can be differentiated neither by the speed of travelling the path nor by the superiority or inferiority of their disciples. Well then, what is the difference?

Within the Mahāyāna in general, the main goals are to benefit others and to achieve enlightenment. Of these two ideals, the principal one is to benefit others. [25] Enlightenment itself is not the principal objective, because enlightenment is desired only as a means of helping others. For example: a person suffering from thirst has drinking as his main interest, but he also takes interest in a vessel so that he may use it to obtain the drink. In a similar way, enlightenment includes within its scope both the *dharmakāya* ('body of truth') and the *rūpakāya* ('body of form') and the main purpose here is to attain the *rūpakāya* because it is this, and not the *dharmakāya*, that possesses the ability to benefit disciples by appearing to them directly. The special practice of meditating on the characteristics of the *rūpakāya* is found on the path of the tantric vehicle and not in the perfection vehicle, and it is this fact that distinguishes the two vehicles.

In brief then, on the side of wisdom there is the understanding of emptiness, and on the side of method there is the arising of the retinue of deities and the maṇḍala palace. The very clear appearance of these two together in one mind is the particular characteristic of the tantric vehicle. [Such a unified appearance of method and wisdom] is not to be found within the perfection vehicle.

As is said in the first chapter of the *Vajra Tent Tantra:*

> If emptiness were the method
> One would never become Buddha
> Since a result cannot be at variance with its cause,
> And method is not emptiness.
>
> In order to reverse the self-grasping of those
> Who seek a view of self

And of those who [wish to] turn away from [false] views,
The Conquerors have shown emptiness.

For this reason, the maṇḍalas and deities
Have been shown as a blissful method.
By union with the pride of Buddhahood
[26] Buddhahood is not far away.

Because the thirty-two marks of the Teacher
And his lordly eighty signs
Are results attained by method,
Therefore method has the Teacher's form.

So it is written, and the significance here is that the wisdom that realizes emptiness was formerly taught as a path simply in order to overthrow the idea of grasping at a self. One might argue that Buddhahood must be attainable on the basis of meditating on this wisdom alone, because this wisdom not only realizes emptiness, and therefore opposes self-grasping, but is also the method for abandoning the mind that grasps at true existence and believes in the reality of phenomenal appearances. To such an argument we reply that enlightenment will not be attained with only the wisdom of realizing emptiness, because this wisdom alone is only the cause for the attainment of the *dharmakāya*, and has no cause whatsoever for the quite different attainment of the body of form.

If one now asks, "Then what is the reason for showing emptiness?", the answer is that the Conquerors have taught emptiness for the benefit of those with views that contradict the selflessness of phenomena, and to reverse the self-grasping of those who are manifestly fond of grasping at a self.

Therefore, if one now asks, "What is the method of attaining the resultant *rūpakāya* of Buddhahood?" we answer that, because the wisdom of realizing emptiness is not by itself the method for attaining enlightenment, one should cultivate the pride of Buddhahood and, on the basis of realizing bliss through this method, one realizes emptiness simultaneously. [27] By this method of deity yoga, producing the divine palace and the maṇḍala circle of deities as inseparable wisdom and bliss, the complete and perfect condition of Buddhahood is attained within a very short time.

Why is it necessary to practise the yoga of the deity adorned with the 112 marks and signs in order to attain the Buddha's Form Body? The reason is that, because it has been established that the enlightened form of the Teacher possesses the 32 marks and 80 signs of lordliness, when one is meditating on a path that aims at establishing this Form Body, the method itself must possess similar characteristics. As it has been said [by Buddhajñānapāda] in [his] *Engaging in the Means of Self-achievement:*

The ordinary methods are not the only ones. By meditating on causes that are dissimilar to complete and perfect Buddhahood,

Buddhahood will not be attained, because the path lacks meditations that accord with the result.

The meaning here is that, although in the perfection vehicle it is explained that generosity and so forth are methods for attaining the Form Body, these are not the only methods, because they themselves do not constitute a path that has characteristics similar to the Form Body. As [the same text] says:

> If the path does not possess characteristics similar to the Form Body, then it is not the unsurpassed method for attaining the Form Body. The profound Truth Body and the vast Form Body are attained by paths that accord with them.

Also, in the same text, it is said:

> For oneself, the result of the profound and vast nature that arises from within one's own being is attained by its own essence.

From this we understand that the *rūpakāya* must be achieved by means of a path that is concordant with it. And, because the *dharmakāya* [28] also needs to be achieved in a similar manner, it is therefore necessary to practise these two in the same way, [making the path like the result in all respects]. As it says in the text:

> For this reason, just as one meditates on selflessness, one should meditate upon the essential nature of the vast as being without difference [from the profound, which is emptiness].

Also, it is said in [Śridhara's][70] *Co-emergent Light, Commentary on the Difficult Points of Black Yamāri:*

> It should not be asserted that one will arise as a Buddha by relying on generosity and the rest as methods and by the power of prayers of aspiration. How can one's mind attain certainty by generating doubt? If it is maintained that the Enjoyment Body and the Emanation Body are produced by the power of prayer, and not by the appropriate meditation, then one could also gain the clarity of selflessness without meditation. Why, then, would one bother to meditate? If it is now agreed that these Bodies arise only after the appropriate meditation, and yet this meditation is not performed, what fault lies in the Enjoyment and Emanation Bodies? Therefore, even when one abides within the perfection vehicle, one should hold the truth of the three Bodies of Buddhahood and then, by means of meditation, the nature of all this will become clear. This is extensively taught.

The Secret Mantra Vehicle

Far superior to the *pāramitāyāna* is the vehicle of tantra, and this is taught in four classes. These four are not differentiated in terms of the result that is attained, nor in terms of their motivation of *bodhicitta*, nor by their practice of the six perfections. They do not differ in their view of realization, nor in their having the practices of deity yoga and so on. So then, [29] if one asks, "How can they be differentiated?" some reply that *kriyātantra* has been taught in order to gather those disciples who follow the ignorant Brahmā, *caryātantra* has been taught in order to gather those disciples who follow the angry Viṣṇu, *anuttarayogatantra* has been taught for the purpose of converting the disciples of the lustful Īśvara (Śiva), and *yogatantra* has been taught in order to gather the disciples of those three in general. Also, some say that these four classes of tantra respectively are taught in order to gather disciples from among the four castes of Brāhmans, Vaiśyas, Kṣatriyas and Śūdras. And again, some also say that because the Buddha's teachings contain the tenets of the four schools, the four different practices of deity yoga have been shown in harmony with those.

According to our own tradition, however, it is the main disciples of these various classes of tantra who are themselves distinguished in accordance with the four different ways in which they employ desire on the path. As it is written in the *Introduction to the Meaning of Highest Tantra*: "There are four doors of entry into the resultant Vajra vehicle of secret mantra, commonly known as Action tantra, Performance tantra, Yoga tantra and Highest Yoga tantra." And, in the *Embrace of the Four Yoginīs Tantra* we read: "Smiling, gazing, holding hands and embracing, these four represent the four tantras in the manner of insects."[71] Also, it is said in the *Vajra Tent Tantra*: [30] "For inferior beings Action tantra is taught, and Performance tantra is superior to that. For excellent beings the excellent Yoga tantra is taught, and Highest Yoga tantra is superior to that." Also, in the *Ornament of the Vajra Essence Tantra*: "By the embrace of the couple, the divisions of tantra are shown. Thus we may know them by the holding of hands, the smile and the gaze." The significance of these words is that, depending on the manner in which disciples take the joy of gazing on the meditational goddess onto the path, there is the distinction between external activities and internal meditative stabilization.

The class of tantra within which are taught mainly outer activities is *kriyātantra*. The type known as *caryātantra* teaches practices of the outer activities of body and speech in equal measure with practices of internal deity yoga. This has been taught for those disciples who are able to take onto the path the joy of smiling at the meditational goddess, as well as the joy of gazing. Similarly, with reference to the inner and outer yogas, that class of tantra which teaches primarily the internal practice of deity yoga is called *yogatantra*. This class is taught for those disciples who, beyond gazing and smiling at a meditational goddess, are able to take the happiness of touching her hand onto their path. *Anuttarayogatantra* is a class of tantra which teaches only internal deity yoga. Doctrines of this class are taught only for those disciples who are capable of taking onto their path the co-emergent bliss arising from the union of the male and female secret organs.

The meaning of all this is that Performance tantra is so called because it uses external activities and internal concentration in equal measure. Yoga tantra is so called because internal yoga is taken as the main practice, and Highest Yoga tantra is so called [31] because no yoga is higher.

Thus, the purpose of these tantric teachings is to lead superior individuals onto the path as disciples. They are not intended for ordinary beings.

It is said in the later chapters on meditation in the *Compendium of Reality Tantra* that disciples are terrified with fear when [these teachings of taking joy onto the path] are taught, but, as has been explained [by Ānandagarbha in his] *Illumination of the Compendium of Suchness*: "From the *anuttara-yogatantra* down to the three lower tantras, it is taught that one should take onto the path those joys that arise from gazing and so forth." So this is a pervasive teaching that exists right down to the lowest tantras. For example, taking the happiness of gazing onto the path of *kriyātantra* is explained in the *Detailed Rite of Amoghapāśa*: "One should look upon the face of the Bhagavatī Bhṛkuṭi."

It is also said:

> One should gaze to the right with joy and faith upon the beautiful goddess Tārā, she who bends down with a gesture of supreme generosity. One should gaze to the left with joy and faith upon the beautiful Padmakula in accordance with the doctrines of secret mantra, and one should gaze upon Amoghapāśa.

In *caryātantra* it is the happiness of smiling which is taken onto the path. As it is said in the *Perfect Enlightenment of Great Vairocana Sūtra:*

> The goddess on the right, whose face is gently smiling, encircled by a halo of light one full armspan across, is called Buddhalocanā. Her incomparable body is radiantly shining and she is the consort of Śākyamuni.

In *yogatantra* it is the happiness of touching hands which is taken onto the path. In the *Vajra Peak Tantra* it says: "The goddess murmuring with *vajra* passion, embracing [32] one's head, is one's personal goddess. Bowing down her head, she takes hold of the Buddha's hand." These quotations all make the meaning clear.

Now I will explain the four classes of tantra in detail: Action, Performance, Yoga and Highest Yoga tantra. The first of these is Action tantra, and this I will explain in three parts: (1) the inner classification, (2) an explanation of the empowerments and vows and (3) the stages of practising the path.

Action Tantra

INNER CLASSIFICATION

Inner classification is twofold: firstly there is the classification into families and, secondly, the general divisions of each of the families. Families are classified into three groups: the Tathāgata family, the Lotus family and the Vajra family.

THE TATHĀGATA FAMILY

With regard to the Tathāgata family, there are eight divisions of subject matter. There are [tantras concerning]: (1) the principal of the Tathāgata family, (2) the lord of the Tathāgata family, (3) the mother of the family, (4) the 'crown protrusion' [deity] of the family, (5) the wrathful gods and goddesses, (6) the group of obedient messengers, (7) the bodhisattvas, and (8) the nāgas and yakṣas of the Tathāgata family.

(1) The principal of the Tathāgata family is the Teacher Śākyamuni. Without the request of his entourage, he spontaneously taught the benefits of the 100-syllable mantra,[72] and, upon the request of his entourage, he arose as the Lord of the maṇḍala and taught the tantras of the Conqueror, including the *Establishment of the Three Commitments* of the teacher and the explanation of the maṇḍala.

The [33] abbreviated, medium and extensive *Golden Light Sūtras* are included within this category because they teach similar subjects. Some claim that these texts are sūtras, whereas others say that they are both sūtra and tantra. The reason we find these views unacceptable is because the *Great Glorious Sūtra* is taught within this group of texts, as well as the *Sādhana of the Four Great Kings* and the methods of drawing their *maṇḍala*.

(2) The overlord of the Tathāgata family is Mañjuśrī. The tantras in this group are the extensive *Root Tantra of Mañjuśrī* in 36 chapters, which explains the 12 deeds of the Tathāgata and so forth, and the abridged tantra in four chapters which gives only the *Sādhana of the Heroic Mañjuśrī* [*Tantra of the Solitary Hero Mañjuśrī*]. In their first chapters, these texts teach the Buddhas' and bodhisattvas' system of dream analysis, together with rites which ensure protection from lightning, and the *sādhana* of the nine deities of Jambhala. In the fourth chapter are taught rituals of subjugation which rely on Kurukullā, and methods of a protective circle in which are united the male and female entourages of yakṣas.

Some say that the practice taught in the *Heart of Wisdom Sūtra*, in which the meditator first dissolves the world and all its inhabitants into clear light and then sees himself arising as Buddha Śākyamuni from that state of emptiness, is to be included within this division of scriptures. Also included in this category are a *sādhana* by Nāgārjuna[73] which focuses on the Great

Mother (Prajñāpāramitā) together with all the Buddhas of the ten directions as her retinue of children, and a short empowerment ritual said to have been written by Pha dam-pa sangs-rgyas[74] concerning the eight clear realizations.[75] The large and small rituals of the Medicine Buddhas[76] should also be included here, [34] even though they have been classified by some as belonging to the class of sūtras. Ratnakīrti,[77] however, has shown clearly that they belong to the class of Action tantra because, even though they include an ethical conduct section of confessions, they teach a square maṇḍala with four doors and so forth.

(3) The mothers of the Tathāgata family are Mārīci and the five Vidyārājñī.[78]

For Mārīci there are both rituals and a knowledge mantra [the *Chapter of the Tantra Arisen from the Radiant Lady of Illusion* and the *Dhāraṇī of the Radiant Noble Lady*, respectively], and also a text known as the *Seven Hundred Stanzas of the Radiant Noble Lady of Illusion*, which seems to be a mixture of Highest Yoga tantra and Action tantra, as it teaches the generation and completion stages, and the channels (*nāḍi*), winds (*prāṇa*) and drops (*bindu*).

As for the five Vidyārājñī, these are Mahāsāhasrapramardanī, Mahāmayūrī, Mahāpratisarā, Mahāśītavatī and Mahāmantrānusāriṇī. Śāntipa wrote a maṇḍala ritual for these five and also a *sādhana* for their practice.[79] Jetari[80] wrote a *sādhana* for each of them individually, and also a combined practice.[81]

(4) The crown protrusion [deities] of the Tathāgata family are Uṣṇīṣavijayā, Sitātapatrā, Vimaloṣṇīṣa and Uṣṇīṣaprabhā. With regard to the first of these, Indra requested Vijayā for a teaching in order to protect the Devaputra Susthira. This is contained in the text *Dhāraṇī of the Crown Protrusion Victor Who Completely Purifies All Those in Lower Births*. There is also a practice associated with this.[82] The text *Chapter of the Dhāraṇī of the Crown Protrusion Victor of All Tathāgatas and Related Topics* [Toh.596] teaches the construction of the Victorious *stūpa*[83] and the making of the small cast images which are placed inside.

Regarding Sitātapatrā, there are four texts; *Praise to She Who is Unconquerable by Others*, the *Lady of Supreme Attainment* and two smaller texts called *Arisen from the Land of Gods*, [35] one of which has an introductory section, and one of which does not. The first two of these are a little different in their translation but not in their meaning, the second of them being the more accurate translation. Śūraṅgamavarma wrote a commentary [called *Commentary on the Lady with a White Parasol, Arisen from the Crown Protrusion of All Tathāgatas*] to this latter text, dealing with the secret mantra, knowledge mantra, essence mantra and the near-essence mantra. Candragomin[84] wrote a collection of 14 commentaries on this text, including a maṇḍala ritual (*Sādhana of the Noble Lady with the White Parasol Called She Who is Unconquerable by Others*), a *bali* ritual (*Bali Ritual of the Noble Lady etc.*), a ritual for the protection wheel (*rakṣācakra*), a fire offering (*homa*) and so forth. Maṇḍala rites were also written by Vajrāsana, Tīkṣṇavajra and Vajrāṅkuśa. Although maṇḍala rites were also written by Padmāṅkuśa[85] and Vajravarma, these are not suitable to be included within this category because they contain explanations concerning the taking of vows of the five Buddha families and so forth. There are many Tibetan commentaries that supplement the rituals of Candragomin, and there are also instructions for the preparation of *bali* (Tib: *gtor ma*), which are said to have come from India. The first Tibetan text following the tradition of this ritual was written by Pho-rog mgon-po rdo-rje.

With regard to Vimaloṣṇīṣa, texts devoted to her include a method of drawing her maṇḍala using scented water, and a teaching explaning the layout of 108 *stūpas*. There are also two texts by Sahajalalita: the *General Compendium* and the *Specific Compendium*.[86]

Fourthly, with regard to texts concerning Uṣṇīṣaprabhā, it seems that in this case we must take separately the first chapter of the *Root Tantra of Mañjuśrī*. With regard to the text known as *Kālyuṣṇīṣā*, we can definitely say that this was written by a non-human spirit of Tibet. Of this there is no doubt.

(5) There are two texts dealing with the wrathful gods and goddesses of the Tathāgata family: the *Secret Rite of Victory Over the Triple World (Secret Tantra Rite of Complete Wrathful Victory)* and the *Dhāraṇī of the Goddess of Invocation*. [36]

(6) Concerning the class of obedient messengers of the Tathāgata family, there are the *Parṇaśabarī Dhāraṇī* (the *Rite of the Leaf-clad Noble Hermit Lady*)[87] and others.

(7) With regard to bodhisattvas of the Tathāgata family, we find texts such as the *One Hundred and Eight Names of Avalokiteśvara* and others,[88] all of which are to be considered separately.

(8) As for tantras of the nāgas and yakṣas of the Tathāgata family, there are the *Kubera Tantra* [*Dhāraṇī of the Continuity of Wealth*], and the *Arising of Nectar Tantra* (*Dhāraṇī*) which explains such things as water libations and *bali* offerings.

THE LOTUS FAMILY

The second family is the Lotus family, and this will be discussed under five headings: (1) the principal, (2) the overlord, (3) the mother, (4) the wrathful gods and goddesses and (5) the obedient messengers.

(1) The principal of the Lotus family is Amitāyus. Regarding him there are two tantras[89] which came from the impure god realm, and there is also one tantra known as the *Immortal Drum-roll of Amitāyus*[90] which was spoken in the pure land of Sukhāvati (Paradise of Great Bliss).

(2) The overlord of the Lotus family is Avalokiteśvara and, with regard to him, the three volume root tantra of Avalokiteśvara in 12,000 verses called *Lotus Net* was not translated into Tibetan. A shorter redaction of this tantra in 1,000 verses, however, does exist in Tibetan and this teaches two maṇḍalas of 1,227 deities who have Avalokiteśvara as their lord. There also exists a partial translation of the vision of Avalokiteśvara with 11 heads,[91] and the longer and shorter *dhāraṇīs* called *Lion's Roar of Avalokiteśvara.*

(3) The mother of the Lotus family is Ārya Tārā and, regarding her, there is the tantra in 35 chapters [called *Tārā, Mother of All Tathāgatas, Arising of Various Actions Tantra*] which explicates 108 maṇḍalas. Chapter III of this text is identical to the text now known as the *Twenty-one Homages to Tārā.* Some argue that these cannot be the same because [37] the third chapter of that tantra must be classified as an Action tantra, whereas Candragomin explains the *Twenty-one Homages to Tārā* in the manner of the Highest Yoga tantras. This argument is invalid however, because, in the same way, [Puṇḍarīka's][92] great commentary [called *Stainless Light*] comments on the *Expression of the Ultimate Names of the Wisdom-being Mañjuśrī* according to the system of the Kālacakra (Wheel of Time) teachings and [Āryadeva] interprets it in terms of the Guhyasamāja (Secret Assembly) cycle in his *Lamp Compendium of Practice*, whereas the masters Līlāvajra[93] and Mañjuśrīkīrti[94] comment upon that text using the terminology of the Yoga tantras.

(4) The wrathful deity of the Lotus family is Hayagrīva, and concerning him there is the abbreviated *Hayagrīva-tantra* (the *Dhāraṇī of Hayagrīva Avalokiteśvara*), but the extensive *Hayagrīva-tantra* was not translated into Tibetan.

(5) Regarding the obedient messengers of the Lotus family, there are the texts of the *Great Glorious Mother Tantra* (*Sūtra of the Noble Great Glorious Great Mother*) and so forth.

THE VAJRA FAMILY

The third family is the Vajra family, which also has five divisions as given above.

(1) The principal of the Vajra family is the Tathāgata Akṣobhya. The text that relates to him is the *Vajrākṣobhya-tantra* (*Dhāraṇī Purifying All Obscurations of Karma*), which teaches the maṇḍala that purifies the lower realms of existence.

(2) The overlord of the family is Vajrapāṇi, and he has the three tantras known as the *Root Tantra of Vajrapāṇi* (*Glorious Fierce One*), the *Explanatory Tantra* (*Explanatory Tantra of the Secret Mind of the Glorious Vajra Fierce One*) and the *Subsequent Tantra* (*Subsequent Tantra of the Secret Mind of the Glorious Vajra Fierce One*).[95] There are also the *Vajrapāṇi Bhūtadāmara-tantra* (*Great*

King of Tantras, Subduing the Elemental Forces) and the *Tantra of the Complete Vajra Conqueror.*

It is said that the *Tantra of the Complete Vajra Conqueror* was put into 21 verses by the translators, who claimed that it was taught at Bodhgayā. In the view of the *paṇḍit* Buddhaguhya, however, this claim is not acceptable because Bodhgayā is the site of the subjugation of Māra and the attainment of enlightenment. It is not the place where the wheel of the Dharma was turned. If this is the case, where then was it taught? It was taught to the southeast of Mount Meru in the cave of the Vajra Mountain, [38] a place of the Holders of Knowledge Mantras (*vidyāmantra-dhara*). The circumstances of the discourse were that King Ajātaśatru, having killed his father Bimbisāra, had become known as the 'heart of perversity' and many non-virtues were being committed throughout the world. Thus a great famine arose. Because of this, the four great kings supplicated the Blessed One who then gave instructions to Vajrapāṇi. Vajrapāṇi subsequently manifested in the form of Vajravidāraṇa (the Complete Vajra Conqueror) and taught that tantra. This is the manner of its origin and, including the chapter in which the Blessed One says "Well done! Well done!", it has 108 chapters.

(3) The mother of the Vajra family is Analapramohanī (She of the Blazing Flames) and, for her, there is one tantra (the *Dhāraṇī of the Completely Enlightening Invincible Vajra*).

(4) The tantra of the wrathful gods and goddesses of the Vajra family is the *Dhāraṇī of the Fourth Application of the Hearth and Nectar.*

(5) The tantras of the oath-bound messengers of the Vajra family are the *Great Powerful One Mahāyāna Sūtra* and the tantra *Commitment of the Nāgas, Vajra Lips.*

It should be known that the two tantras by the names of *Vajra Hook* (*rdo rje lcags kyu*) and the *Vajra Garuḍa Wing Tantra* (*khyung gshog 'bar ba*) are both spurious.

GENERAL CLASSIFICATION

Now, secondly, I will explain the general classification of the three families as taught in the *General Secret Tantra,* the *Accomplishment of Goodness Tantra,* the *Tantra Requested by Subāhu* and the *Subsequent Concentration Tantra.*

In the first of these texts, the ritual procedures of the maṇḍala are shown in accordance with the system of *kriyātantra,* all the way from the initial blessings of the site to the final bestowal of empowerment. This text also describes 3,500 maṇḍalas based upon those three families.

The second tantra explains the procedures of a meditational retreat for the invocation of the wrathful deity Susiddhi (Accomplishment of Goodness) and provides details of his ritual activities. It also shows the necessity of supplementing the empowerment found in the *General Secret Tantra.*

The third text, the *Tantra Requested by Subāhu,* shows the retreat practice of the deities mentioned in the above two tantras, [39] together with methods for the accomplishment of myriads of profound activities.

The final text, the *Subsequent Concentration Tantra* (*Kriyātantradhyānottara*), teaches general aspects of the path of Action tantra such as the meditative stabilizations of the four branches of mantra repetition, the meditative stabilization of abiding in fire, the meditative stabilization of abiding in sound, and the meditative stabilization of the liberation beyond sound, as well as the procedural methods before and after these meditative stabilizations. This text also teaches rituals for achieving magical attainments (*siddhi*), the fire offering ritual (*homa*), and describes the methods of investigating the sites suitable for meditation.

EXPLANATION OF EMPOWERMENTS AND VOWS

Secondly, now that the inner classification of the Action tantra has been dealt with, I will go on to explain the empowerments and vows. This explanation has two parts.

EMPOWERMENTS IN KRIYĀ- AND CARYĀTANTRA

Firstly I will show how the empowerments are given in the systems of Action and Performance tantra. The ritual must begin with activities to bless the site (*bhūmividhi*), then preparatory practices (*adhivāsana*) and the actual entering into the maṇḍala (*maṇḍalapraveśana*), all of which precede the empowerments (*abhiṣekha*) known as the flower garland (*puṣpamālā*), water (*udaka*), crown (*mukuṭa*), vajra, bell (*ghaṇṭā*) and name (*nāma*) empowerments. After these come the permission (*anujñā*) for the performance of the rites, the prophecy (*vyākaraṇa*) of one's success, the bestowal of the transmission (*āgama*) and the encouragement (*ucchvāsana*). By these methods alone, the empowerment is granted.

The empowerment of the vajra master (*ācārya*) is not applicable at this level, as is seen in this quotation from the *Vajra Garland* [by Abhayākaragupta[96]]: "After receiving just these empowerments, it is taught that one is permitted to listen to, to meditate upon and to teach the path of Action and Performance tantra, but the master's consecration is not explained [at this time]." Also, the masters Buddhaguhya, Lwa-ba-pa[97] and Ratnākaraśānti did not teach the master's empowerment. If we find a contradiction here because the *ācārya* Jetāri taught the vajra master empowerment in the Action tantra, actually there is no contradiction, because Jetāri referred to the permission and encouragement as the vajra master empowerment, but these are not the actual vajra master empowerment in which the three-fold commitment (*samaya*) is conferred. "So," you may ask, "what is the master's consecration of the three-fold commitment?" This consists of: (a) the vajra commitment, in which one abides in the *mudrā* of holding the vajra whilst maintaining the wisdom of one's own mind as inseparable from the Buddha's mind; [40] (b) the bell commitment, in which one abides in the *mudrā* of holding the bell with mindfulness of the emptiness which is the non-inherent existence of all phenomena; and (c) the mudrā commitment, in which one abides in meditation upon oneself as Vajrasattva in union with Vajradhātviśvarī and, ascertaining emptiness by means of this bliss, one unites the bliss and emptiness. These three commitments constitute the actual *vajrācārya* empowerment.

As it says in the *Hevajra-tantra*:

> Holding in one's arms
> The sixteen-year old wisdom [seal],
> The vajra master empowerment is understood
> As the union of vajra and bell.

In the system of Yoga tantra, the first two commitments of the vajra master empowerment are taught as above, but the mudrā commitment consists of meditation upon the inseparability of the profound [emptiness] and clear appearance, with oneself generated in the form of Vajrasattva. This is the essential feature of the *vajrācārya* empowerment.

Although there is a vase empowerment (*kalaśābhiṣekha*) in the lower three [classes of] tantra, the vase empowerment found there does not have the same significance as that encountered in the Highest Yoga tantra. In Highest Yoga tantra, the vase empowerment is conferred by sprinkling water upon the head of the disciple and placing water for him to drink in his mouth. The vase water used in this case is actually *bodhicitta* which has been caused to flow by the heat of great desire from the male and female deities. In the lower three [classes of] tantra, the vase empowerment is given by means of vase water which consists of a flow of nectar falling from the single body of the male or female deity.

Now, although there is an empowerment called the knowledge empowerment (*vidyābhiṣekha*) in the lower three classes of tantra, the conferral of an inner empowerment is not found. This is because this empowerment consists of the disciple being produced from the light of a syllable HŪṀ in the heart of the guru who is, himself, inseparable from the principal deity. [41] The deity then places the disciple in his mouth and sends him through the central channel to his vajra. From there he is placed within the lotus of the mother, from whence he is born in the form of the deity. Following that, empowerment is granted by the initiating deities, all of whom are invited for this purpose. They bestow the actual empowerment by means of *bodhicitta* which is melted in the heat of great desire. They cause this to descend and fall onto the crown of the disciple's head. This empowerment is not found here [in the three lower classes] because in these systems there is no inseparable union of guru and deity.

EXPLANATION OF VOWS

There is no tradition of holding to the vows of the five Buddha families in Action and Performance tantra. Abhayākaragupta, Lwa-ba-pa and Ratnākaraśānti, who are skilled in Highest Yoga tantra, Śākyamitra, Buddhaguhya and Ānandagarbha, who are skilled in Yoga tantra, and Buddhaguhya and Varabodhi,[98] who are skilled in Action and Performance tantra, never mention the holding of these vows in the Action and Performance tantras. Therefore we say that whoever has the vajra master empowerment also holds the vows of the five Buddha families, and similarly, one who holds the vows of the five Buddha families also holds the vajra master empowerment.

Also, in Action and Performance tantra there is no self-empowerment by the guru prior to conferring empowerment upon others. This is because the purpose of self-empowerment is to keep oneself within the vows of the deity and, in order to keep oneself within these vows in the context of Action and Performance tantra, it is not necessary to perform the self-empowerment because there is no vajra master empowerment in these two classes of tantra. In these two classes of tantra there is no vow other than the holding of the bodhisattva vow. Therefore, since the vows of the five Buddha families are not upheld, the tantric *saṁvara* vows do not form part of this system and it is said that any downfall of the bodhisattva vows is counted here as a fundamental downfall. There is, however, a necessity to keep the various *samaya* commitments in order to protect oneself in the Action and Performance tantras.

[42] As is said in the *Accomplishment of Goodness Tantra*:

> The guru who reveals the maṇḍala
> Even if he performs a bad action
> Should never be belittled
> By means of either speech or mind.

Countless other such quotations from Action tantras support this view. In the *Perfect Enlightenment of Great Vairocana Sūtra* we read:

> O child! From today onward
> You must never abandon
> The holy Dharma and *bodhicitta*
> Even at the cost of your life.

So it is stated in texts of the *caryātantra* class, as well as in texts of the *kriyātantra* class. This is because, within both Action and Performance tantra in common, these are the things that must be protected.

In all classes of tantra, up until the fourth, it is said that to one who takes the bodhisattva vows but cannot keep them, and to one who cannot even take the bodhisattva vows, it is permitted only to show the face of the deity and to allow such a one to enter the maṇḍala, but the details of the maṇḍala and its secrets must not be revealed. Also, it is not permitted to grant such a one the knowledge empowerment. It is only proper to confer the empowerment of knowledge upon one who is capable of holding and protecting the vows of *bodhicitta*.

Over and above this, in the two higher tantras it is considered proper to confer the vajra master empowerment to those persons who are capable of taking and protecting the tantric vows. Beyond that, in the Highest Yoga tantra, there are three additional higher empowerments which it is appropriate to bestow upon those persons who are capable of meditating on the completion stage.

STAGES OF PRACTISING THE PATH

In the three lower classes of tantra there is no generation stage. This is because the pure ground (i.e. the mind itself) is not mentally developed into the form of the maṇḍala and deity in accordance with the three processes of death, intermediate state and birth and thus the generation by the mind of the maṇḍala and the deity in harmony with the utter purity of the resultant [enlightenment] is not included [within the scope of the three lower tantras].

Also, there is no completion stage in the three lower classes of tantra because here there is no yoga of the clear light of inseparable bliss and emptiness gained through the absorption of the winds into the central channel. [43] Nor are the pure and impure illusory bodies that derive from that practice to be found here, nor the method of contemplating those illusory bodies with the yoga of penetrating the vital points of the vajra body. None of these practices are included within the three lower tantras.

Certain Tibetan lamas of former times have said that the Action tantras have meditation on the deity [generated] in front, but not the process of self-generation. In the Performance tantras, they say, the meditator himself arises as the divine commitment being (*samayasattva*) and generates the wisdom being (*jñānasattva*) to be present in front. In this class of tantra, however, the wisdom deity does not enter into the commitment deity.

As it is said in the *Compendium of the Vajra Wisdom Tantra*:

> Experiencing fear and grasping tightly,
> Lacking the true bliss of the wisdom being,
> And not having the pride of oneself as the deity;
> This is not the mode of action of the excellent ones.

This kind of religious practice involves a fundamental flaw in its view and yet it is claimed that one who practises in this way abides upon the stage of Action tantra. In Action tantra, it is explained, there is neither self-generation nor any entry of the wisdom deity.

Examples of Performance tantra texts are the *Perfect Enlighten-ment of Great Vairocana Sūtra* and the *Empowerment of Vajrapāṇi Tantra,* within which it is said: "Proclaiming the generation of oneself as the deity, but not teaching the descent of the wisdom being." Also, in the Indian commentary on Kṛṣṇayamāri called the *Co-emergent Light,* in the *Commentary on the Difficult Points of the Secret Assembly Tantra* by Jinadatta,[99] and in the *Complete Explanation of the Condensed Tantra of Heruka Cakrasaṁvara* attributed to Indrabodhi,[100] it is taught that there is no self-generation in Action or Performance tantra. Other authors also agree with this view, and yet we say that it is not correct because, in this system, the practitioner relies on deity yoga and the view that realises emptiness in order to accomplish the religious rites of pacification and the rest.[101]

The necessity of meditating upon oneself as a deity in Action tantra has been demonstrated in Varabodhi's *Condensed Means of Accomplishing the Accomplishment of Goodness,* which quotes from both the *Empowerment of Vajrapāṇi Tantra* and the *Ten Verses on Suchness,* [44] and says that: "It is inappropriate to hold the view that there is no self-generation in Action tantra because in the *Perfect Enlightenment of Great Vairocana Sūtra* and in the *Empowerment of Vajrapāṇi Tantra* it is clearly explained that one meditates upon oneself as a deity." Also, Buddhaguhya, in his *Extensive Commentary Gradually Unfolding the Subsequent Concentration Tantra,* quoted extensively from the *Dhāraṇī of the Complete Vajra Conqueror* and spoke of the generation of oneself as a deity through the six-fold deity process. Furthermore, self-generation and the entry of the wisdom being are explained in Ārya Asaṅga's *Sādhana of Maitreya,* the *Sādhana of the (Thousand-armed) Eleven-faced Avalokiteśvara* by Nāgārjuna and the *Sādhana of the Exalted Eleven-faced Avalokiteśvara* by Bhikṣuṇī Lakṣmī, [102] as well as in the Tārā *sādhana* by Candragomin [called *Sādhana of Tārā Who Gives Refuge from the Eight Fears*] and in the *sādhana* of Vimaloṣṇīṣa by Atiśa [103] [called *Ritual of the Dhāraṇī of Stainless Crown Protrusion*], all of which ritual texts are relied upon as belonging to the class of Performance tantra.

Again, in the *Subsequent Concentration Tantra,* it says: "One should abide on the basis of sound and mind." The commentary, when dealing with the words 'abide on the basis', refers to both the abiding on the basis of oneself and the abiding on the basis of the other [i.e. the deity generated in front]. The 'abiding on the basis of oneself' is explained clearly as the generation of oneself as a deity.

Well then, we must now accept the quotation from the *Compendium of the Vajra Wisdom Tantra* as being in agreement with our own tradition. Why? Because this quotation indicates that self-generation together with the invitation and merger of the wisdom beings are not accepted in Action tantra, whereas in Performance tantra[104] these two are not rejected. Thus there is no fault in this view.

THE WAY OF PRACTISING ON THE PATH

Although the generation and completion stage practices are not found in the three lower classes of tantra, in their place are the yoga with signs [45] and the yoga without signs. Here, 'yoga with signs' means deity yoga performed by a mind that does not cognize emptiness. Signless deity yoga, on the other hand, is engaged in by a mind possessing a clear cognition of emptiness with respect to [divine] confidence, and a clear cognition of the deity and his entourage with respect to appearance. Deity yoga with signs, furthermore, consists of three concentrations (*dhyāna*): concentration on the four aspects of recitation, concentration on abiding in fire, and concentration on abiding in sound. Deity yoga without signs consists of the concentration which bestows liberation at the end of sound.

Now [I will explain] those four *dhyāna*: (a) the four branches of recitation, (b) abiding in fire, (c) abiding in sound, and (d) bestowing liberation at the end of sound.

(a) The four branches of recitation are divided into two parts: the preliminary requirements and the manner of proceeding through the main stages of the practice.

The preliminary rites consist of establishing the general seals of the three families, offering oneself to the Tathāgatas, taking refuge and generating *bodhicitta*. Then, going outside, one blesses the earth and water and performs the ritual ablutions and sprinkling. Returning inside, the meditator sits upon a comfortable cushion, dons a robe and performs appropriate *mudrā* and *mantra* in order to protect both himself and his place of meditation. The *mudrā* and *mantra* required on this occasion are similar to those employed whilst making offerings to the assembly tree (*tshogs zhing*)[105] and meditating upon the circle of protection in the two higher tantras.

Having completed the preliminary requirements, one proceeds to the main part of the practice. Here, for the full meditation on the deity in both Action and Performance tantras, it is necessary to actualise the so-called 'six deities'. [46] This has been made clear by Buddhaguhya who liberally quotes from the *Tantra of the Complete Vajra Conqueror* in his work, the *Extensive Commentary Gradually Unfolding the Subsequent Concentration Tantra*:

> Yogins should first perform the ablutions
> And then, established on the vajra throne,
> Should make offerings and faithfully pray,
> Meditating on the six deities.

The six deities, as mentioned in this text, are: "Emptiness, letter, sound, form, seal and sign; these are the six." Just as it says here, the deity of the ultimate condition (*tathatā*), the deity of letters, the deity of sound, the form deity, the seal deity and the sign deity are the six deities. Here, meditation on the 'ultimate deity' consists of establishing the emptiness ('lack of ultimate truth') of both one's own mind and the generated deity. 'Letter deity' refers to the radiant forms of the long mantra, the essence mantra, the near-essence mantra and so on, visualized upon the moon. 'Sound deity' is the sound arising from these mantras, and one concentrates on that. The 'form deity' arises from the transformation of lights radiating from these mantras. The lights make offerings to the noble ones and fulfil the purposes of sentient beings before being reabsorbed into the mantras in one's heart. The final transformation of these lights into the complete body of the deity is the actual form deity. The 'seal deity' is the blessing of the three places (channel-wheels or *cakra*) of the crown, throat and heart by the mudrās of the three families, and the 'sign deity' is the concentration of one's mind upon the deity and the mantra. In this manner, achieving the practice of six-fold deity generation, one brings the life force under control (*prāṇāyāma*) and thereby promotes the clear appearance [of the deity].

Now, about *prāṇāyāma*: although we speak here of 'bringing the life force under control' and also in the Highest Yoga class of tantra 'bringing the life force under control' is explained, although the same term is used in both cases, the words are understood differently [in the two systems] with regard to their meaning, time, purpose and method.

[47] There is a difference with regard to meaning because, in the *Secret Assembly Tantra* of the Highest Yoga class of tantra, 'life' refers to wind and 'force' is explained as that particular wind which prolongs the lifespan. Furthermore, in the *Wheel of Time Tantra*, 'life' means wind and 'force' is explained as that which stops the movement of air within the right and left channels and concentrates it within the central channel. Here, in Action tantra, 'life' refers to wind and 'force' means conceptualization. The combination of wind and conceptualization must not be allowed to wander outside. Rather, these two must be controlled and kept securely within. That is the rule.

There is a difference with regard to time because, in Highest Yoga tantra, one engages in this practice only on the completion stage, whereas in Action tantra it is practised only at the time of deity yoga with signs.

There is a difference with regard to purpose because, in Highest Yoga tantra, its purpose is to gather the winds into the central channel, whereas here its purpose is to stop the movement of winds towards the outside and thus prevent the conceptual mind from wandering toward external objects. It is through the power of these [concentrated winds] that one generates the clear appearance of the deity.

There is a difference with regard to method because, in the Highest Yoga tantras, one concentrates on visualizing the upward and downward movement within the central channel. Here in the Action tantras, on the other hand, by stopping the movement of winds to the outside and through the power of keeping them inside, one's conceptual mind is forced to cease wandering toward objects and becomes, instead, firmly fixed upon the clear appearance of the deity.

In this way, through the practice of *prāṇāyāma*, one generates the clear appearance of the deity and then performs the mental recitation and the whispered recitation.

With regard to this [mental recitation and whispered recitation] it is said in the *Subsequent Concentration Tantra*:

> Abiding on the basis of sound and mind
> One rests on the foundation of unchanging secret mantra.
> Recite the [four] branches of *guhyamantra* without fault
> And relax when tiredness arises.

As is said here, the *dhyāna* of the four branches of recitation must be performed without fault. [48] The basis [of sound and mind] referred to here has two branches: abiding on the basis of oneself and abiding on the basis of another.

The former means that one performs the meditation of the six aspects of the deity as oneself, and the latter means that one generates the deity with a similar appearance to oneself [in the sky] before one. Abiding on the basis of mind means that one generates the maṇḍala of the moon as one's own mind within the heart of the deity. Abiding on the basis of sound means that one places the letters of the meditation mantra upon that moon disc.

The method of recitation is of two kinds: recitation whilst visualizing the form of the letters, and recitation whilst imagining their sounds. When visualizing the form of the letters, one either whispers the recitation and concentrates one's mind single-pointedly upon the form of the letters, or one merely concentrates single-pointedly upon the form of the mantra with the mind free of agitation and dullness, by virtue of the winds inside being well controlled.

When imagining the sounds of the letters, one either whispers the recitation and concentrates single-pointedly on the light radiating from the letters of the mantra upon the moon disc within the heart of oneself visualized as the deity, or one simply recites mentally whilst concentrating single-pointedly upon the radiance of the letters with a mind free of all agitation and dullness, due to having controlled the winds within.

As for the number of recitations, it is said in the *Accomplishment of Goodness Tantra*:

> For less than 15 letters, or, in general, however many letters there are, one should recite the mantra 100,000 times for each letter. When the mantra is up to 32 letters, it is said that one recites it

> 300,000 times. A mantra with more than that number of letters should be recited 10,000 times.

And it is just as stated here.

As one recites the mantra, if one feels drowsy, yawns, or needs to urinate, expectorate or defecate, one should arise from one's seat and, leaving one's rosary inside, should go outside briefly [49] and then again resume one's seat and practice. It is further-more explained in the *Accomplishment of Goodness Tantra* that, when taking up the rosary once more, it is necessary to resume counting at the beginning.

(b) The concentration of abiding in fire is the concentration of one's mind upon the sound of the mantra which emanates from the midst of a lamp-like brightness upon the moon at the heart of oneself clearly visualized as the deity.

(c) The concentration of abiding in sound is the concentration of one's mind upon the sound of the mantra situated on the moon at the heart of oneself clearly visualized as the deity.

In these two cases, the mantra is not recited audibly but is recited as if one were listening to someone else's recitation. This, however, is not the same as the mental recitation that has been discussed above in the context of the four branches of recitation.

(d) The concentration bestowing liberation at the end of sound is performed by meditating on emptiness, after having performed the previous three [concentrations]. In this regard, it is also said in the *Subsequent Concentration Tantra*:

> The secret mantra practice of abiding in fire bestows attainment (*siddhi*), and we should remember that abiding in sound bestows yoga. The end of sound bestows liberation. These are the three.

So it is said.

> This which has been presented clearly
> In accordance with the views and explanations
> Of the learned masters of India and Tibet,
> After careful consideration of their intentions,
> Bestows the sole eye to perceive Action tantra to its end
> —The source of joy for all fortunate beings.

(This is a verse inserted between chapters.)

Performance Tantra and Yoga Tantra

EXPLANATION OF PERFORMANCE TANTRA

Under this heading it is explained that the three families—Tathāgata, Lotus and Vajra—all possess tantras belonging to the class of Performance tantra. As an exemplary tantra of this class belonging to the Tathāgata family, we may cite the *Perfect Enlightenment of Great Vairocana Tantra,* [50] and the *Extensive Hayagrīva Tantra* as an example of the second family. This tantra, however, has not been translated into Tibetan. A representative tantra belonging to the third family is the *Empowerment of Vajrapāṇi Tantra*, and the list could go on.

All the empowerments, commitments, modes of practice on the path and so forth are, in Performance tantra, just as has been explained above for Action tantra. Now follows an explanation of Yoga tantra.

EXPLANATION OF YOGA TANTRA

First of all I will give an explanation [of Yoga Tantra] in accordance with the various texts of this class, and then I will show the methods of practice according to the viewpoint of these texts.

EXPLANATION IN ACCORDANCE WITH TEXTS

Authoritative texts in the class of Yoga tantra include the *Compendium of the Reality of All Tathāgatas,* the later continuation of that tantra,[106] the explanatory *Vajra Peak Tantra,* and other related texts such as *Supreme Glory* and so forth. The *Compendium of the Reality of All Tathāgatas* explains the attainment of the state of Vairocana in its introductory part, and then proceeds to describe the four-fold method of achieving this state based upon the generation of the wish for its attainment. Similar topics are also discussed in the other texts mentioned above.

Of the four parts of the method to attain the state of Vairocana, the first is the [practice of the] Vajra Sphere (*vajradhātu*), the second is Conquering the Three Worlds (*trailokyavijaya*), then there is the Training of Beings (*jagadvinaya*) and, finally, the method of Accomplishing Attainment (*arthasādhana*). The first practice relates to the Tathāgata family, the second to the Vajra family, the third to the Lotus family and the fourth to the Jewel family. If one asks, "Why are only four families mentioned here, when we know there to be five families?", Buddhaguhya explains that, in order to fulfil the wishes of disciples, the agent of actions is associated with the Jewel family while the activity itself is associated with the Action family. [Thus the two, agent and action, may be subsumed together under the Jewel family.]

In the later extension of the *Compendium of the Reality of All Tathāgatas*, this four-fold method of the four families is explained as being for the benefit of those disciples who are meditating on the inner yoga of the deity [51] and is applied in order that they may attain the supreme attainment. This extensive method also serves to make good any omissions [in their practice]. Also, the four families are taught in the extension of this tantra for the benefit of disciples who are afraid to meditate on the inner yoga of the deity and who rely, instead, simply on the physical activity of making offerings and the verbal activity of recitation. Thus it is shown that these four methods are related to the extensive method of attaining worldly attainments, and as means of augmenting any omission.

Although it is taught in this way, this does not contradict those Yoga tantras which are meant for disciples whose main practice is that of inner deity yoga because, although the principal disciples meditate chiefly on inner deity yoga, there are also other, ordinary disciples, for whom this is not the main practice.

Now, with regard to these four aspects of method; should they be practised by four different types of disciple, or should they all be practised by each disciple in successive stages? Śākyamitra expounds upon this point in his commentary to *Supreme Glory* (*Ornament of Kosala, Commentary on the Compendium of the Reality of All Tathāgatas*) when he says:

> For disciples who utilize the three root poisons in equal measure, there is the family of the Tathāgata. Also, for those disciples who utilize mainly desire, again, the path of the Tathāgata family is explained. The family related to Akṣobhya is expounded as a path for those who utilize mainly anger. For those disciples who make use of ignorance and wrong views, the way of the family of Amitābha is taught, and for those who utilize mainly miserliness and jealousy, there is explained the family of Amoghasiddhi.

[52] Thus we see that these practices are taught for the benefit of four different types of disciples.

Further, in this commentary it is also demonstrated that these four aspects of method are to be connected, respectively, with the Nature Body (*svabhāvikakāya*), the Body of Fully Matured Karma (*vipākakāya*),[107] the Enjoyment Body (*sambhogakāya*) and the Emanation Body (*nirmāṇakāya*). Further, they are also linked with the wisdom of equality, the mirror-like wisdom, the discriminating wisdom and the all-accomplishing wisdom, as well as with the four perfections of *bodhicitta*, generosity (*dāna*), wisdom (*prajñā*) and effort (*vīrya*) which are explained as attainments.

Each of these four aspects has the three meditative stabilizations of the preliminary practice (*ādiyoga*), the supreme victory maṇḍala (*maṇḍalarājāgri*) and the supreme victory activities (*karmarājāgri*),[108] in either extensive, intermediate or abridged form, as suitable for the various disciples. The three extensive meditative stabilizations related to each of the four aspects of method have four divisions: the original root maṇḍala, the maṇḍala of the *dhāraṇī*, the Dharma maṇḍala and the action maṇḍala. Thus, the three meditative stabilizations called preliminary practice, supreme victory maṇḍala and supreme victory activities, are each taught in these four divisions.

In the *Illumination of Suchness* (*Illumination of the Compendium of the Reality of All Tathāgatas*) [by Ānandagarbha[109]] it is said that these four aspects of method are to be united with the body, mind, speech, and activities of all the deities. Thus, the first of these is concordant with the *mahāmudrā* of the body, and the second is concordant with the *samayamudrā* of the mind. The third is concordant with the *dharmamudrā* of speech, and the fourth is concordant with the *karmamudrā* of activities.

Although, in the three lower classes of tantra, aspects of the stages of birth and death of beings within cyclic existence are not included within the system of teaching meditation on deity yoga, [53] deity generation is taught there by means of the five clear realizations which are in harmony with the stages of awakening.

In order to perfect the generation of the deity in this way, it is necessary to seal [the deity] with the four mudrās. How is this to be done? The four seals must be fixed by inviting the wisdom being to be present within the commitment being, but not merely partially. The union must be total, because its purpose is to mix indivisibly the body, speech, mind and activities of the wisdom and commitment beings by means of these four mudrās. This is also the reason for the similarity of the self-generated and front-generated deities. With regard to this, the *Supreme Glory* says: "With whatever seal it is to be sealed, that must possess its very nature." Also, in the *Vajra Peak Tantra* it is said: "Abandoning all distinctions of higher and lower." The meaning of these two quotations is that, in the application of the seals, one should not differentiate between the *jñānasattva* as superior and the *samayasattva* as inferior.

Each of the four mudrās is also said to be of three kinds. Thus there are the four basis mudrās which are to be purified, the four path mudrās which perform the purification, and the four fruit mudrās of resultant purity.

The four basis mudrās are the ordinary body, speech, mind and activities. The four path mudrās are the union of these with the four aspects of method. The first aspect of method is to be connected with the path of the great seal of the body. The second aspect is to be connected with the path of the commitment seal of the mind and the third is to be connected with the path of the Dharma seal of speech. [54] The fourth aspect is to be connected with the path of enlightened activities.

Each of these four aspects demonstrates the three meditative stabilizations. The *mahāmudrā* is important principally for the three meditative stabilizations of the original root maṇḍala, the *samayamudrā* is important principally for the three meditative stabilizations of the *dhāraṇī* maṇḍala, the *dharmamudrā* is important principally for the three meditative stabilizations of the Dharma maṇḍala, and the *karmamudrā* is important principally for the three meditative stabilizations of the action maṇḍala.

The symbolic meaning of the mudrās is that the body of Vairocana is the great seal, his mind is the wisdom [seal] that is free of all conceptualization, his speech has the 60 melodious qualities [of the Dharma seal], and his enlightened activities bring benefit to all sentient beings [as the action seal]. In order to symbolize these, one performs the ritual hand gestures that correspond to the body of Vairocana, and places in one's hands the symbol[110] that corresponds with the arising mind of Vairocana. Then, with oneself clearly visualized as the deity, one places Vairocana's speech upon one's tongue in the form of letters. Then, for the purpose of bringing benefit to all sentient beings, one performs once more the hand gestures that correspond with Vairocana's body. These four are the outer symbolic mudrās.

The four inner symbolic mudrās are the vivid contemplation of one's own body as it arises in the form of Vairocana, the vivid contemplation of one's own mind arising as Vairocana's hand symbol, the contemplation of one's own speech arising as the speech of Vairocana in the form of letters, and the vivid contemplation of one's body in the form of Vairocana bringing benefit to sentient beings by leading them all to his divine state. [55] This is the manner in which one becomes sealed with the four mudrās.

Now, if one asks, "What is the sequence of application of these four mudrās?", according to the tradition of *ācārya* Ānandagarbha their order is as follows: the commitment seal first, the Dharma seal second, and then the action seal, followed by the great seal. They should be contemplated in this order because, as it is said in his text *Commentary on the Difficult Points* [*of the Secret Assembly Tantra*]: "Having gained accomplishment by means of the *samayamudrā*, apply it by means of the *dharmamudrā*, perform divine activities with the *karmamudrā* and achieve the final goal by firmly abiding within the *mahāmudrā*."

Or, on the other hand, according to the tradition of the *ācāryas* Buddhaguhya and Śākyamitra, the great seal is to be applied first, followed by the commitment seal, the action seal and the Dharma seal.

The reason for Ānandagarbha's arrangement is that one must first achieve inseparability with the deity, as this has not been done before, and then one must single-pointedly place one's mind within thusness. That is the commitment seal, and this is shown first. Abiding in thusness, so long as one's speech has not become powerful, one will not have the ability to invoke deities beyond the level of the worldly gods, and therefore the Dharma seal is shown second. The action seal is shown third, and this consists of single-pointedly abiding within thusness in full possession of the power of speech which is able to invoke deities beyond the level of worldly gods. The great seal is shown as the fourth because, until one achieves the complete non-duality of oneself and the deity, one is not able to dwell within this great union.

In the tradition of the latter two *ācāryas* it is said that the *dharmakāya* must be gained on the basis of the *saṁbhogakāya* [56] and, therefore, their arrangement places the great seal first. The commitment seal is shown next because, without the attainment of the *dharmakāya*, one is unable to invoke the deities. The action seal is shown third because attaining the *dharmakāya* enables one to induce those deities above the worldly level to act. The Dharma seal is shown fourth because one must act for the welfare of one's disciples by means of a voice with the 60 melodious qualities of benefitting others.

METHODS OF PRACTICE

Secondly, for the stages of practising the path, initially one must prepare oneself as a suitable vessel. Then, as a fit vessel, one must keep the commitments and vows completely pure. Next, abiding within this commitment, one must carry out, in proper fashion, the procedures for meditational retreat and, after the retreat, one must know the methods for achieving attainments and put these into effect. Thus there is a great deal to be said here on these and other topics but I am not writing all of it down at this time. Instead, the details can all be learned from [Tsong-kha-pa's] *Great Exposition of Secret Mantra.*[111]

I have set down here, briefly and simply,
The significance of the glorious Yoga tantras
In accordance with the clear explanations of the learned
—a treasury of instructions on the realization of *yogatantra*.

(This is a verse between chapters.)

Highest Yoga Tantra

The fourth class of tantra, the *anuttarayogatantra*, can be analysed in two different ways: (a) in terms of the way in which the different names of Highest Yoga tantra arose and (b) by pointing out the distinctions between the two [types of Highest Yoga] tantra in terms of both name and meaning.

EXPLANATION BY WAY OF NAME

Firstly; the terms 'Highest Yoga tantra' and 'non-dual tantra' are simply different names [for the same thing]. Likewise, 'Father tantra', 'yogi tantra', 'method tantra' and '*ḍāka* tantra' are synonymous, as are the terms 'mother tantra', 'yoginī tantra', [57] 'wisdom tantra' and '*ḍākinī* tantra'.

Those tantras called 'father tantra' and 'mother tantra' were given their different names by gurus of the past. The names 'yogi tantra' and 'yoginī tantra' are found in the *Source of Commitment Tantra,* where it is said, "Yogi tantras number 60 million and, in the same way, there are 16 million yoginī tantras." The names 'method tantra' and 'wisdom tantra' are found in the *Stainless Light.* The names '*ḍāka* tantra' and '*ḍākinī* tantra' are found in the *Ornament of the Vajra Essence Tantra,* where it is said that "the most recent of all tantras are the *ḍāka* and *ḍākinī*."

EXPLANATION BY WAY OF DISTINCTION

Secondly, I will show the difference between the pairs [of Highest Yoga] tantra by raising particular points of controversy, and then I will explain the various views concerning these.

If the texts of *anuttarayogatantra* may be divided into method and wisdom categories, then one may ask whether the texts of those two divisions are really tantras of inseparable method and wisdom. If both method and wisdom are not found together in each category, then the significance of the method tantras would be distinct and separate from that of the wisdom tantras and it must follow that the two types of tantra would stand in contradiction to the tantric ideal which is based on the inseparability of the two. This being so, the tantras could not be classified as texts possessing inseparable method and wisdom. This plainly stands in contradiction to the Highest Yoga tantra explanation of the meaning of yoga as given in the *Subsequent Tantra of the Secret Assembly* where it says: "Yoga is so called because of the union of wisdom and method."

I will now explain the various views on this controversy. This will be discussed in two parts; the views of other schools, and the view of our own school.

VIEWS OF OTHER SCHOOLS

[58] Regarding others' views, it has been said by some Tibetan lamas that the Highest Yoga tantra is divided into three classes: father tantra,

mother tantra and non-dual tantra. The distinctions between these three boil down to differences in their mode of expression, differences in their definitions of the words used, differences in the arrangement of both speech and activities, and differences in the disciples who request [the teachings].

With regard to the mode of expression, a father tantra is defined as a text that explains the meaning of *evaṁ mayā śrutam* ("Thus have I heard"), such as, for example, the *Secret Assembly Tantra*. The definition of a mother tantra is that it takes as its subject for discussion the bliss of the supreme secret, such as, for example, the *Supreme Bliss Tantra*.[112] The definition of a non-dual tantra is that it discusses both of these subjects together, such as, for example, the *Hevajra Tantra*. In the two-fold root tantra of Hevajra we read the words: "Thus have I heard." The significance of these words is expounded in the uncommon explanatory tantra (*Vajra Tent Tantra*) whilst, in the common explanatory *Union Tantra*, their meaning is taught together with the bliss of the supreme secret.

Secondly, distinguishing the texts according to the meaning of their words relates either to the generation stage or to the completion stage. In the first case, the definition of a father tantra is that it presents mainly male deities and entourage, whereas a mother tantra will display mainly female deities and entourage. The definition of a non-dual tantra is that it shows both. Examples are as before. In the second case, the definition of a mother tantra is that it describes the manifest maṇḍala and entourage, whereas a father tantra deals predominantly with the subtle *bindu* (blood and semen). That which describes both is a non-dual tantra.

Thirdly, the distinction based upon both speech and activities together is as follows: any tantra which explains the personal aggregates (*skandha*), sense spheres (*dhātu*) and sense organs with their objects (*āyatana*) is a father tantra, whereas one which describes the arrangement of the channels is a mother tantra. A non-dual tantra deals with both.

[59] The fourth distinction, in terms of the disciple who makes the request, considers father tantras to be those requested by male deities and mother tantras to be those requested by female deities. Non-dual deities are given at the request of both as, for example, the *Hevajra Tantra* in which the first section is requested by Vajragarbha and the second by Nairātmyā.[113]

So it is said, but we refute these views. In the first place, the distinction of names is untenable because, in keeping with this definition, the *Supreme Bliss Tantra* would have to be classified as a non-dual tantra because, in the root tantra, the bliss of the supreme secret is explained whereas, in the uncommon explanatory tantra *Explication of the Highest Tantra*, 'thus have I heard' is explained. Also, in the common explanatory *Union Tantra*, these two topics are both explained.

The second and third distinctions are also untenable because, once again, according to their way of reasoning the *Supreme Bliss* would have to be classified as a non-dual tantra.

The distinction based upon the interlocutor must also be wrong because, in accordance with this definition, the *Secret Assembly Tantra* would have to be classified as non-dual, since the root tantra is requested by a male deity and the explanatory tantra by a female.

Furthermore, some say that the division of Highest Yoga tantra into three groups has a provisional purpose (*neyārtha*) whilst, in the final analysis (*nītārtha*), all Highest Yoga tantras must be non-dual and the three categories cannot be accepted separately because they contradict each other.

Also, Kṛṣṇācārya [114] says, "In terms of the generation and completion stages, [60] the yogin is shown as generation and completion is taught as yoginī." On the basis of what is said here, any text which describes the generation stage is a father tantra while any text which describes the completion stage is a mother tantra. But this is not correct because, for example, in the *Secret Assembly Tantra* both generation and completion stages are shown in full. The *Secret Assembly Tantra* further explains that a father tantra is defined as one having the practice of the generation of the illusory body (*māyādeha*) from the four emptinesses, whereas a mother tantra reveals the stages of arousing the bliss of the innate (*sahajānanda*) through the profound contemplation of thusness which is complete from the very beginning.

THE VIEW OF OUR OWN SCHOOL

Now, secondly, I will state the view of our own school on this matter. When we speak of 'method' in the context of tantras of non-dual method and wisdom, although that method has the same name as the method which is spoken of in the method tantras, the meaning is not the same. 'Method', in the context of the non-dual tantras, refers to the co-emergent bliss, whereas, in the method tantras, the 'method' that is spoken of is the illusory body.

Similarly, although the 'wisdom' that is spoken of in the tantras of non-dual method and wisdom and the 'wisdom' that is spoken of in the wisdom tantras have the same name, the meaning in each case is different. When we speak of wisdom in the context of the non-dual tantras, this refers simply to the mind that cognizes emptiness, whereas, in the wisdom tantras, wisdom means the inseparable bliss and emptiness which is the realization of emptiness by means of co-emergent bliss.

The significance of the words 'wisdom and method' and 'non-dual' withinin the non-dual tantras are explained in the *Stainless Light*: "In its own natural state, everything consists of the method and wisdom of the Yoga tantras." In order that we may comprehend this, it is said in the *Hevajra Tantra*:

> '*He*' means great compassion, and '*vajra*' means wisdom.
> This tantra has the nature of wisdom and method.
> Listen and I will explain.

[61] Also, it is said in the *Wheel of Time Tantra*:

> If there is no yoga of the body as skilful method
> Wisdom alone will not effect the transformation.
> Wisdom and method together in union
> Is the yoga the Buddha taught.

Again, in the *Subsequent Tantra of the Secret Assembly*, it says 'wisdom and method together' and so forth. These three quotations clearly show the intention.

DIFFERENTIATING BETWEEN FATHER AND MOTHER TANTRAS

Well then, how can father and mother tantras be differentiated? Generally, the difference between these two may be discerned from the point of view of the stages of generation—in terms of whether or not the aspect of the deity's form with face and hands and so forth purifies the intermediate state. In particular, however, the distinction between them is to be understood with respect to the completion stage. Thus, a mother tantra primarily emphasizes the wisdom of inseparable bliss and emptiness through the cognition of *śunyatā* on the basis of co-emergent bliss, which is the cause that corresponds with the Truth Body. It does not lay stress on the attainment of the pure and impure illusory bodies which are the causes that correspond with the Form Body. Such a Highest Yoga tantra or a similar tantra is identified as a mother tantra. A father tantra, on the other hand, is distinguished as one which emphasizes not only the inseparable bliss and emptiness which is the cause that corresponds with the Truth Body, but also the method of attaining the pure and impure illusory bodies as a causal path that corresponds with the Form Body. Such a Highest Yoga tantra or a similar tantra is classified as a father tantra.

The 'wisdom' referred to in the term 'wisdom tantra' is said to be the wisdom of inseparable bliss and emptiness. [62] Thus, as it is said in the *Vajra Tent Tantra*:

> The Blessed One was asked, "Why is it called yoginī tantra?" and the holder of the vajra replied, "It is because of the method of transcendental wisdom that it is known as yoginī. By the union of *mahāmudrā* one enters suchness, and this is known as the tantra of the yoginīs."

The meaning of these words is that, by means of the great seal which, itself, is the inseparable union of co-emergent bliss and emptiness, one enters the sphere of the ultimate transcendental wisdom of the natural condition. This is the causal method corresponding to the Truth Body and was taught by the Buddha as the empty characteristic of wisdom. For that reason it is known as 'mother'.

The 'method' referred to in the term 'method tantra' is the illusory body. This is stated in the *Ocean of Ḍākinīs Tantra*:

> All the yogas in the King of Tantras
> Can be discriminated and their rituals known.
> I teach the clear light and illusion—
> Illusion is explained for the world.

Now, as for the meaning of the word 'explained' in this quotation: where is it said? In the King of Yoga tantras. What is it that is being explained? It is the illusory body. To whom is it explained? To the disciples of the world. Who explains it? The Teacher himself. How does he explain it? He says that the illusory body is attained by means of the four progressive emptinesses, that is, by means of the clear light and the three preceding emptinesses. Who will achieve this attainment? One who thoroughly understands the subjects taught in this tantra together with the specific characteristics of their rituals.

SUMMARY OF FATHER TANTRA

[63] There are three kinds of father or sacred method tantras: tantras that utilize the methods of desire, hatred and ignorance. An example of the first is the *Secret Assembly Tantra.* Examples of the second include the *Tantra of the Destroyer of the Lord of Death* and for the third there are the *Great King of Tantras, Vajra Arali* and so forth. These examples have been taken from the teachings of Bu-ston rin-po-che.[115]

DESTROYER OF THE LORD OF DEATH TANTRA

Further, with regard to those tantras pertaining to the Destroyer of Yama, the Lord of Death, there are three divisions: the Black Enemy of the Lord of Death (Kṛṣṇayamāri), the Red Executioner of the Lord of Death (Raktayamāntaka) and the Terrifier (Bhairava). Each of these three, furthermore, has both a root tantra and a condensed tantra. From among these, the extensive root tantra of the Black Enemy of the Lord of Death has 25,000 verses, and the two extensive root tantras of the Red Executioner of the Lord of Death are about the same length. These are said to be in Oḍḍiyāna. Condensed from these there are the *Black Destroyer of the Lord of Death Tantra* in 18 chapters, and the *Red Destroyer of the Lord of Death Tantra* in nine chapters, both of which have been translated into Tibetan.

In a similar way, the extensive root tantra called *Vajra Terrifier, Opponent of the Lord of Death* contains 300 chapters in 100,000 verses, and it remains in Oḍḍiyāna, while the seven chapters extracted from this have been translated into Tibetan. It is said that these seven chapters have not been condensed from the root tantra, but rather constitute a separate text which was brought from Oḍḍiyāna by the *mahāsiddha* Lalitavajra.[116] In fact, however, they are a part of the extensive root tantra in the same way that the abbreviated empowerment of the Wheel of Time is taken from the root text. Counted together with these seven there are the *Musk Shrew Chapter,* [64] the *Three Chapter Explanatory Tantra* and the *History Chapter.* There is also another chapter on the Lord of Death, King of Dharma (Yamadharmarāja), and a section on attainments in the *Opponent of the Lord of Death Tantra* (called *Ritual Procedure Tantra of the Vajra Terrifier*), which covers four chapters.[117]

As for the seven chapters themselves, in the first of these the maṇḍala is revealed, the second chapter deals with the accomplishment of all desires, in the third chapter the mantras are assembled and arranged upon a device wheel (*yantra*), the fourth chapter concerns the meditation of deity yoga, the fifth chapter is on drawing the sacred image, the sixth on the methodology of the fire offerings, and the seventh is a chapter on the yoga of divine activity.[118]

In the extensive root tantra [the maṇḍala is described in many ways], the Solitary Hero (*ekallavīra*) Vajra Terrifier [is the smallest, and then there are] a retinue of eight zombies (*vetāla*), nine deities, 13 deities and 49 deities. There is no doubt that all of these are shown in the extensive root tantra, but in the text of the *Seven Chapters* only the eight zombie maṇḍala and the 49 deity maṇḍala are shown clearly. Although the 13 deities are not explicitly discussed in this text, however, their significance is fully explained in the [third] chapter on the *yantra* wheel.

The purpose of both root and explanatory tantras is to expound the steps of the four yogas of the completion stage.

Now, if one asks, "Who taught this tantra?", it was taught by Buddha Mañjuśrī as he remained within the meditative *samādhi* called Vajra which Destroys all Māras, Slayer of the Lord of Death (*sarvamārasūdanayamāntakavajra*). [65] The reason he taught this tantra was in order to subdue Yama Dharmarāja, the Lord of Death, who held sway over 16 gateless iron cities. This has been explained in the *History Chapter.*

Just as the *Supreme Bliss Tantra* was requested by Vajravārāhī, so too, this tantra was requested by Vajravetālī (Adamantine Zombie), consort of the Vajra Terrifier. In the root tantra it is written: "The glorious Viśvarūpā (Universal Form) respectfully requested the Vajra Terrifier," and it is said that Vajravetālī, Viśvarūpā and Vajraḍākinī are three names for the same goddess.

With regard to the time of the teaching, there are two traditions. Some say that it was taught during the second era (*dvāparayuga*), at the time of the subjugation of Īśvara, whilst others contend that it has been taught only during this present era of strife (*kaliyuga*). It was taught in the place where most of the Highest Yoga tantras were taught, glorious Dhānyakaṭaka.[119] This is true in outward appearance, but the secret place where this tantra was taught was within the lotus of the consort Vajraḍākinī, as has been said in the great Wheel of Time commentary, *Stainless Light*, in a quotation from the intro-ductory preamble of the root tantra: 'Abiding in the lotus of the Vajraḍākinī.'

[66] In the succession of those who have elucidated the intention [of this tantra], both Akṣobhyavajra and Kumāravajra have written commentaries on the difficult points of the *Vajra Terrifier*. There are also two commentaries on the *Black Enemy of the Lord of Death* called the *Co-emergent Light* and the *Precious Lamp*. Bu-ston rin-po-che maintains that the first of these was written by the *mahāsiddha* Śrīdhara and the second by Śāntipa (Ratnākaraśānti).

As for *sādhanas*, there are *sādhanas* of the Red and the Black by Śrīdhara and by *Jagbhadra ('Gro-bzang snying-po, who wrote *Sādhana of the Destroyer of the Lord of Death*) and so forth. There is also a *sādhana* of the eight zombie maṇḍala of Vajrabhairava written by Lalitavajra (possibly the *Sādhana of the Glorious Vajra Terrifier*, Toh.1999), and a *sādhana* of the 49 deities (*Sādhana of the Forty-nine Deities of Vajrabhairava*, Toh.1998). Amoghavajra[120] wrote a *sādhana* for the nine deities (*Brief Heroic Mind, Sādhana and Ritual of Activities of the Glorious Vajra Terrifier*) and for the solitary hero Vajra Terrifier there are *sādhanas* by Śrīdhara (*Buffalo-face Sādhana*), Śrībhadra (*Condensed Sādhana of the Glorious Vajra Terrifier*), Śāntijñāna (*Ritual of Accomplishment*), Mañjuśrījñāna (*Sādhana of the Vajra Terrifier*) and *ācārya* Mañjughoṣa (*Sādhana of the Vajra Terrifier with One Face and Two Hands*). By the term 'solitary hero' (*ekallavīra*) we understand only the father deity, as opposed to the 'co-emergent' (*sahaja*) form of the union of the father and mother deities.

From among the Tibetan commentaries, the five most popular traditions are those of Rva,[121] sKyo[122] and Zhang,[123] plus the gNyos and Mal.[124] From among these, the tradition of Rva lo-tsā-wa is considered to be the best. This translator wrote a series of five clear realizations, which are the *Vajra Terrifier with one face and two arms*, the *Vajra Terrifier with one face and four arms*, the *Vajra Terrifier with three faces and six arms*, the *Solitary Hero Opponent of the Lord of Death* with the complete number of faces and arms, and a clear realization of the 13 deities. The *paṇḍit* Vairocanarakṣita[125] composed a *sādhana* concerning the 13 deities called the *Vajra Light* [67] and it is believed that Rva lo-tsā-wa rDo-rje grags, gNyos lo-tsā-wa Yon-tan grags and others also composed *sādhanas* concerning these 13 deities.

As has been explained above, this tantra is derived from the chapter on the wheel of devices. Within this chapter it is said that, by combining, inviting and mixing the mantras, one should generate 12 deities and four skull-cups on 16 seats. We must understand, however, that this is done mainly by the Vajra Terrifier himself.

SUMMARY OF MOTHER TANTRA

Texts identified as belonging to the category of mother tantra include the *Two Examinations* (*dviparīkṣita*, i.e. the two sections of the *Hevajra Tantra*), the *Supreme Bliss Tantra*, the *Wheel of Time Tantra* and so forth. Among these, the *Two Examinations* stresses the special nature of co-emergent great bliss, whereas *Supreme Bliss* emphasizes mainly the characteristics of the external action seal and the skilful methods that rely upon her. The *Wheel of Time* lays most stress on the immutable supreme bliss, which is caused by the union of form and emptiness of the inner wisdom seal.

THE HEVAJRA TANTRA

For Hevajra there is a root tantra, as well as exegetical and related tantras. In [Abhayākaragupta's] commentary *Vajra Garland* it is said that the root tantra was taught in Jambudvīpa, but Karmadhenu adds that, after this tantra was taught once in Jambudvīpa, it was then taught in the peerless pure land and then once again in the Realm of Controlling Others' Emanations (*paranirmitavaśavartin*). This root tantra is extracted from the extensive tantra of Hevajra in 500,000 verses, and it is this root tantra [in two parts] that is known as the *Two Examinations.* With regard to exegetical tantras, there is a commentary on the extensive root tantra, another on the continuation tantra (*uttaratantra*) called *Drop of the Great Seal* [68] and, commenting on the abbreviated *Two Examinations,* there are the common exegetical *Union Tantra,* and the unshared [with other tantras] explanatory tantra *Vajra Tent Tantra.* As for related tantras, these include the *Drop of Wisdom Tantra* and the *Lamp of Suchness, Great Yoginī Tantra.*

The explanatory *Union Tantra* comments on both *Hevajra* and *Supreme Bliss*. The way in which it explains the generation stage of the *Hevajra Tantra* is by means of the deity with one face and two arms without consort, as well as by means of the deity with 16 arms. This text also teaches a maṇḍala of 17 deities, a Nairātmyā maṇḍala of 23 goddesses and so on, the appropriate places [and times] and so on for the assembly and performance of the rites, and it explains a little about the ripening empowerments. With regard to the completion stage, it covers, in general, the arrangement of the channels and, in particular, it explains extensively the process of inner fire (*caṇḍālī*) through placing the seed syllables upon the four channel-wheels (*cakra*), as explained in the root tantra.

The manner in which the exegetical *Vajra Tent Tantra* explains the stages of generation and completion for Hevajra is as follows: the generation stage is explained by means of the six branches of yoga and the three meditative stabilizations. The protection wheel of the ten wrathful deities is also explained, as well as the ascending sequence of meditation on the elements. The questions of the *nāga* king Unwarmed[126] are answered, the blessings of body, speech and mind are given, and the triple stack heroic minds[127] and other themes are explained. The completion stage is explained in terms of the wisdom of great bliss in all its parts from beginning to end, which is also the chief subject matter of the root tantra.

The *mahāsiddhas* Saroruha[128] and Ḍombipa[129] both teach the completion stage Hevajra in terms of these six branches of yoga, following the method of the *Vajra Tent Tantra.*

[69] Although it is necessary to learn in detail the manner of attaining the illusory body from the teachings of father tantra, even so, by quotations such as "Like an illusion and a dream, it is like the intermediate state," we can understand it briefly.

During the course of successive interpretations of [the Buddha's] thought, two distinct traditions of explanation have developed. The bodhisattva Vajragarbha[130] wrote one commentary (the *Very Extensive Commentary on the Condensed Meaning of the Hevajra Tantra*), and his tradition is followed by Nāropa[131] in his commentary on the difficult points, *Single Vajra Word of the Oral Lineage,* and by others. The commentaries in this tradition are in accordance with the explanations of the *Wheel of Time Tantra.* The second tradition follows those commentaries that were written by Indian paṇḍits before the three cycles of the *Vimalaprabhā* appeared in India from Śambhala. In this tradition there is a commentary called *Lotus Bearer* by the *mahāsiddha* Saroruha, who was a disciple of Anaṅgavajra,[132] and a commentary called *Kumutri* (*Lily Commentary*) written by the scholar Durjayacandra,[133] a holder of the oral tradition of Ḍombipa, a disciple of the *mahāsiddha* Virūpa.[134] Our own school explains the meaning of the *Two Examinations* in reliance on both of those traditions.

THE SUPREME BLISS TANTRA

For Supreme Bliss there are also root tantras, exegetical tantras and supplementary tantras. The extensive root *Abhidhānottara Tantra* in its full version consists of 300,000 verses, and from this a 100,000 verse version has been condensed. Then there is another more condensed version that consists of 700 verses contained within 51 chapters. These are the three root tantras.

[70] As for exegetical tantras, according to Jyotirājacandra (sKar-rgyal zla-ba) there are four of these: "The *Exaltation of Vajravārāhī,* the *Conduct of the Yoginī,* the *Explication of the Highest Tantra* and the *Embrace of the Four Yoginīs Tantra* are the four to be known as explanatory tantras." As he says, for Supreme Bliss there are the four uncommon tantras: the *Source of Commitment Tantra,* the *Explication of the Highest Tantra,* the *Vajraḍāka Tantra* and the *Conduct of the Yoginī,* and these together with the common explanatory *Union Tantra* make five. The *Exaltation of Vajravārāhī* is not included here because it seems that this text is simply the third chapter extracted from the 12 chapters of the *Explication of the Highest Tantra* and is not a separate text.

The supplementary tantras are the *Ocean of Ḍākinīs Tantra*, the *Embrace of the Four Yoginīs Tantra* and the *Exaltation of Heruka*, these three.

Now, as for the manner in which the explanatory tantras comment on the root tantra, this is explained under three headings: (1) recognizing the main purpose of explaining the root tantra, (2) the way it is explained in the uncommon explanatory tantras, and (3) the way it is explained in the common explanatory tantra.

(1) Although there are many reasons for explaining the root tantra, the main points are related to the completion stage yoga. In the completion stage practice of the *Supreme Bliss* cycle there are six branches[135] whereas, in the *Secret Assembly Tantra*, the path is presented in terms of five stages.[136] All of these are commented on, because, as it says in the *Ocean of Ḍākinīs Tantra*:

> Isolation and, likewise,
> Concentration, life force and retention,
> Recollection, and meditative stabilization:
> These are the six aspects of yoga.

So it is said. And also:

> One's [71] body is like an illusion,
> Self-empowerment is subtle and this is
> The definitive characteristic of vajra recitation.
> Complete enlightenment is the treasure of the mind
> And, apart from that, what remains is union.

From this citation we may know that definitive signs of mantra recitation is the first stage (*krama*), and this is known as vajra recitation. The second stage is the treasure of the mind, which is seeing [the purity of] the mind. One's own body is like an illusion and, by striving to realize this, it becomes subtle. The blessing of this within oneself is the third stage, which is known as the illusory body (*māyādeha*). Complete Buddhahood is the meaning clear light (*prabhāsvara*) and this is the fourth. The fifth is all that remains, which is union.

Apart from this, commentaries such as that concerning the *mahāyoga* of the completion stage in the tradition of the *mahāsiddha* Lūipa (*Realization of the Glorious Bhagavat*), the five stages in the tradition of Ghaṇṭāpāda[137] (*Five Stages of the Glorious Cakrasaṁvara* and the *Commentary on the Five Stages of the Glorious Cakrasaṁvara*), the four stages taught by Kṛṣṇapāda (*Four Stages* and the *Discrimination of the Four Stages*) and other such teachings illuminate the meaning of this tantra.

(2) As for the way in which it is explained in the uncommon explanatory tantras, this has four divisions. First, according to the *Explication of the Highest Tantra*, the generation stage is explained by saying that the body of

the father-mother Supreme Bliss, the speech of the father-mother Supreme Bliss and the mind of the father-mother Supreme Bliss are each surrounded by a maṇḍala of 28 deities. The maṇḍala of the Solitary Hero and the maṇḍala of 68 deities are also explained in a variety of ways. For example, there is a tradition of generating the deity after generating the measureless mansion and so forth.

The completion stage practice is explained in the fourth chapter and it is at this point that Ghaṇṭāpāda comments on the process of self-empowerment. [72] In the 14th chapter the yoga of inner fire is explained as the fourth *krama* of the completion stage and, in the 25th and 26th chapters, the great yoga of Lūipa is taught.

Secondly, the *Vajraḍāka Tantra* explicates the root tantra by commenting in various ways on the generation stage yoga in its 12th and 14th chapters. The abbreviated completion stage yoga of inner fire is explained in the 11th chapter, and this topic is explained extensively in terms of the four channel-wheels in Chapter XV.

The third text, the *Source of Commitment Tantra,* explains the generation stage in its second chapter, in response to questions asked about it in the first chapter. Meditations are given which accord with the stages of birth, death and the intermediate state and then, in Chapter XIII, the actual meditation of the generation stage yoga is explained in a manner consonant with these three.

In this tradition the simultaneous generation of both the deity and the maṇḍala is taught in a manner similar to that of Lūipa.

The yoga of the completion stage is explained in Chapter III as meditation on the spontaneous arising of the deity. The unification of the meaning clear light as the ground from which the illusory body arises is also shown. In the fifth and sixth chapters, the vajra recitation is explained. In the fifth chapter, the completion stage yoga of meditation upon the mantra seed within the heart is shown, as well as the retention of breath (*kumbhaka*) within the heart. In the 31st chapter are taught salient points of the inner fire practice that relies on the four channel-wheels. Also, in the same chapter, the various characteristics of the four seals are taught and a different method for the enjoyment of each of them is explained.

[73] The fourth exegetical tantra is the *Conduct of the Yoginī*. In Chapters I-XIV, this text explains the generation stage and all its branches, teaching the method of simultaneously generating both the deity and the maṇḍala palace. The completion stage yoga is explained in its 12th chapter, in which are described the innate wisdom and the great yoga of the completion stage.

(3) The shared exegetical *Union Tantra* explains the generation stage in terms of the maṇḍala of the three-faced, six-armed Supreme Bliss with his retinue of 28 deities, and of another maṇḍala with a retinue of 37 deities. For the completion stage, the four blisses are explained as being generated on the basis of the yoga of inner fire.

These above-mentioned explanatory tantras of Supreme Bliss were all requested as teachings by Vajravārāhī, but Virūpa claims that they were requested by Vajrapāṇi.

The place where they were taught was the summit of Mount Meru and the beings to be tamed by these teachings are the residents of Jambudvīpa, as is explained in the *Explication of the Highest Tantra.* However, in the commentary to the root tantra which is said to have been written by Indrabodhi (*Commentary on the Condensed Root Tantra of Heruka Cakrasaṁvara*), it is said that these teachings were given first of all upon the summit of Mount Meru and subsequently taught a second time at the *stūpa* of Dhānyakaṭaka.

> According to the *Ocean of Ḍākinīs Tantra,*
> The time of these teachings
> Is a time of strife in the world
> As prophesied by the *bhagavat* Ananta (Limitless).

This is found in the tantra taught by Śākyasiṁha (the Lion of the Śākyas), and thus it is said that these teachings occurred during an age of conflict.

The graduated series of commentaries explicating the cycle of Supreme Bliss begins with the higher commentary as taught by Vajrapāṇi[138] (*Oral Instructions on the Stages of the Highest Tantra*). [74] Next there are the teachings in the lineage of the father and son Āryas in India. The three *siddhas* Lūipa, Kṛṣṇa-pāda (Kṛṣṇācārya) and Ghaṇṭapāda greatly extended the commentarial tradition related to Supreme Bliss and, finally, there are the 14 different traditions of explanations that have arisen in Tibet in accordance with the teachings of various translators.

THE WHEEL OF TIME TANTRA

In the Wheel of Time teachings, there also exists an extensive root tantra in 12,000 verses, a condensed tantra and a continuation tantra, making three. The extensive root tantra was taught to King Sucandra of Śambhala at the glorious *caitya* of Dhānyakaṭaka, who subsequently condensed and rewrote it. He also wrote a commentary known as the *60,000 Verses*. [Upon his return home, the king] showed this teaching to the people of Śambhala and built a Wheel of Time maṇḍala entirely of precious materials. Following his reign, his son Sureśvara and a succession of six generations of sons continued to reveal the root tantra for 100 years each. At the end of that time it was prophesied that:

> Six hundred years hence
> As the prayers of the sages ripen
> The one known as Mañjughoṣa
> Will appear in the land of Śambhala.

This prophecy is found in the root tantra and, as it is said here, *kalki* Mañjughoṣa propagated the teaching of the root tantra widely for 100 years.

He also wrote a condensed tantra in 30,000 verses abbreviated from the root tantra. Following him, his son Puṇḍarīka propagated the condensed tantra for 100 years, and composed the extensive commentary *Stainless Light* in 12,000 verses.

The manner in which these root and explanatory tantras came to India is described in two traditions. [75] According to the tradition of Rva lo-tsā-wa, *paṇḍit* Cilupa[139] travelled to Śambhala where he heard the teachings from a bodhisattva. On his return to India he taught them to a *paṇḍit ācārya* who, in turn, passed them on to Kālacakrapāda the elder,[140] who transmitted them to Kālacakrapāda junior.[141] From him they passed to the three: Mañjuśrīkīrti,[142] Somanātha[143] and the Tibetan Sangs-rgyas grags-pa.[144] They were received from Mañjuśrīkīrti by the Nepali Samantaśrībhadra.[145]

The second tradition is that of the translator of 'Bro.[146] Here it is said that, on his way to Śambhala, Kālacakrapāda the elder met a bodhisattva from whom he heard both the root tantra and exegetical tradition. He passed these teachings on to the younger Kālacakrapāda, also known as the *jinaputra* Nalendrapāda, and from him the teachings passed to Somanātha of Kashmir.

The way these teachings were brought to Tibet was, according to the translator 'Bro, that Somanātha went to Tibet and passed on the entire lineage to sGom-pa dKon-mchog-srungs,[147] and then the teachings gradually passed to sGro-ston gnam-la-brstegs and then to Grub-chen yu-mo who transmitted them to his son Dharmeśvara, thence to Grub-chen Nam-mkha'-'od,[148] Nam-mkha' rgyal-mtshan,[149] and to 'Jam-dbyangs gsar-ma bla-ma rgva-lo,[150] and from here the two traditions of Rva and 'Bro merged and continued.

According to Rva lo-tsā-wa, Rva Chos-rab[151] went to Nepal and received these teachings from Samantaśrībhadra, and from him they passed successively to Rva Ye-shes seng-ge, Rva 'Bum seng-ge, Bla-ma rGva-lo, Rong-pa Shes-rab seng-ge, Bla-ma rDo-rje rgyal-mtshan, Bu-ston rin-po-che,[152] Chos-kyi dpal-ba, rJe Rin-po-che[153] and thus to mKhas-grub-rje.[154]

Now, with regard to the scholars who translated these teachings: there are Gyi-jo [76] zla-ba 'od-zer,[155] Sangs-rgyas grags-pa, Shong-ston rDo-rje rgyal-mtshan, Shong Blo-gros brtan-pa, lo-tsā-wa mChog-ldan[156] and so forth. There have been many translators.

Three tantras of the Highest class have been analyzed.
In particular, the mother tantras—
Wheel of Time, Supreme Bliss and *Hevajra.*
The meaning of the root tantras
And the arising of the commentaries and the rest
Have been shown clearly as they were taught
By Tsong-kha-pa and his sons.

(This is a verse between chapters.

The Secret Assembly Tantra

Secondly, in discussing the *Secret Assembly Tantra* separately, there are five sections: (1) An explanation of what is meant by the term 'root tantra' of the Secret Assembly. (2) Explaining the greatness of this text. (3) How the commentaries came into being. (4) How the commentarial tradition of this tantra came to Tibet. (5) The actual meaning of these precious precepts.

MEANING OF THE TERM 'ROOT TANTRA'

For the *Secret Assembly Tantra* there is an extensive root text in 25,000 verses. There is also a version condensed from this in 1,800 verses, contained in 18 chapters.

Although the extensive root tantra was taught first, because it was thought to be too difficult for those disciples of the future, who are inferior in both habits and wisdom, to understand immediately, the second tantra arose in an abbreviated form. This later tantra, however, is not the equal of the original root text.

The differences between them can be illustrated in the following three ways: just as the root of a tree is the basis for all its leaves and branches, in the same way, the root tantra is so-called because it is the basis upon which the later teachings arose. It is also called 'root' because it arose first in time. Furthermore, the original tantra is known as the root tantra because of the exegetical commentaries that arose concerning it.

[77] With regard to the first of the above three illustrations, it is also said that the *Secret Assembly Tantra* is the root of all tantras and, with regard to the second, that the version in 17 chapters is the root of the version in 18 chapters. Some people say that the 18th chapter was taught later than the first 17 chapters because it establishes the meaning of these 17 chapters. Yet, with this reasoning, it could be said that all the chapters from the second to the 17th are also later additions, because they all establish the meaning of the first chapter.

The view of our own tradition is that the first 17 chapters must be considered as the root tantra, with the 18th as the *Subsequent Tantra*. The reason for this is that the final chapter clarifies all the difficult points of both words and meaning. It also clarifies the difficult points raised in each separate chapter, by means of 53 questions and answers.

According to Nāropa's commentary on the *Subsequent Tantra* (called the *Condensed Ultimate Meaning, Explanation Showing the Abbreviated Empowerment*) and [Āryadeva's] *Lamp Compendium of Practice*, the *Compendium of the Reality of all Tathāgatas* is the root tantra, the 17 chapter tantra is the *Subsequent Tantra* and the 18th chapter is a further continuation of this. Others reply that it is illegitimate to consider the *Compendium of the Reality of all Tathāgatas* to be the root tantra of the 17 chapter version of the *Secret Assem-*

bly Tantra simply because it is a general root tantra for, if we were to consider it so, this would mean that it would have to be classified as the root tantra of all the tantras of the four classes.

[78] Our own tradition considers that both the *Compendium of the Reality of All Tathāgatas* and the tantra in 17 chapters are united in being tied to the name Yoga Tantra, and that some important points of empowerment and so forth for the *Secret Assembly Tantra* must be understood with reference to the *Compendium of the Reality of All Tathāgatas.* This can be seen from the 16th chapter of the *Secret Assembly Tantra* where it says, "One should know the tantra by its Lord," and, "Drawing should be done with the ritual of the vajra," and so forth.

With regard to the third point [that the original tantra is known as the root tantra because of the exegetical commentaries that arose concerning it]: there are six later commentaries to the *Secret Assembly Tantra.* These are: the *Vajra Garland,* the *Revelation of the Intention Tantra,* the *Compendium of the Vajra Wisdom Tantra,* the *Questions of the Four Goddesses Tantra,* the *Questions of Indra,*[157] and the *Subsequent Tantra of the Secret Assembly.* All of these analyse and comment upon the 17 chapter *Secret Assembly Tantra* as the root tantra.

Of all the commentaries, it is understood that the *Subsequent Tantra* is both an integral part of the *Secret Assembly Tantra* proper and also an exegetical tantra in its own right. The *Vajra Garland* and the rest of the five other texts are all commentaries on the *Secret Assembly Tantra* but are not parts of it. The reason that the *Subsequent Tantra* is considered to belong to both categories is because Vajradhara taught all 18 chapters [i.e. the 17 chapter *Root Tantra* and the *Subsequent Tantra* which is chapter 18] together at one time, in one place and to one group of disciples. The other five teachings were given to different disciples in different places at different times [and therefore they cannot be considered to be parts of the same tantra].

Similar to the *Secret Assembly Tantra* are the *Ornament of the Vajra Essence Tantra* and the *Web of Illusion Tantra.*

How do the six exegetical tantras comment on the root tantra? [79] The special theme of the *Vajra Garland* is to reveal and clarify the hidden meaning of the 40 introductory syllables of the root tantra. The remaining chapters all amplify this basic theme as well as teaching 20 rituals for the empowerment and 49 'suchnesses' for the generation stage, together with six yogas, four yogas and three meditative stabilizations. For the completion stage, the root tantra is explained by means of five stages, and this is the particular way in which the *Vajra Garland* teaches the root tantra. Such a system is not found elsewhere.

The *Revelation of the Intention Tantra* reveals and explains the meaning of the root tantra which is concealed in words that have an indirect meaning and cannot be interpreted directly. This is the special way in which the

Revelation of the Intention Tantra comments on the root text, and this method is not found elsewhere.

The *Compendium of the Vajra Wisdom* explains this root Highest Yoga tantra by means of a teaching called 'the seven ornaments of the oral instructions'. This teaching is also unique, and is not found in the other commentaries.

The *Questions of the Four Goddesses Tantra* clearly explains such topics as the 'life force', the *dhāraṇī maṇḍala* and the meaning of the five precious colours. This method of explanation is not found in the other texts.

The *Questions of Indra* establishes the meaning of the introductory word *evaṁ* by means of questions and answers. Having this as its main topic of discussion is the distinctive feature of this text, not shared by the other commentaries.

EXPLANATION OF THE GREATNESS OF THIS TEXT

[80] The greatness of the *Secret Assembly Tantra* is established by showing the many special qualities of this text. The very title itself indicates that within this tantra are *assembled* all the *secrets* of the body, speech and mind of all the Tathāgatas. Also, in the *Subsequent Tantra* it is written:

E-ma-ho! So very difficult to find!
This is the means of attaining enlightenment,
The highest of the high tantras,
This tantra called the *Secret Assembly*.

Because of the very rare qualities of this text and its enormous significance, if one practises the yoga of the *Secret Assembly* four times per day and listens to the text and recites it and makes offerings to it, it is said that one reaches the stage of 'the Vajra of Enlightenment' (*bodhivajra*) just like Vajradhara and becomes a worthy recipient of prostrations. It is also said that those who practise this tantra will become objects of respect for all who see, hear, think of or come into contact with them. Even those who hold only a fraction of this tantra should thenceforth be seen as Vajradhara, worthy of obeisance. Also, Mañjuśrī himself has praised this tantra with words from his own lips:

This tantra of the assembly of all the Buddhas is
A secret, greater than the greatest of great secrets.
It is the unsurpassed secret instruction.

Indeed, it is said with regard to the coming and going of this tantra that, whether or not the very essence of the teaching remains in the world depends on its existence or disappearance:

When the meaning of this teaching enters one's ear,
As long as it remains there
The precious teaching of the Buddha is alive.

When this lineage succession is broken
[81] The Buddha's teachings disappear.
This should be well understood by everyone.

Thus it is written. And not only are such statements to be found in texts belonging to the cycle of this tantra for, in others such as the Red and Black [*Destroyer of the Lord of Death*] Tantras as well we find the praise:

The ultimate tantra is the Secret Assembly;
Without it no other exists.

Also, in [Padmavajra's[158]] *Secret Attainment* it says:

There is nothing to surpass the glorious *Secret Assembly*,
The most precious jewel of the three-fold world.
It is the supreme quintessence,
The highest of all high tantras.
So long as this teaching and explanation abide
The yoga of perfection will exist.

How can one who is ignorant of the *Secret Assembly*
Ever attain *siddhis*?
Cutting asunder all doubts
And clearing away the mists of unknowing,
This is a basket of Buddha-gems!

In turning aside from this glorious tantra
One becomes ensnared in endless conceptions.
Such an ignorant one, desirous of success,
Like pounding one's fists on the air
Just drinks the water of mirages.

HOW THE COMMENTARIES CAME INTO BEING

Now, with regard to the manner in which the commentaries to the *Secret Assembly Tantra* arose: the three commentaries of king Indrabodhi, Nāgayoginī and Bhūmipati Visukalpa[159] are not found in Tibet. The *Secret Attainment* (*Guhyasiddhi*) in nine chapters, however, written by the glorious lord Mahāsukha, otherwise known as Padmavajra, [82] establishes the purpose of the *Secret Assembly* and the principal topics with which it deals. The order in which the tantra is discussed here is, firstly, the generation stage yoga of placing the letters and, secondly, on the basis of the action seal he shows the symbols of thusness. Thirdly, he teaches the meditation of relying on the wisdom seal in order to stabilize the mind and, fourthly, he teaches the meditation and activity of manifest enlightenment in terms of the great seal.

This *Secret Attainment* is widely renowned as 'the quintessential practice'. It is a later teaching than the other six:[160] the *Attainment of Method and Wisdom* (*Prajñopāyaviniścayasiddhi* by Anaṅgavajra), the *Attainment of Non-duality* (*Advayasiddhi* by Lakṣmiṅkarā), the *Attainment of Wisdom* (*Jñānasiddhi* by Indrabhūti), the *Attainment of the Clarity of Phenomena* (*Vyaktabhāvānugata-tattvasiddhi* by Yoginī Cintā), the *Attainment of the Innate* (*Sahajasiddhi* by Ḍombī Heruka) anld the *Instruction on Reality* (*Tattvopadeśa* by Dārika-pāda).[161] It is also later than the cycle of *dohās* by the great Brahmin Saraha[162] and later than Maitrīpa's 26 categories beginning with A. This text is also important in order to attain the essence of the path—the wisdom of inseparable bliss and emptiness.

The great Ārya Nāgārjuna also wrote a commentary explicating the meaning of the *Secret Assembly Tantra*. In his treatise, the generation stage yogas are as taught in the *Abbreviated Sādhana* and the *Integration of the Sūtras and the Method of Meditating on the Generation Stage of the Great Yoga of the Glorious Secret Assembly*. The completion stage is shown by the five levels of mental placement, with the exception of one lower part (i.e. the vajra recitation). A further commentary is the one by Bodhisattva. As for the lower part of the stages of mental placement (i.e. the vajra recitation), this has been commented upon by Śākyamitra [in his *Explanation for the Oral Instructions on Entering the Yoga of the Great Seal*].

Āryadeva wrote a commentary called *Lamp Compendium of Practice* which explains very little about the yoga of the generation stage but concentrates mainly on the completion stage. [83] Another text written by Āryadeva, which deals exclusively with the yoga of the completion stage, is called *Discriminating the Stages of Self Blessing*.

Nāgabodhi[163] wrote the *Twenty Maṇḍala Rituals of the Glorious Secret Assembly*, a second text [called *Treatise of Oral Instructions, Summarizing the Generation Stage of the Glorious Secret Assembly*] in which he deals mainly with the generation stage and only briefly with the completion stage, and a third text entitled *Discrimination of Karma and its Extremes* in which he teaches solely the completion stage.

Candrakīrti wrote a *sādhana* of Vajrasattva in which he explains the generation stage, and a text called *Commentary on the Six-branched Preliminaries* that teaches the completion stage. He also wrote a commentary known as the *Extensive Commentary, the Elucidating Lamp*, in which he teaches all the branches of yogic praxis for both the generation and completion stages.

There are also five texts that are said to have been written by Nāgārjuna: the *Commentary on the Secret Assembly Tantra*, the *Twenty Maṇḍala Rituals of the Glorious Secret Assembly*, a *Treatise on the Four Empowerments*, *Establishing the Four Seals* and a ritual practice of the syllable HŪṀ (the *Abbreviated Sādhana*). Three other texts claim Āryadeva as their author: the *Oral In-*

structions on the Stages of Realizing Enlightenment, the *Secret Assembly Ritual of Cremating a Corpse,* and an explanation by means of the four syllables YA, RA, LA and VA [called *Gone to the End, Completion Stage of the Glorious Secret Assembly*]. There is also an exegetical treatise called the *Extensive Explanation, Lamp Compendium of Practice,* said to have been written by Śākyamitra. Three texts attributed to Nāgabodhi are: a commentary on the five stages called the *Jewel Rosary,* the *Clarifying the Meanings of the Five Stages* and the *Treatise of Oral Instructions on the Inner Condensed Five Stages.* Candrakīrti is also said to have written an auto-commentary on the root text of the *Ornament for Clear Realization*[164] [called the *Commentary on the Ornament for Clear Realization of the Secret Assembly*] but [in my opinion] all of these texts were not necessarily written by those authors to whom they have been attributed.

Texts which follow the tradition of Nāgārjuna and Āryadeva (known as the Ārya lineage) include Nāropa's exegesis on the *Subsequent Tantra,*[165] his *Clear Compendium on the Five Stages* and another extensive text [called the *Jewel Light*] on the five stages, dubiously attributed to Nāropa.

Further, Alaṅkakalaśa[166] composed a commentary to the first 44 of the 68 chapters of the *Vajra Garland* [84] and there is a commentary on the five stages called *Precious Garland, Commentary on the Abbreviated Sādhana,* which is said to have been written by Śāntipa. Vibhūticandra wrote a *Commentary on the Difficult Points of the Abbreviated Sādhana* and Abhayākaragupta wrote a commentary to the five stages, incorporating the *Abbreviated Sādhana,* called *Moonlight.* Kṛṣṇasamayavajra and Bhavyakīrti[167] wrote commentaries on just the difficult points of these stages. Another commentary called *Captivating the Minds of Yogins, Condensed Explanation of the Meanings of the Five Stages,* which teaches only four of these stages, omitting the second, was written in an abbreviated fashion by Muniśrī-bhadra.[168] Commentaries on the difficult points of all five stages were written by Vīryaśrīmitra[169] and the Kashmiri Śrīlakṣmī [who wrote *Clarifying the Meanings of the Five Stages*]. Commentaries on the Vajrasattva *sādhana* were written by Tathāgatarakṣita[170] and Līlavajra.

Bhavyakīrti wrote a commentary to the *Elucidating Lamp* called the *Explanatory Commentary, Illuminating the Thought of the Elucidating Lamp,* and Karuṇāśrī wrote another by the name of *Commentary on the Difficult Points, Elucidating the Elucidating Lamp.* Kumāra wrote the *Mirror of the Essential Condensed Explanation,* which also comments on the *Elucidating Lamp,* and Kuladhara wrote a combined commentary to the *Elucidating Lamp.* A further commentary called *Explanation of the Condensed Difficult Points of the Elucidating Lamp* is said to have been written by Bhāvaviveka, and there is yet another which is said to have been written by Āryadeva [called *Commentary Explaining the Elucidating Lamp*]. Thus, in general, there are six commentaries to the *Elucidating Lamp.*

Śraddhākaravarma[171] wrote an explanation of the Vajrasattva recitation [called *Very Extensive Explanation of the Vajra Recitation*] taken from the *Revelation of the Intention Tantra.* [85] He also wrote the *Explanation to Completely Clarify the Seven Ornaments, Arisen from the Compendium of the Vajra Wisdom Tantra.*

*Ekādaśasvara (sGra-dbyangs bcu-gcig) wrote the *Secret Nectar of Oral Instructions, Stages of the Path of Vajradhara* and Rāhulaśrīkalyāṇamitra[172] wrote the *Clear Placement in Union, Practice of Empowerment.* Kṛṣṇasamayavajra[173] wrote a maṇḍala ritual for the *Secret Assembly Tantra,* and an offering ritual for Vajrasattva. All of these texts follow in the tradition of the 'father and his four sons'.[174]

The *ācārya* Līlavajra [in his *Explanation of the Guru's Oral Instructions on the Introduction to the Secret Assembly Tantra*] writes only about the introductory topics, without giving any special teachings on the generation and completion stages. His disciple, *ācārya* Buddhajñānapāda, however, was taught the meaning of the *Secret Assembly Tantra* by Mañjuśrī, and this tradition now bears his name. He wrote a *sādhana* called *Completely Good* which shows the maṇḍala of 19 deities, with Mañjuvajra as their principal, and this teaches the yoga of the generation stage. He also wrote a maṇḍala ritual in 450 verses dealing with the subject of empowerment.[175] The completion stage yoga he discusses in his text *Liberating Drop* and also in his *Revelation, on Meditating the Suchness of the Two Stages,* in which he transmits the teachings he recieved from the worshipful Mañjuśrī. According to the *Revelation,* his instructions on the completion stage are based on teachings contained within the *Subsequent Tantra of the Secret Assembly,* but out of the six branches found there he teaches only the final four. The topics of withdrawal and concentration, which are the two he omitted, he teaches as part of the generation stage. [86] Also, with regard to the completion stage, he wrote a condensed technique based on the *Questions of the Four Goddesses Tantra* and the *Ornament of the Vajra Essence Tantra.*[176]

The *ācārya* Ānandagarbha wrote a commentary [called the *Very Extensive Commentary on the Secret Assembly Tantra*] in which he explains the *Secret Assembly Tantra* in terms of yoga.

Ācārya Śāntipa wrote a commentary on the root tantra called *Handful of Flowers* in which he explains that the first chapter of the root tantra shows itself to be a resultant tantra (*phalatantra*) arisen from skilful means. The next 16 chapters are the tantra of method (*upāyatantra*), and this is divided into four parts. Four of these chapters (III, VII, XI, XV), collectively known as 'possessing three [qualities]' (*tretā*), deal with the procedures of service (*sevā*). Another four chapters (II, VI, X, XIV), collectively known as 'possessing two [qualities]' (*dvāpara*), reveal the near-attainment (*upasādhana*). Four (IV, VIII, XII, XVI) are known as 'perfection' (*kṛta*) and these show the attainment (*vratasaṁbara*) and four chapters (V, IX, XIII, XVII) are known as 'happiness' (*nandin*) and these show the great attainment (*mahāsādhana*).

Śāntipa states that all of this is clarified in the *Subsequent Tantra* (Chapter XVIII) *of the Secret Assembly.*

Śāntipa teaches the generation stage in terms of the maṇḍala of 19 deities with Akṣobhya in the centre, and the completion stage in terms of the six branches. He explains the significance of these topics in his seventh chapter in accordance with the *Subsequent Tantra of the Secret Assembly*, a system completely different from that taught in the Jñānapāda tradition, the Ārya tradition or the Kālacakra tradition. Thus, in India, there were many different traditions of commentaries on the *Secret Assembly Tantra*, the most popular among them being the Ārya and Jñānapāda.

HOW THE TEACHINGS CAME TO TIBET

[87] Now, with regard to the manner in which the oral lineage of these teachings reached Tibet, the succession of masters who transmitted this tantra began with the lord Vajradhara himself. Vajrapāṇi was the second in succession, and from him the line passed to Indrabodhi, the yoginī who was an emanated *nāga*, the Lord of the Earth Visukalpa, the glorious Saraha and then to the master Nāgārjuna. Nāgārjuna transmitted it to four of his disciples: Āryadeva, Śākyamitra, Nāgabodhi and Candrakīrti. Candrakīrti passed it on to his disciple Śiṣyavajra and from him it went to the *mahāsiddha* Kṛṣṇācārya, who transmitted it to both *ācārya* Vimalamati and Gomiśra. Gomiśra had five disciples: Yoṣa, Abhijña, Śāntipa, Śrīgupta and Dīpaṅkarabhadra. From Vimalamati the teachings went to Jñānagarbha, *paṇḍita* of the western pure land, and it was from him that Marpa, the translator of lHo-brag,[177] heard them. It is widely known that Marpa held seven different Indian lineages of explanations in the Ārya tradition of the *Secret Assembly*. Although he received teachings on the *Elucidating Lamp* from both the Kashmiri Jñānākara and Nāropa, he did not establish these teachings in Tibet. The oral instructions on the five stages that he brought back from India, however, became widely disseminated in Tibet. This peerless translator travelled to India 12 times, receiving instructions from a total of 70 *paṇḍita* gurus and two *ḍākinī* gurus. With particular regard to the Ārya lineage of the *Secret Assembly Tantra*, however, he received these teachings from the Bengali scholar Abhijña, the scholar from Zahor Yoṣa; [88] the scholar of Kong-ka-ṇa Meghavegin, the scholar of Shrinagar in Kashmir Cundrahari,[178] Jñānākara [of Kashmir] who was blessed by Mañjuśrī, Cahadu[179] from the lowlands of Nepal, Nāgakoṭi[180] from the Fortress of Nepal, the *paṇḍita* Saraha, Kṛṣṇasamayavajra the scholar of Vajrāsana, and Dīpaṅkaraśrījñāna the scholar of Vikramaśila. These last two also visited Tibet and gave teachings there. Marpa received the complete cycle of the *Secret Assembly* empowerments and teachings from each one of these teachers, and yet the three that he considered to be the most important of them

all are Yoṣa, Abhijña and Kṛṣṇasamayavajra. Marpa's teachings, therefore, are based mainly on the traditions of these three.

Marpa had 12 particularly learned disciples: four during the early period of his life, four during the middle period and four during the later. Among all of these, the one most skilled in the explication of texts was Mang-rab seng-ge rgyal-mtshan. The one most skilled in composition was Chos-kyi shes-rab of mGar; the one most skilled in enumeration was rTog dge-ser; and the one most skilled in a number of ways was bZi-dga' of dBus. The lineages of explanation deriving from these four remain to the present day.

From Mang-rab seng-ge rgyal-mtshan the teachings passed on to rTog ye-shes seng-ge, and were then transmitted to rTog mu-ner grags-pa nyi-ma seng-ge. From him they passed to Glan-rtsang-tsa nyi-ma-lcam, and then to both rTog Āryadeva and Thur-lha-ba tshul-khrims-skyabs. Thur-lha-ba passed the teachings on to Thang-spe-ba 'phags-pa-skyabs, and from him they were transmitted to gSer-sdings-pa gzhon-nu-'od. Then they were recieved in turn by Kun-mkhyen chos-sku 'od-zer and Kun-mkhyen 'phags-'od, from whom [89] they passed to the omniscient Bu-ston rin-chen-grub. From him they were received by the glorious holy guru bSod-rnams rgyal-mtshan, who passed them on to the translator Nam-mkha' bzang-po. From him they passed to the unequalled great worshipful Red-mda'-ba.[181]

The next in succession was rJe Tsong-kha-pa himself, and he received the complete transmission of empowerments, exegesis and oral instructions of the *Secret Assembly Tantra* from three gurus: Red-mda'-ba, Khyung-po lhas-pa gzhon-nu bsod-nams (who was himself a direct disciple of the venerable Bu-ston) and Gong-gsum bde-chen chos-kyi-dpal-ba. Although rJe rin-po-che then had countless worthy disciples, the most excellent holder of the instruction lineage following him was mKhas-grub shes-rab seng-ge, from whom the teachings were passed on to rDo-rje 'dzin-pa sbyin-pa-dpal and thence to rGyud-pa chos-rje drung-grags and rJe-btsun kun-dga' don-grub. The direct disciples of these two teachers, and the succession of those who followed after them, then caused this tantra to flourish and spread so that nowadays the whole of this snowy land of Tibet is filled with monks who hold both the words and the meaning of this lineage of the *Secret Assembly Tantra.*

EXPLANATION OF THE ACTUAL MEANING OF THESE PRECIOUS PRECEPTS

With regard to the actual meaning of the precious teachings: the essence of the path consists of two stages (the *utpattikrama* or generation stage and the *saṁpannakrama* or completion stage), and then there is the practice of what should be adopted and what should be abandoned. These two divisions of path and practice will be shown separately. At this juncture I will explain the empowerments that ripen the disciple into a suitable vessel for the teachings, and the commitments and vows which are taken at the time of empowerment.

The Explanation of Empowerment

The explanation of empowerment has six parts: (1) showing the principal features of the empowerment that opens the door of tantra, (2) defining the qualities of the vajra master who grants the empowerment, (3) defining the qualities of the disciple upon whom the empowerment is to be bestowed, (4) defining the maṇḍala within which the empowerment takes place, (5) the number of empowerments and commitments which are to be bestowed at this time, and [90] (6) defining the ritual procedures of the empowerment. [These six parts are explained as follows:]

THE PRINCIPAL FEATURES OF EMPOWERMENT

In order to enter into the secret mantra path of the Mahāyāna it is necessary to receive the proper empowerment in accordance with the teachings of the appropriate tantra. As it is written in the *Vajra Garland*:

The most important thing is the empowerment,
The permanent abode of all attainments.
Therefore, listen well from the outset and
I will explain the significance of the way things are.

At the beginning, when the disciples
With perfect intelligence are empowered,
By the completion stage yoga
They then become suitable vessels.

Also, from the *Drop of the Great Seal*:

When the master first fully empowers the disciple
And then reveals the great secret,
The definitive vessel is produced.
Without empowerment there are no attainments,
Just as there is no butter to be squeezed from sand.

If one confers empowerments without
The oral transmission and divine confidence,
Immediately after death,
Even a master possessed of *siddhi*
Will go with his disciples down to hell.

Therefore, with all effort one should strive
To receive empowerments from a qualified guru.

Again, it says in the *Vajra Garland*:

Just as the milk of a lion
Is not to be kept in a clay pot,

So the tantras of *mahāyoga*
Must not be given to unsuitable disciples,
Or such disciples will immediately die.

In this life and in the future one will be ruined
If the teachings are imparted to an unsuitable vessel,
And the attainments of the master will decline.

Thus, if the secrets of mantra are exposed to a disciple who is not a suitable vessel for empowerment, it is said that for both the master and disciple many misfortunes will accrue.

DEFINING THE QUALITIES OF THE VAJRA MASTER

Regarding the qualities of the vajra master, it is written in Aśvaghoṣa's *Fifty Verses of Guru Devotion*:

Reliable, disciplined and intelligent,
Patient, straightforward and without deceit,
Knowing the application of mantra and tantra,
Compassionate, an expert in the explanatory texts,
Learned in the ten categories[182]
And skilled in drawing the maṇḍala,
The master must know the exegesis of mantra,
Be full of faith and have his senses under control.

Also, in the *Vajra Tent Tantra* it is said:

Skilled in the drawing of maṇḍalas
And having completed the required recitation,
With all root downfalls completely overcome.

Thus, ideally, the perfect vajra guru should possess all the excellent characteristics mentioned above. If, however, all of the good qualities listed in the tantras are not to be found in the guru upon whom one relies, then at least he must have the most important of them and possess fewer faults and more good qualities than oneself. As said [by Puṇḍarīka] in *Approaching the Ultimate Meaning*:

Owing to the time [of the five degenerations],
Faults and virtues are mixed in the guru.
No-one is found to be completely perfect.
But one who is recognized as having superior qualities
May be relied upon by his children.

DEFINING THE QUALITIES OF THE DISCIPLE

Regarding the disciple upon whom the empowerment may be bestowed, such a one should have practised on the path of the outer vehicle and now have strong faith in the special qualities of the vajra vehicle. In the *Vajra Garland* it is said:

> What are the qualities of a disciple
> Who wishes to receive the yoga tantras?

And the reply to this question is given:

> Faithful and full of respect for the guru,
> Abiding always in the practice of virtue,
> With wrong views completely abandoned, [92]
> Such a one must have received many teachings.
>
> Free of the faults of killing and harming,
> With his mind intent on liberating beings,
> Always diligent and very pure,
> These and others are the virtues he should have;
> But the best of all is strong faith.

DEFINING THE MAṆḌALA

With regard to the maṇḍala within which the empowerment is conferred, these are of two kinds. Firstly, there is the type of maṇḍala within which is bestowed the vase empowerment that prepares the disciple as a suitable vessel for meditation upon the generation stage and, secondly, there is the type of maṇḍala in which is bestowed the higher empowerment that prepares the disciple as a suitable vessel for meditation upon the completion stage.

In the first case there are four types of maṇḍala that may be used: the maṇḍala painted upon cloth, the maṇḍala drawn in coloured powder, the maṇḍala generated by *samādhi* and the inner body maṇḍala.

In the second case there are three types: the maṇḍala of the female secret organ, the maṇḍala of conventional *bodhicitta* and the maṇḍala of ultimate *bodhicitta*.

Thus, in general, we can speak of seven types of maṇḍala. Among these, it is explained in the 17th chapter of the *Secret Assembly Tantra* as well as in the *Vajra Garland of Maṇḍala Rituals* that the maṇḍala of meditative stabilization is used only when the master has strong deity yoga, the disciple has very sharp faculties, and when the coloured powders and other materials necessary for the drawing of a visible maṇḍala cannot be obtained. This type is not for general use. Also, it is said that when a beginner is to become empowered as a suitable vessel for the very first time, it is vital to use a created maṇḍala. In this regard, Ghaṇṭāpāda has said that a created maṇḍala can be defined as one painted on cloth or drawn with coloured powder. It is also said that empowerment bestowed within a maṇḍala painted on cloth is the proper method of bestowing the definitive empowerment. That the ritual of empowerment should be given into a maṇḍala painted on cloth is mentioned in the *Explication of the Highest Tantra* and taught by the *mahāsiddha* [93] Ghaṇṭāpāda as well as by Vāgīśvarakīrti, Rāhulaśrīkalyāṇa-mitra and Abhayākaragupta. Even so, the maṇḍala of coloured powders is the best when empowerment is to be bestowed upon a complete novice because, with respect to the vajra guru, it is said that he "should be skilled in the art of drawing the maṇḍala" and, with respect to the disciple, such a maṇḍala prepared of various substances provides many opportunities for the practice of generosity by making offerings. Therefore this type of maṇḍala is most helpful in maturing the disciple as a suitable vessel for higher religious practice.

Although external maṇḍalas, such as those painted on canvas and so on, and the inner body maṇḍala are both essentially manifestations of one's mind, the reason that we speak of maṇḍalas generated by the mind and maṇḍalas not generated by the mind is because of the difference between that basis of practice which is freshly created and that which is not. In choosing between these two, the latter is to be preferred to the former. As it has been said by Ghaṇṭāpāda:

> What are the natures of the two kinds of creation?
> They exist for the empowerment and practice of disciples,
> Not for the advancement of scholars.
> Perceiving their very pure meaning leads to liberation.

In accordance with tantras such as the *Secret Assembly* and so on, empowerments are conferred within maṇḍalas painted on canvas, drawn with coloured powder, generated by meditative stabilization and the inner body maṇḍala. In the tradition of the *Wheel of Time Tantra*, however, the complete empowerment should be conferred only into the maṇḍala of coloured powder. In the *Concise Explanation of Empowerments* it is said: "The seven empowerments should be [94] conferred within the constructed maṇḍala," and Nāropa, in his commentary to this text [the *Condensed Ultimate Meaning, Explanation Showing the Abbreviated Empowerment*], adds: "These seven empowerments should not be bestowed in reliance upon any other maṇḍala, such as one painted on cloth and so forth, whilst putting aside the maṇḍala of coloured powder." From this we see that there is an explicit objection to using a maṇḍala painted on canvas for this empowerment, and this can also be understood as an implicit objection to the use of a maṇḍala created by meditative stabilization. In the *Wheel of Time Tantra* there is no mention of the maṇḍala palace and its retinue of deities being found within the body.

THE NUMBER OF EMPOWERMENTS AND COMMITMENTS

As for the number of empowerments: there are nine vase empowerments (*kalaśābhiṣeka*), one secret empowerment (*guhyābhiṣeka*), one wisdom empowerment (*prajñājñānābhiṣeka*) and the fourth empowerment (*caturthābhiṣeka*), so that all together there are 12. The nine vase empowerments are listed by Nāgabodhi in his text *Twenty Maṇḍala Rituals*, thus:

> Flower, Water, Complete Buddhahood,
> Vajra, Bell, Mirror,
> Name, Master and Permission.

Now, with regard to the order of the empowerments: before the disciple may receive the fourth empowerment, which ripens him as a suitable vessel for the meditative practice of union, it is necessary that he receive the wisdom empowerment that will ripen him as a suitable vessel for the practice of the clear light. This is because the disciple must already have arrived at the fourth stage of the meaning clear light before he can advance towards the stage of union. Further, before the disciple may receive the wisdom empowerment, it is necessary that he receive the secret empowerment in which he becomes prepared as a suitable vessel for the practice of the illusory body with its three-fold isolation [of body, speech and mind]. This is because one must attain the three isolations of the illusory body before practising the four stages of the meaning clear light. Again, before the disciple receives the secret empowerment, he must have received the vase empowerments which mature him as a suitable vessel for the practice of the gross and subtle [95] meditations of the generation stage. This is because, before one can attain the illusory body with its three isolations, one must have developed perfection in the gross and subtle aspects of the yoga of generation. Now, before the disciple receives the vase empowerments it is necessary to enter the maṇḍala. This is because, before the special secrets of the vase empowerments and so forth are revealed, the disciple should have entered the maṇḍala and become similar to the gods of the maṇḍala, with inner and outer potentialities equal to theirs. Before entering the maṇḍala, however, the maṇḍala itself must have been prepared and the disciple should have offered worship, because it is into that completed maṇḍala of worship that the disciple actually enters. But in order for that maṇḍala of worship to be achieved, it is necessary to construct the maṇḍala of coloured powder and then, on that basis, the commitment being must be generated, residing in his residence. Then the wisdom natures of both the deity and the maṇḍala palace must be invited and dissolved into the commitment being and his residence. Before assembling the coloured powder maṇḍala, however, the lines and measurements should be calculated first because, without these guidelines, one may become confused in applying the colours on the ground.

There are two traditions concerning the laying down of the lines. In the system of Saraha, Kṛṣṇācārya, Abhayākaragupta and Vibhūticandra, the karma lines are drawn first, followed by the wisdom lines. They say that the lines should be drawn in this order because the wisdom lines bless the karma lines in the same way that the wisdom deities bless the commitment beings. Thus, just as we first arise as commitment beings [96] before inviting the wisdom beings to come and take their seats; so, too, the karma lines are to be drawn first and then wisdom lines constructed in the sky. The sequence of drawing the lines, in fact, is the only difference between these two traditions which are otherwise similar in all respects. It is with these ideas in mind that the maṇḍala ritual of the *Vajraḍāka Tantra* and many other texts explain that the preparatory practices (*adhivāsana*) should be completed first and then the lines drawn at the time of the actual ceremony.

The *Vajra Garland Tantra,* however, says that the lines should be drawn before commencing the preparatory practices. In agreement with this view, Nāgabodhi says that the lines should be drawn immediately after the site has been consecrated. Thus there are these two traditions, and our own school follows the latter system.

Kṛṣṇācārya and Lva-ba-pa say, "Perfume should be applied to those places where the preparation deities are to be seated." Also, Durjayacandra has said, "Wherever the maṇḍala is to be established, in that circle five perfumes or colours should be applied." And, as it is said here, the drops of perfume and the bunches of flowers should be arranged wherever the maṇḍala is to be constructed. If, however, the lines have not already been drawn in place, then the areas on the ground for the coloured powders will not be known.

Before the lines themselves are marked out, however, the ritual of consecrating the site (*bhūmividhi*) should be performed. Also, that site itself should be examined with respect to whether or not it is a suitable place for the drawing of the maṇḍala, and if it is suitable, requests must be made to the visible or invisible owner for the use of that site and his permission be obtained. That site which has been granted then needs to be ritually purified and, in order to do this, there are the three requisites of the proper materials, mantra and meditative stabilization. [97] There now follows the ritual of 'seizing the site' (*bhūmiparigraha*) in order that that purified land may become the foundation of the maṇḍala. The seized site should next be protected and blessed by meditating upon oneself as the deity. One then rejoices, invokes the deities with praises, offers prayers and draws the maṇḍala. Standing with the pride of one's own divine nature, one circumambulates the maṇḍala and confidently commands all the interfering hindrances to depart. Those obstructors who disobey one's orders must be vanquished by striking them with the ritual spike (*kīla*). Then, by meditating on the [vajra] fence, tent and so forth, one prevents the entry of any further hindering demons. This is the ritual for quelling all hindering spirits (*vighna*).

In short: the necessary rituals are those of examining the site (*bhūmiparīkṣā*), [requesting and] accepting (*upādāna*) [the site from its owner] and then purifying it (*bhūmiśodhana*). The site must finally be fully appropriated (*bhūmiparigraha*) and protected by the rite of blessing (*adhiṣṭhāna*).

With regard to conferring empowerment into a maṇḍala drawn on cloth, *paṇḍitas* such as Vāgīśvarakīrti and Rāhulaśrīkalyāṇamitra make no mention in their writings of the three preliminary rites of examining the site, accepting it and then purifying it. In view of this circumstance, it appears that such rituals are not required here. On the other hand, however, on whatever base the maṇḍala is established, the site must be fully appropriated through meditation on the complete ritual of the deity, up to the section that prevents the entry of any further hindrances. Abhayākaragupta says that this ritual is necessary even in the case of empowerment into a maṇḍala generated by *samādhi*, and the teachings on maṇḍala rituals by rJe Tsong-kha-pa clearly show the necessity of this ritual in the case of empowerment into a maṇḍala painted on cloth, and also at the time of performing the self-empowerment.

[98] When we speak of 'preparation' (*adhivāsana*) in this context, this refers to the rites of installation (*pratiṣṭhā*) of the deity. In the *Twenty Rituals of the Maṇḍala* by Nāgabodhi and the *Maṇḍala Ritual of the Glorious Secret Assembly* in 450 verses by Dīpaṅkarabhadra, mention is made of the installation of the deity, the installation of the earth goddess, the installation of the deity within the vase and the installation of the deity within the disciple. These four installations constitute the preparation.

According to the writings on maṇḍala ritual by Kṛṣṇācārya, however, he says that the ceremonial installation of the earth goddess forms a part of the ritual for the consecration of the site, and is not part of the preparation. Nāgabodhi's *Twenty Rituals of the Maṇḍala*, on the other hand, definitely says that this is part of the preparatory procedures, and not a part of the consecration of the site. According to [Abhayākara's] *Vajra Garland of Maṇḍala Rituals*, it belongs to both sections. These are the three great traditions of explanation.

With regard to the installation of the deity, this certainly must be performed at the time of preparation, and then the installation of the deity within the vase is performed immediately after the maṇḍala is drawn. The *mahāsiddha* Śrīdhara has said that the installation within the vase should be performed after the construction of the maṇḍala has been completed, and the preparation of the disciple should be performed after that. If, on the other hand, the installation within the vase is performed at the same time as the rest of the preparation, then it has more significance. It is also more appropriate for the installation within the disciple to be performed at the time of preparation.

With regard to those points of controversy: the reason why the earth goddess must be invoked during the initial preparation is because it is necessary to receive her permission for the construction of the maṇḍala on the chosen site. As for the installation of the deity, this should be performed [during the preparation] in order that the deity may be requested to bless the maṇḍala of powdered colours when the appropriate time arises.

The installation within the vase at the time of preparation [99] has two parts. The action vase (*karmakalaśa*) is prepared in order to eliminate any obstacles that may interfere with the disciples, the maṇḍala or the offering materials, and the victory vase (*vijayakalaśa*) has the function of conferring empowerment upon the disciples. [Both rites must therefore be performed at the time of preparation.]

The reason why [the installation of the deity within] the disciple must be performed at the time of preparation is in order that his mental continuum may be purified before he enters the maṇḍala.

With regard to maṇḍalas drawn on cloth: whenever one takes self-empowerment or initiates others it is necessary to perform all these preparation rites, with the exception of the earth rituals of accepting the land, purifying it, expelling hindrances and consecrating the lines and powdered colours of the maṇḍala.

According to Nāgabodhi's *Twenty Rituals of the Maṇḍala,* the *Vajra Garland,* and the *Maṇḍala Ritual of the Black Enemy* by the *mahāsiddha* Śrīdhara, it is said that, whenever the maṇḍala ritual is practised, the deity in front should be inseparable from the deity within oneself. In the tradition of the *mahāsiddhas* Saraha and Dārikapa,[183] however, it is said that oneself as the deity and the deity in front should be meditated upon as separate entities. Thus there are two ways of considering this particular issue.

Again, according to Nāgabodhi's *Twenty Rituals of the Maṇḍala,* it is said that at the time of the initial preparation the commitment being of the three vajras and the wisdom being should be mixed together, and also that the deity of the supreme victory maṇḍala, the commitment being and the wisdom being should be mixed together. Further, the maṇḍala which has been previously meditated upon in the sky should be held firmly in the mind and mixed with the maṇḍala of preparation. Then there follow the two stages of mixing the front-generated deity. The first of these stages is the entry of the wisdom being into the commitment being of the maṇḍala of coloured powder. In this case, light rays radiate from the hearts of oneself and the other commitment deities [100] and these transform themselves into the appearance of iron hooks which reach out to the wisdom beings and draw them forth into the hearts of the triple stack commitment beings. Following that, light radiates from the HŪṂ in one's heart and invokes the wrathful king Sumbha. When he appears he receives instructions to invite the Buddhas to come and grant empowerment to the disciples. In order to fulfil this task, the vajra in his hand is transformed into an iron hook which he casts into the hearts of the wisdom beings who correspond with the triple stack commitment beings so that the wisdom beings are caused to merge and abide within the commitment beings.

In this regard, it is written in the 16th chapter of the *Root Tantra of the Secret Assembly*:

> The wondrous great secret vajras,
> Being summoned by means of the Wrathful King,
> When dissolved, one makes offerings to them.

The meaning here is that all those who are called Buddhas are completely gathered together, and all those who reside in the maṇḍala in the sky are invited to dissolve into their respective individual places, and one makes offerings to them. This is the explanation given in the commentary on the root tantra.

The second stage is the abiding of the wisdom being. Thus, from the blue HŪṂ in one's heart, rays of light radiate in the form of iron hooks and present offerings to all the Jinas residing in the highest pure land. These Conquerors are invited to be present in the sky before oneself, and one offers them all the objects pleasing to the five senses. After that, as one recites the words, "Manifesting clearly the natures of all living beings without exception ..." and so on, the deities are invited to come to the crown of the head of each of the commitment beings, and thenceforth to become absorbed into each of them and reside there. The procedure for this is all in accordance with the 16th chapter of the root text within which it is stated: "One should meditate on the whole of space as being filled with countless Buddhas." [101] Also: "All those belonging to the vajra family and so on should meditate with clouds of incense and the tinkling of bells." The meaning of this is that one should meditate after having first constructed the maṇḍala of coloured powder.

Over and above the five mixings mentioned already, there is the mixing of the maṇḍala generated in front with the maṇḍala of preparation, and thus there are six. This final mixing is necessary whenever the empowerment is given, whether it be into a maṇḍala painted on cloth or maṇḍala constructed of coloured powders.

In the tradition of *mahāsiddha* Dārikapa it is said that all the six maṇḍalas are to be combined into one by inviting the wisdom being to be present within the maṇḍala in space, and then this maṇḍala abides as the secret within the commitment being. Thus, at the time of the earth rituals, the wisdom being and the commitment being are mixed, and they are also mixed at the time of preparation. Finally, the invited wisdom being and the commitment being of the maṇḍala of coloured powder are mixed, and this makes six.

In the *Vajra Garland* system, only five mixings are mentioned because, after the maṇḍala of preparation that is generated in the sky is mixed with the commitment being of the maṇḍala of coloured powder, there is no further invitation of any new wisdom being. [In other respects there is no difference between this and the above tradition.]

Mahāsiddha Saraha speaks of the mixing of only four maṇḍalas. Firstly there is the mixing of the wisdom being with the commitment being of the maṇḍala of preparation, and then there is a new wisdom being who is invited and mixed with the commitment being of the maṇḍala of coloured powder.

[102] In the tradition of Lalitavajra (Līlāvajra) it is taught there are the wisdom being and the commitment being of the maṇḍala of preparation, and these two abide within the commitment being of the maṇḍala of coloured powder. Thus there are three to be mixed.

Lva-ba-pa and the *mahāsiddha* Śrīdhara teach only the abiding of the wisdom being within the commitment being of the maṇḍala of coloured powder. Thus in their tradition there are only two to be mixed.

In the tradition of Dinodbhava, no mixing whatsoever is taught in one maṇḍala.

By followers of the Ārya tradition of the *Secret Assembly Tantra*, the maṇḍala of coloured powder which is utilized at the time of empowerment is to be realized in terms of the body maṇḍala, as described in Chapter XVI of the root tantra:

> In the centre abides Vairocana, and
> Akṣobhya and the rest are also drawn.

And for the speech maṇḍala it says:

> In short, all those worthy of salutation
> Are drawn in accordance with the rite.

These quotations show the necessity of the two maṇḍalas of body and speech in the realization of the maṇḍala. The method of preparing the maṇḍala is fully explained in this 16th chapter. If the two maṇḍalas of body and speech are not shown here, they are not shown anywhere.

The supreme victory maṇḍala within the mother's lotus is also shown here in the 16th chapter, both as part of the teachings on the body maṇḍala:

> By deep meditation on the vajra secret
> Offerings are made by the knower of mantra.

And within the section on the speech maṇḍala: [103]

> Within complete clarity in accordance with the ritual
> One prepares the holy maṇḍala
> And then makes the secret offering.

Also, in Chapter IV it says "the radiantly lovely maiden" and so forth, which shows the same thing. When the lovely maiden is mentioned, this is understood by Nāgabodhi to refer to the time of constructing the maṇḍala but, according to the *Elucidating Lamp*, it refers to the time of making offerings.

The rite of purification should be performed with one's mind in the meditative state of clear realization, even in the case of the maṇḍala painted on canvas. This is the proper method. Despite this fact, however, Abhayākaragupta, Vāgīśvarakīrti and Rāhulaśrīkalyāṇamitra all say that during the ritual of the maṇḍala painted on cloth, offerings are to be made but none of the other practices appropriate to the maṇḍala of coloured powder are to be performed.

Some people, when practising the maṇḍala painted on cloth, raise the painted wisdom deity up into the sky and then arise as commitment beings. Since it is not acceptable to say that these painted deities subsequently descend and melt into the commitment beings, this procedure cannot be correct. If the deities of the maṇḍala painted on cloth were the actual wisdom beings, it would be contradictory to invite wisdom beings to descend into such a maṇḍala during the process of its consecration. There is no fault in generating oneself as the commitment being without inviting the wisdom beings painted on cloth to descend. If there were any fault here, then, when practising within a maṇḍala of coloured powder, [104] one would have to be blessed by wisdom beings of coloured powder. Also, when the maṇḍala is drawn, it would be necessary to bless the generated maṇḍala and retinue of commitment beings by inviting wisdom beings of coloured powder. Also, because the crown empowerment of Ratnasambhava follows after the water empowerment of Akṣobhya, then, whenever empowerment was being bestowed upon a disciple, or a statue was being consecrated, it would be logical for one to arise as the commitment being Ratnasambhava and then to be blessed by the descent of Akṣobhya. Clearly this is wrong.

Regarding the maṇḍala of meditative stabilization, practising this is similar to the meditation of generating oneself as the deity.

Regarding the practice of the body maṇḍala, Ghaṇṭāpāda says that the basis of this is "... the nature of sentient beings. There is no maṇḍala of practice other than this." This refers to the practitioner's own body. Of all bodies, however, the body of the vajra master is the most excellent basis. It is by the vajra master that the disciple is invited to enter the maṇḍala for the practice of the retinue of deities of the body, and it is by him that the empowerment is conferred. The disciple enters the maṇḍala by meditating on the deities arising from the guru. The meaning here is clarified by Ghaṇṭāpāda who says, "In the first instance it is the vajra master who is the three wheels of activity, and then the disciple meditates on himself as being like that."

At the time of the practice of the maṇḍala, there are four sets of offerings: those connected with the vase empowerment, those connected with the secret empowerment, those connected with the wisdom empowerment and those connected with the fourth empowerment.

The first set of offerings consists of four kinds of water,[184] the five offerings,[185] offerings to please the five senses, the seven precious symbols of royalty[186] and so forth. [105] The second set of offerings are the inner offerings, which are blessed as nectar. Thirdly, the bliss of the inner contents of the five offerings and the five sense organs is offered together with the great bliss generated by sitting in union with the consort. The fourth offering is composed of indivisible bliss and emptiness, as the subjective great bliss experiences objective emptiness arising as a result of sitting in union with the consort.

There are 17 stages in the rite of entering this maṇḍala of offerings and practice: (1) preparation, (2) blessing, (3) questions and answers, (4) taking the common and uncommon vows, (5) generating the *bodhicitta* of yoga, (6) taking the oath of secrecy, (7) the ritual of entering the gates of the maṇḍala, (8) offering flowers, circumambulating the maṇḍala and saluting the deities, (9) abiding within the commitment, (10) descent of the wisdom beings, (11) the question "What colour do you see?", (12) recitation of the words of the power of truth, (13) the disciple arises as Vairocana and arranges the deities on his body, (14) the actual entering of the maṇḍala (the 13th and 14th stages should be examined carefully!), (15) the empowerment of the flower garland, (16) the removal of the blindfold, and (17) the revelation of the outer and inner maṇḍalas.

The most important stages of all of the above are the taking of vows, generating the *bodhicitta* of yoga, the two parts (i.e. stages 13 & 14) of actually entering into the maṇḍala and the flower garland empowerment. The other stages are like branches of these. All the stages from the preparation up to that of actually taking the oath of secrecy (stages 1-6) [106] are merely preparations for the later stages (stages 7-17) which constitute the actual entry.

THE RITUAL PROCEDURE OF EMPOWERMENT

With regard to defining the ritual procedure of empowerment, there are four kinds of empowerment to be bestowed at the time of entry into the maṇḍala, as explained above. These are: (1) the vase empowerment, (2) the secret empowerment, (3) the wisdom empowerment, and (4) the fourth empowerment.

THE VASE EMPOWERMENT

The vase empowerment has both the common empowerment of the vajra disciple and the uncommon empowerment of the vajra master. The common empowerment of the disciple consists of the five empowerments: water, crown, vajra, bell and name, plus [the optional empowerment of] the eye [ointment], spoon and mirror. They are known as common empowerments because they are held in common by all four classes of tantra, and because they can be given either with or without the vows of the five Buddha families.

The uncommon empowerment is so-called because it is not found in the two lower [classes of] tantra and, even in the two higher [classes of] tantra, it is only bestowed upon those who accept the vows of the five families.

Whenever an empowerment is given, it is necessary for the disciple to actually request it from the master, and it is also necessary for the master himself to make a similar request to the deities of the maṇḍala. Thus there are two who actually confer the empowerment—the guru and the maṇḍala deities.

The guru must continue to bestow upon the disciple the empowerments of all the deities of the maṇḍala of coloured powder until the empowerment is completely finished. At the end of each section of the empowerment, the deities are dissolved into the disciple. The main deities are not dissolved into the disciple until the end because, according to the teachings of the *mahāsiddhas* of India, it is the various deities who are newly invited during the ritual that are dissolved into the disciple first.

[107] The essential features of the water empowerment include placing the vase upon the head of the disciple, the sprinkling of water and the giving of water to drink. The main point here, however, is for the disciple to arise as Akṣobhya and for the Akṣobhya who is generated within the water of the ritual vase to become assimilated into him. Although, in this way, it is the deities of the practice maṇḍala who give purpose (*abhiprāya*) to the bestowal of empowerment upon the disciple, it is the newly invited deities who actually perform the ritual and it is the guru in the external world who physically places the vase upon the crown of the disciple's head, sprinkles him with water and places water into his mouth for him to drink. By these means, the disciple's fundamental aggregate of consciousness becomes transformed and he is purified of the stain of hatred. Thus the disciple attains the wisdom of the Realm of Truth and gains the attainments of Akṣobhya and his family. This is the water empowerment of the *tathāgata* Akṣobhya.

Following that paradigmatic example, the crown empowerment of Ratnasambhava, the vajra empowerment of Amitābha, the bell empowerment of Amoghasiddhi and the name empowerment of Vairocana should all be understood.

The empowerment known as eye, spoon and mirror liberates the view of the disciple from the cataracts of ignorance and opens the eye of wisdom. By the example of a reflection in a mirror, one must understand that all phenomena in general, and in particular the Vajrasattva situated within one's own heart, are empty of inherent existence, like the images in a mirror.

Now, with regard to the inner empowerment: by the light which radiates from the HŪṀ at the heart of the guru indivisibly united with the deity, [108] all the disciples are summoned and taken inside the mouth of the guru. Being swallowed by him, they pass down inside his body and are ejected through his vajra into the lotus of the consort, from whence they are reborn.

Secondly, the manner in which the empowerment of the vajra master is conferred is as explained already in the section on the common and uncommon traditions of the lower classes of tantra.[187]

THE SECRET EMPOWERMENT

Now I will explain the secret empowerment, the second of the four empowerments. This has two parts: the supreme secret empowerment and the ordinary secret empowerment.

In former times, certain masters have said that the supreme secret empowerment is given to those disciples whose faculties are sharp and the ordinary secret empowerment is given to those of lesser capacity. This view is incorrect, however, bec.use the teachings of the *Elucidating Lamp* and the *Root Tantra of the Secret Assembly* both state: "The disciple upon whom the ordinary secret empowerment is conferred is that same disciple upon whom the supreme secret empowerment is conferred."

The secret empowerment is bestowed within the maṇḍala of conventional *bodhicitta*. In this regard, Ghaṇṭāpāda has said:

> The *bodhicitta* of conventional reality
> Is the site for the bestowal of the secret empowerment.

The conferral of the supreme secret empowerment is shown in the eighth chapter of the root tantra, where it says:

> The stable, intelligent being with open eyes
> Should take the liquid and drink it.

The ordinary secret empowerment is shown in Chapter XVI:

> Begin the conferral of the secret
> By blessing according to the ritual
> Either the impurities or seminal fluid.
> On drinking these with a vajra mind
> Attainments are not hard to accomplish.

The manner of bestowing this empowerment [109] is:

> By *bodhicitta* overflowing from the blazing jewels
> Of all the Jinas without exception
> Onto the bodies of the parched ones,

By means of the waters of wisdom
Arisen from their utterly pure vajras,
The empowerment is conferred by
The descent of precious gifts from the vajra.

This accurate description of the conferral of the empowerment is taken from the [tantra] *Drop of the Secret Moon.*

As for the supreme secret empowerment, the *Drop of the Secret Moon* says:

The vajra master, full of resolve,
Touches one's mouth with the vajra.
Thus, with the help of great beings,
The mind gains the great bliss of awakening.
This is the supreme secret.

The *Subsequent Tantra of the Secret Assembly* enlarges on this quotation by commenting that, if the rite is performed in this way, each secret empowerment is bestowed twice. Thus [the disciple receives] the secret empowerment from the guru and the secret empowerment from the consort.

THE WISDOM EMPOWERMENT

Thirdly, I will explain the wisdom empowerment. In the *Vajra Garland* explanatory tantra it is said that, following the ritual questions and answers and so forth, the disciple sits in union with the *vidyā* (consort). *Bodhicitta* then descends from the crown of his head to the secret organ, and thus this empowerment is conferred by arousing the wisdom of emptiness and bliss. With regard to this, in Chapter XVI of the root tantra we find the verse:

These four are great secrets but
Having the vajra is the most secret.
The mantra wheel takes the form of a woman
And one abides there for the benefit of all sentient beings.

THE FOURTH EMPOWERMENT

Bestowal of the fourth empowerment is described in the *Vajra Garland* where it says, "the meaning of the fourth is purity" and, "the fourth is to be understood as the resultant fruit." This is confirmed by the *Subsequent Tantra of the Secret Assembly* which says, "... the fourth is just like that." [110] Again, in the *Vajra Garland* it is written: "meditation on the stage of generation should be understood by means of oral instructions." And in the empowerment ritual by Ghaṇṭāpāda it is written: "it is to be understood through oral instructions from the guru of the third awareness empowerment." The above quotation from the *Vajra Garland* also indicates that one should rely on the precepts of the guru for practising meditation on the generation stage with oneself arising as the father-mother deity of desire. As a result of this, the fourth empowerment manifests in the form of the male and female deities face to face in the embrace of union. The view of Ghaṇṭāpāda, as demonstrated in his empowerment ritual, is also in agreement with this.

In brief, as it is written in the *Union Tantra*:

One who aspires towards the vast and profound truth
Should receive the empowerment of the precious word.

As it is said here, the ultimate tantric attainment is to reach the stage of union which has the seven aspects of the face to face kiss [known as the seven special qualities of Vajradhara]. The precious word of explanation given by the guru to the disciple helps one to gain an understanding of the nature of this union, and this is the actual fourth empowerment as conferred upon a suitable vessel. The disciple himself is only capable of receiving this fourth empowerment if his mental continuum is a proper vessel, suitable to contain such an understanding.

With regard to the seven special qualities of Vajradhara, these are explained by *paṇḍita* Vāgīśvarakirti as: the attainment of the Enjoyment Body (*saṁbhogakāya*), great bliss (*mahāsukha*), being [perpetually] in the embrace [of union] (*saṁpuṭa*), non-inherent existence (*niḥsvabhāva*), being filled with love and compassion (*maitrīkaruṇatā*), being free of hindrances (*anācchedya*) and with an unceasing nature (*aniruddha*).

The benefits of receiving these four empowerments in a pure manner are such that the supreme disciple will attain Buddhahood in this very lifetime, the middling disciple will either attain enlightenment in the intermediate state (*antarābhava*) or within seven lifetimes, and even the inferior disciple [111] will attain the supreme result within 16 lifetimes.

Saraha, in his *Explanation of the Difficult Points of the Buddha Skullcup*, cites this quotation from the *Treasury of Secrets*:[188]

If one possesses the pure empowerment,
Then in life after life one will become empowered
And within seven births, even without meditation,
The attainments will be accomplished.

Vibhūticandra also says:

Even without meditating, if no downfall occurs
Within 16 lifetimes, the goal will be achieved.

The point here is that everything depends on the vows remaining unimpaired. In the *Source of Commitment Tantra* it is written:

Relying closely on the precepts,
If one desires the supreme attainment
Then to sacrifice one's life

Or to face death presents no problem,
But one must always protect one's vows!

Vase empowerment, birth in the six realms and the nirmāṇakāya

Now, taking all that has been said heretofore with regard to the meaning and purpose of empowerment and arranging it in accordance with the stages of the path: the result, which is called Buddhahood, consists in the realization that the six classes of beings are the actual manifestation of the circle of deities. The proximate cause of this realization is the completion stage meditation on the circle of deities as the manifestation of the beings of the six classes. Prior to this, one must complete the generation stage meditation on the circle of deities as the circle of the six classes of beings. In order to become a suitable vessel for such a meditation, however, one needs to receive the vase empowerment. The particular purpose of the vase empowerment, therefore, is to plant the seed of the Emanation Body and purify all bodily defilements.

The resultant state of Buddhahood, furthermore, has the mind of the Emanation Body [112] possessing the wisdom that realizes emptiness. This wisdom mind completely eradicates delusions (*kleśa*), as well as the very instincts (*vāsanā*) of delusion, and directly realizes the five wisdoms. The proximate cause of that realization is the completion stage meditation and, in order for the result to arise in just this way, it is necessary for that cause also to possess all these qualities. The proximate cause of that is the generation stage meditation. The practitioner, therefore, must possess similar qualities at the generation stage as well and, in order to become a fit vessel capable of containing such qualities, must be purified of the stains of the five delusions by means of the water empowerment and the rest. The five aggregates must be transformed and the seeds of the five wisdoms must be planted.

During the vase empowerment, the wisdom deities are invited and then melted into the body of the disciple. The guru subsequently presents offerings to the deities which the disciple must accept. Thus, at the time of the result, an enjoyment of the objects of the five senses is engendered within the disciple with an understanding of their nature. It is through the bestowal of the first empowerment—the flower garland—that the power to become a Buddha in one of the five families is granted, and one's future Buddha-name is prophesied at that time. The water empowerment of Akṣobhya washes away all impurities that may prevent the disciple from being born into that family. Having attained the crown empowerment of Ratnasambhava, the lord of the family himself will meet the disciple at the time of Buddhahood and place the crown upon his head, and he will have the potential to attain the *uṣṇīṣa* and the other marks of a great being. [113] The vajra empowerment of Amitābha confers the power for the disciple's mind to attain the wisdom of indivisible bliss and emptiness. The bell empowerment of Amoghasiddhi bestows the power for disciples to turn the wheel of Dharma by means of speech with the 60 melodious qualities. It is due to the name empowerment of Vairocana that the disciple has the capacity to become a Buddha with such-and-such a name. The eye, spoon and mirror empowerment confers the power to attain the mirror-like eye and gain a comprehensive realization of the meaning of emptiness. Thus, in general, the disciple gains the power to understand that all phenomena are illusory and, in particular, that the Vajrasattva within his heart is just like the image in a mirror.

By bestowing these prophetic blessings (*anujñā*) of the four families before conferring the vajra master empowerment, the disciple is given the power to turn the wheel of Dharma within any of the four families when the result is attained. The conferral of the prophetic blessing of the mantra before the vajra master empowerment gives one the power to recite mantras during the generation stage, and to accomplish specific worldly attainments (*siddhi*) in dependence upon that recitation. Conferring the prophetic blessing of the wheel and so forth enables the disciple to turn the wheel of the Dharma, blow the conch shell of the Dharma, recite the tantric mantras, proclaim emptiness, gain a comprehensive realization of the meaning of emptiness, and achieve victory over the four demons[189] at the time of the result. The blessing of the prophecy to final awakening makes it possible for the disciple, whilst he is still on the path, [114] to hear the name of the Buddha he will eventually become.

Secret empowerment, the intermediate state and the sambhogakāya

On the level of Buddhahood, also, there is the actual Enjoyment Body which is similar in aspect to [the body of] the intermediate state. Before that, the pure illusory body must be attained, adorned with the major and minor signs, and this is to be preceded by the attainment of the impure illusory body with the major and minor signs. Before that, one attains a similitude of the illusory body during the time of the three isolations and this, in turn, must be preceded by meditation on the Enjoyment Body of the primordial Lord (*ādinātha*), generated by means of the five clear realizations whilst practising upon the stage of generation. In order to become a suitable vessel for such meditations as these, the disciple must receive the secret empowerment. The particular purpose of the secret empowerment, therefore, is to plant the seed of the Enjoyment Body and purify all the defilements of speech.

Wisdom empowerment, death and the (jñāna)dharmakāya

Further, on the level of Buddhahood there is the actual Wisdom Truth Body, which is similar in aspect to the moment of death. This must be preceded by the meaning clear light which is a direct realization of emptiness by means of the great bliss of the innate. Before this, the disciple needs a comprehensive understanding of emptiness which must be gained through the clear light of mind isolation and, prior to this, one must practise the Truth Body meditation of gathering up all the excess (*pariśeṣa*) clear light during the generation stage yoga. In order to be able to serve as a suitable vessel for these meditations, one needs to receive the wisdom empowerment. The particular purpose of the wisdom empowerment, therefore, is to plant the seed of the Truth Body [115] and purify all the defilements of the mind.

The fourth empowerment and the stage of no more learning

When these two bodies just described—the Wisdom Truth Body and the Enjoyment Body—are fully united on the level of resultant Budhahood, the disciple attains union on the stage of no more learning. The proximate cause of this is the union on the stage of learning and, in order to become ripened as a suitable vessel for this meditation, it is necessary to receive the fourth empowerment. The fourth empowerment, therefore, plants the seed of union and simultaneously purifies all the stains of body, speech and mind.

The meaning of the root tantra
Of the glorious *Secret Assembly*,
Explained in the manner of the six great commentaries
And in accordance with the view
Of the great scholars of India and Tibet
With a clear explanation of the ripening empowerments
Are all given here from the tradition
Of father Tsong-kha-pa and his sons.
Fortunate and intelligent beings should adopt this now.

(This is a verse between chapters.)

Explanation of the Commitments and Vows

Now I will discuss the way in which the disciple protects the commitments (*samaya*) and vows (*saṁvara*) that he promised to uphold at the time of receiving empowerment.

FOURTEEN ROOT TANTRIC DOWNFALLS

The disciple who has received the four empowerments in a pure and proper manner and who now strives to preserve intact the commitments and vows should recognize from the outset that the three main areas within which the 14 root downfalls (*mūlāpatti*) and eight branch downfalls (*sthūlāpatti*) are commited are with respect to: (1) the vajra master, (2) the friends of the religious practitioner, and (3) the teachings.

(1) In order to prevent any violation of the oath made with respect to the vajra master, [116] the disciple must realize that the guru himself is Vajradhara and that all attainments come from him. With this in mind, if one belittles or despises one's guru, the first of the root vows is broken. 'Guru' in this context refers to any teacher who bestows empowerment, explains the tantras, or transmits the oral tradition and so forth, and a fault committed toward any such teacher constitutes the breaking of this root vow.

(2) Regarding the friends of the religious practitioner, these fall into two categories: pure friends and perverse friends. Pure friends include both vajra brothers and sisters and all sentient beings with faith. The downfall with respect to vajra siblings is to feel angry with one of them. This constitutes the third root downfall. A vajra sibling is any disciple with whom one receives an empowerment from the same guru, or any disciple who possesses the tantric vows. So, if one knowingly speaks in anger to such a person about their faults, and if they hear and understand the meaning, then, as the five factors are present, this downfall is committed.

Sentient beings with faith include those who have faith in the supreme vehicle as well as those who are suitable vessels for the Mahāyāna. Regarding them it is said: "Disturbing the minds of those who have faith is the 12th." Thus, if one performs any action which is intended to disturb the mind and shake the faith of such a being, and if the evil act of actually destroying their faith is completed, then this root downfall is committed.

'Perverse friends' are those impure or bad friends whose influence is harmful to one's practice and, in order to prevent any violation of one's vows, one should avoid their company. [117] As it is said: "Having a close friendship with an evil being is the tenth." 'Evil beings' in this context are wicked persons who manifestly despise the Three Jewels or one's guru, or who try to destroy the teachings of the Buddha, and so forth. To show affection with body and speech toward such a person and treat that person as a friend constitutes a root downfall.

(3) Downfalls concerning the teachings are related either to the scriptures or to the teachings of insight. The term 'scriptures' refers to those teachings spoken by the Buddha, and a transgression against them would be to scorn or slander them, or to say that they are not the teachings of the Buddha. It is also an offence to disclose the secrets of tantra to an improper vessel. Of these three faults, in order to prevent the first one should remember: "Neglecting the teachings of the Buddha is the second root downfall." This means that if one knowingly and with scornful intention breaks any of the precepts contained within the three categories—individual liberation (*prātimokṣa*), bodhisattva or tantric vows—then this root downfall is committed.

In order to prevent the second one should remember that: "To disrespect the Dharmas which are one's own or another's tenets is the sixth." 'One's own tenets' are the teachings of the tantras, whereas 'others' tenets' refers to the teachings of the Perfection vehicle or the teachings of any of the three vehicles. If one says that any of these teachings are not really the teachings of the Buddha, [118] and if one believes this to be true, then this root downfall is committed.

The third can be stopped by the thought, "Disclosing secrets to a completely immature being is the seventh." This refers to those beings in whom no faith has been aroused and whose minds have not become mature, even if they have previously received tantric empowerment. If one knows a person to be of this type, and yet one still discloses the extraordinary secrets of tantra to that person without any great hope of conversion, and if that person understands the meaning of what has been said, then the presence of all six factors causes this root downfall to be committed.

Secondly, with regard to the teachings of insight, there are also three types of offence. The first relates to the basis of the path, the second to the essence of the path, and the third to the branches of the path.

(i) *Bodhicitta*, generated for the benefit of all sentient beings, relies upon all sentient beings as its sphere of operation and this is the basis of the path. In order to prevent any downfall in this regard, one should remember: "Abandoning love for all beings is the fourth. Thus spake the Buddha." This means that to hold any single sentient being in mind with the thought, "May this person be separated from happiness," and thus to abandon love for this being, is to commit this root downfall.

Furthermore, in order to prevent any downfall with respect to the essence of *bodhicitta*, one should remember: "The root of Dharma is *bodhicitta*. To abandon it is the fifth." In fact, even in the absence of other circumstantial factors, one transgresses this root vow by giving up the *bodhicitta* of aspiration due to feeling incapable of benefitting all the infinite sentient beings of the universe through the attainment of enlightenment. [119]

(ii) Secondly, offences committed in relation to the nature of the path pertain either to the generation stage or to the completion stage. With regard to the generation stage, in order to prevent any violation of the deity generated on the basis of one's own aggregates it is necessary to remember that: "The aggregates have the nature of five Buddhas. To abuse them is the eighth." This means that to impose any torment upon one's body and so forth,[190] or to think of it as impure and low, would cause one to break this root vow.

There are two faults that may be committed with regard to the completion stage. The first is to abandon from the outset that emptiness which is the particular concern of the completion stage, and the second is to abandon emptiness after realization has been achieved. In order to prevent any downfall with respect to the first of these, one should remember: "Harbouring doubt with regard to phenomena which are pure by nature is the ninth." This means that this downfall is committed through disbelief in the nature of profound emptiness.

Also, in order to prevent any transgression with respect to the second, one should remember: "All phenomena are free of imputation and the rest. To have concepts about them is the 11th." As it is said here, to pass even one day and night without maintaining the continuity of the view of selflessness (*nairātmya*) constitutes a root downfall.

(iii) Thirdly, downfalls relating to the branches of the path are concerned either with the various oaths (*samaya*) which are the basis of the path, or with one's companions in practising the path. Firstly, in order to prevent the misdeed of not relying properly on the commitments which are the basis of the path, one should remember: "Failure to uphold the words of honour as they were obtained is the 13th." [120] This means that during an offering assembly (*gaṇacakra*), or whenever there is a festival of the *ḍākas* and *ḍākinīs* or such-like ritual, to have doubts about the sacred articles of food and drink such as the five meats and so forth which are shared at this time, and to have the idea that these things are unclean and therefore to refuse them, is to transgress this root vow. This is the interpretation of the vow only in Highest Yoga tantra. In the Yoga tantra, what is the use of vajra and bell? They are used merely in the various hand gestures and so on during meditation. Thus, [in Yoga tantra] one commits a root downfall by remaining in the company of others and belittling them.

Secondly, in order to prevent any transgression with regard to those women who are the friends of practitioners on the path, one should bear in mind: "To despise women, whose nature is wisdom, is the 14th." As it is said here, if one uses any derogatory or abusive words towards Vajravārāhī, or any other goddess who has gone beyond the world but appears in the form of an ordinary woman, in order to expose supposed faults in them, then this root vow is violated, both for the Yoga tantras and for the Highest Yoga tantras. If one has the desire to criticize any woman at all, and then uses words that imply a criticism of all women in general, then the fundamental downfall specific to the Highest Yoga tantra is committed.

In order to determine the gravity of any root downfall, consider the following factors: if the wish to repeat the action in the future is present from the second moment of being engaged in the action up until the action is completed, and if joy is taken in the activity itself, [121] these are the first two requisites for the vow to be broken. Further, if one does not recognize the fault of the action thus committed, and feels neither shame nor regret for what has been done, these are the third and fourth factors. In the absence of all four binding factors, no root downfall has been committed.

EIGHT SECONDARY TANTRIC DOWNFALLS

The second section on vows is the group of eight subsidiary vows. The first downfall here is said to be "taking wisdom by force", which means that one takes a consort for one's own use when she is not properly qualified for such practices.

The second is called "taking her nectar by force", which means that one uses a consort in the absence of divine pride (*divya-māna*), in the presence of people who have no faith, or at an improper time.

The third downfall is "revealing secrets to improper vessels". This means that one shows the painted image of a deity, the sacred text, the six bone ornaments or any other secret material or ritual method of the hand gestures and so on to one who has received no empowerment whatsoever, or even to one who has received an empowerment but is lacking in faith.

The fourth is called "arguing in the assembly". Thus, if one is seated in the assembly during the time of making offerings, or whenever there is a celebration of the heroes and yoginis and, instead of maintaining the confidence of the deity with an attitude of love and compassion for all beings and the wish to accumulate merit for the sponsor of the ritual, one argues with others, or displays antagonism toward them and so forth, this is the fourth branch downfall.

Concerning the fifth, this is "to show other Dharmas to those who have faith". This means that if someone were to ask for teachings on the ultimate truth, for example, and one were to reply by showing only the relative truth, this vow would be broken.

The sixth [122] is "abiding with Hearers for a week". The meaning here is that one is allowed to remain in the home of those who disparage the tantras, such as Hearers, for only six days. To stay with such people for seven days is a fault— except when one is there in order to protect life, or when one is obliged to remain there under law.

The seventh secondary downfall is "to have the pride of a false yogin". Thus, one who proudly displays knowledge of ultimate suchness while merely relying on the practice of deity yoga commits this fault.

The eighth secondary downfall is "to reveal the Dharma to those without faith". This means that to confer an empowerment on someone who has no faith in the vehicle of secret mantra and whose mind will not become ripened by the empowerment, or to display the secrets of tantra to unripened disciples who are without faith, even though they have been initiated, but who merely aspire to acquire the outer trappings of Dharma, is to commit this downfall.

It is also a transgression to act without the proper backing of one's practice. Thus, to teach the tantras or confer an empowerment or any other such thing for no special reason, when one has allowed one's previous commitment to degenerate and has not taken the vows afresh is a gross offence. Also, not properly completing the retreat—either by not completing the mantra count or the prescribed time, or achieving the signs of success, or correctly performing the concluding ritual of fire offerings, or maintaining the deity yoga, or for whatever reason—and then to confer empowerment upon another is also a gross infraction. It is also a downfall for a *tāntrika* to transgress any of the vows of the three ordinations without a valid reason. For example, should a vajra-holding *bhikṣu* perform the fire rite without at the same time being mindful of the *vinaya* injunction against touching fire, or without blessing the offerings properly first, [123] that *bhikṣu* would break this secondary tantric precept as well as his own vows of individual liberation. These three additional downfalls together with the eight secondary vows discussed above make 11.

If, in this way, one properly receives an empowerment and then holds the 14 root and the eight or 11 secondary vows without defilement and makes effort in meditation on the stages of generation and completion yoga, one can attain the state of *yuganaddha* Vajradhara in this very lifetime.

This topic, which has a most attractive form,
Is adorned with a precious explanation.
Showing a smile to scholars in many ways,
It is seen to captivate the minds of fortunate beings.

How could those teachers whose minds' eyes
Are covered with the mists of jealousy
Bear to see this incomparably eloquent speech
Of masters possessed of so many excellent qualities?

Even toward masters and their excellent speech
It is the nature of some people to be jealous.
In that case, what can I possibly do for them?
May the holy beings witness this truth!

Now, in this period of the final 500 years
Of the Buddha's teachings,
Ignorant beings are revered more highly than the wise.
It is extremely difficult to find a witness for my actions.
Oh, root and lineage gurus, you know this!

[124] [But look] here! In this degenerate age
Vajradhara has assumed the guise of a monk in robes.
He has abridged the profound path
And made it abundantly clear.
He and his lineage of sons are the objects of veneration!

By my effort with regard to this overview of the tantras
And all my accumulation of the two-fold merit,
May the supreme lineage of the mighty Jina—
bLo-bzang grags-pa and his sons
Go on to the end of cyclic existence!

May I also, from now and throughout my future lives,
Diligently pay attention to the words of the wise
With faith in the teachings and love for all beings.
May all my good qualities increase!

Colophon

This overview of Buddhist tantra, called *Captivating the Minds of the Fortunate Ones,* relies for its authority upon teachings handed down in the lineage of Father [Tsong-kha-pa] and his sons. Added to this is a mass of material gathered together from a wide range of important exegetical commentaries concerning Cakrasaṁvara, Hevajra and Kālacakra, as well as Tsong-kha-pa's *Great Exposition on Secret Mantra*. It was composed by Paṇ-chen bSod-nams grags-pa, a disciple of the *vajrācārya* Chos-ldan blo-gros, in the place of solitude called Byams-pa-gling.

Appendix I
Vows and Commitments of a Bodhisattva

THE ROOT DOWNFALLS OF A BODHISATTVA

1 Praising oneself and scorning others.
2 Not giving wealth or the Dharma.
3 Not accepting other's aplogies.
4 Abandoning the Mahāyāna.
5 Stealing the property of the Three Jewels.
6 Abandoning the Dharma.
7 Causing monks or nuns to disrobe.
8 Committing any of the five heinous actions.
9 Holding wrong views.
10 Destroying places such as towns.
11 Explaining emptiness to those who are likely to misunderstand.
12 Causing others to abandon the Mahāyāna.
13 Causing others to abandon their vows of individual liberation.
14 Belittling the Hīnayāna.
15 Speaking falsely about profound emptiness.
16 Accepting property that has been stolen from the Three Jewels.
17 Making bad rules.
18 Giving up *bodhicitta*.

SECONDARY DOWNFALLS OF A BODHISATTVA

Downfalls that obstruct the perfection of giving

1 Not making offerings to the Three Jewels every day.
2 Indulging in worldly pleasures out of attachment.
3 Being disrespectful to anyone who received Bodhisattva vows before oneself.
4 Not replying to others.
5 Not accepting invitations.
6 Not accepting gifts.
7 Not giving the Dharma to those who desire it.

Downfalls that obstruct the perfection of moral discipline

8 Forsaking those who have broken their moral discipline.
9 Acting in a manner that will not inspire faith in others.
10 Doing little to benefit others.
11 Not believing that the compassion of bodhisattvas ensures that all their actions are pure.
12 Acquiring wealth or fame through wrong livelihood.

13 Indulging in frivolity.
14 Claiming that bodhisattvas need not abandon cyclic existence.
15 Not avoiding a bad reputation.
16 Not helping others to avoid negativity.

Downfalls that obstruct the perfection of patience

17 Retaliating to harm or abuse.
18 Not apologizing when the opportunity arises.
19 Not accepting the apologies of others.
20 Making no effort to control one's anger.

Downfalls that obstruct the perfection of joyous effort

21 Gathering a circle of followers out of desire for profit or respect.
22 Not trying to overcome laziness.
23 Indulging in senseless conversation out of attachment.

Downfalls that obstruct the perfection of mental stabilization

24 Neglecting to train in mental stabilization.
25 Not overcoming obstacles to mental stabilization.
26 Being preoccupied with the experience of mental stabilization.

Downfalls that obstruct the perfection of wisdom

27 Abandoning the Hīnayāna.
28 Studying the Hīnayāna to the detriment of one's own Mahāyāna practice.
29 Studying non-Dharma subjects without a good reason.
30 Becoming engrossed in non-Dharma subjects for their own sake.
31 Criticizing other Mahāyāna traditions.
32 Praising oneself and scorning others.
33 Making no effort to study Dharma.
34 Preferring to rely on books rather than on one's Spiritual Guide.

Downfalls that obstruct the moral discipline of benefitting others

35 Not going to the assistance of those in need.
36 Neglecting to care for the sick.
37 Not acting to dispel suffering.
38 Not helping others to overcome their bad habits.
39 Not returning help to those from whom benefit has been received.
40 Not relieving the distress of others.
41 Not giving to those who seek charity.
42 Not taking special care of disciples.
43 Not acting in accordance with the inclinations of others.
44 Not praising the good qualities of others.
45 Not acting wrathfully when appropriate.
46 Not using miracle powers, threatening actions, and so forth.

EIGHT RITUAL PRECEPTS OF MAINTAINING BODHICITTA

1 To remember the benefits of *bodhicitta* six times a day.
2 To generate *bodhicitta* six times a day.
3 Not to abandon any living being.
4 To accumulate merit and wisdom.
5 Neither to cheat nor deceive one's Preceptors or Spiritual Guides.
6 Not to cause others to regret their wholesome actions.
7 Not to criticize those who have entered the Mahāyāna.
8 Neither to pretend to have good qualities nor to hide one's faults without special, pure motivation.

Appendix II
Vows and Commitments of the Tantric Path

ROOT DOWNFALLS OF THE TANTRIC PATH

1 Abusing or scorning the Spiritual Guide.
2 Disregarding any precept.
3 Criticizing one's vajra brothers or sisters.
4 Abandoning love for any being.
5 Giving up aspiring or engaging *bodhicitta*.
6 Scorning the Dharma of Sūtra or Tantra.
7 Revealing secrets to an unsuitable person.
8 Abusing one's body.
9 Abandoning emptiness.
10 Relying on non-beneficial friends.
11 Failure to recollect the view of emptiness.
12 Destroying another's faith.
13 Failure to keep the *samaya* articles.
14 Scorning women.

SECONDARY COMMITMENTS OF THE TANTRIC PATH

1 To abandon negative actions, especially killing, stealing, sexual misconduct, lying and taking intoxicants.
2 To rely sincerely on the spiritual *guru*, to be respectful toward one's vajra brothers and sisters, and to observe the ten virtuous actions.
3 To abandon the causes of turning away from the Mahāyāna, to avoid abuse of the deities, and not to step over sacred objects.

GROSS DOWNFALLS OF THE SECRET MANTRA PATH

1 Relying on an unqualified consort.
2 Engaging in union without the three awarenesses.
3 Showing secret substances to an unsuitable person.
4 Fighting or arguing during an offering assembly.
5 Giving false answers to questions asked in good faith.
6 Staying seven days in the home of anyone who scorns the Vajrayāna.
7 Pretending to be a yogin whilst remaining imperfect.
8 Revealing holy Dharma to those with no faith.
9 Engaging in maṇḍala actions without completing a close retreat.
10 Needlessly transgressing the precepts of individual liberation, or those of a bodhisattva.
11 Acting in a manner contrary to the *Fifty Verses on the Spiritual Guide*.

SPECIAL COMMITMENTS OF MOTHER TANTRA

1 To begin all physical actions with the left, to make offerings to the Spiritual Guide, and never to abuse him.
2 To abandon union with those who are unqualified.
3 While in union, never to be separated from the view of emptiness.
4 Never to lose appreciation for the path of desire.
5 Never to forsake the two kinds of *mudrā* (relative and absolute).
6 To strive with enthusiasm in the outer and inner methods.
7 Never to release seminal fluid; to maintain pure behaviour.
8 To abandon repulsion when tasting *bodhicitta*.

Notes

1. A reference to the author's teacher, rJe tsong-kha-pa blo-bzang-grags-pa (1357-1419) who founded the dGe-lugs-pa school of Buddhism in Tibet.
2. *Śrāvaka* (Tib: *nyan thos pa*): 'one who heard' the original teachings of the Buddha. Later disparaged as following an 'inferior way' (*hīnayāna*) for the purpose of self-liberation alone.
3. A follower of the *mahāyāna* (Tib: *theg pa chen po*) or 'Great way' strives to attain Buddhahood for the sake of all living beings through the cultivation of wisdom and skilful compassion.
4. Written by Vasubandhu, *circa* 6th century.
5. Tib: rNam-gzigs, 'Perfect Vision'.
6. Tib: *byang chub sems*. The mind of enlightenment intent on the welfare of all sentient beings.
7. Tib: Shā-kya thub-pa chen-po, 'Great Mighty One of the Śākyas'.
8. Tib: Rin-chen gtsug-tor-can, 'He With Jewelled Headcrest'.
9. Tib: Mar-me-mdzad, 'Acting as a Lamp'.
10. The first of the five paths, 'the path of the accumulation of merit and wisdom' (*saṁbhāramārga, tshogs lam*) was completed by the *bodhisattva* during the previous three immeasurable aeons. Then, during the night, he completed paths 2-4: the *prayogamārga (sbyor lam), darśanamārga (mthong lam),* and *bhāvanāmārga (sgom lam).* The final path of 'no more learning' (*aśaikṣamārga, mi slob lam*) he attained at dawn when he arose as a complete and perfect Buddha.
11. An 'ordinary' *bodhisattva* dwells in the world due to the force of his previous *karma,* traversing the paths to full awakening as outlined above. A 'noble' (*ārya*) *bodhisattva* is one who, having attained such awakening, continues to dwell in the world for the benefit of others.
12. There are ten levels for a *bodhisattva* on the path of meditation: these are: (1) Joyous (*pramuditā, rab tu dga' ba*); (2) Immaculate (*vimalā, dri ma med pa*); (3) Illuminating (*prabhākarī, 'od byed pa*); (4) Radiant (*arciṣmatī, 'od 'phro ba*); (5) Difficult to Master (*sudurjayā, sbyangs dka' ba*); (6) Approaching (*abhimukhī, mngon du gyur ba*); (7) Far Advanced (*dūraṅgamā, ring du song ba*); (8) Unshakeable (*acalā, mi gyo ba*); (9) Excellent Intelligence (*sādhumatī, legs pa'i blo gros*); and (10) Cloud of Dharma (*dharmameghā, chos kyi sprin*).
13. Of the ten *bhūmi* listed above, the first seven are considered impure because they include the possibility of regression, whereas the eighth, ninth and tenth levels are considered pure because they do not. Until the *bodhisattva* reaches the eighth level he remains afflicted by obstructions to liberation: delusions and their cause, grasping at inherent existence. Above the eighth level he is free of these and progressively

removes even their subtle imprints which act as obstructions to omniscience. When these also are eradicated, a *bodhisattva* achieves the state of Buddhahood

14. Akaniṣṭhaghanavyūha, Tib: 'Og-min stug-po bkod-pa'i zhing.
15. The five certainties (*pañcaniyata, nges ba lnga*) of the *saṁbhogakāya* are the certainties of: (1) place—always residing in the peerless pure land; (2) body—always being adorned with the 32 major marks and 80 minor signs of a Buddha; (3) time—remaining for as long as there is even one being still caught in cyclic existence; (4) teaching—always proclaiming the Mahāyāna teaching; and (5) disciples—always teaching to superior *bodhisattvas*.
16. The 12 deeds of a Buddha are traditionally enumerated as: (1) descending from the Tuṣita pure land; (2) entering his mother's womb; (3) taking birth; (4) displaying his skill in the worldly arts; (5) enjoying the women of his harem; (6) renouncing worldly life and taking vows of chastity; (7) practising austerities; (8) meditating under the Bodhi tree; (9) conquering the hordes of Māra; (10) attaining full enlightenment; (11) turning the wheel of Dharma; and (12) passing into the ultimate *nirvāṇa*.
17. For an outline of Buddhist cosmology and the position of our world within it see Martin Boord, *Maṇḍala Meaning and Method*, Kailash Editions, London, 1995.
18. Tib: Shā-kya bshes-gnyen, *circa* 1387.
19. Tib: Sangs-rgyas sbas-pa, *circa* 920, disciple of Buddha-jñānapāda.
20. Tib: Kun-dga' snying-po, *circa* 1100, disciple of Atiśa Dīpaṅkaraśrījñāna and teacher of Tha-ga-na.
21. It is by means of four *dhyāna* (levels of meditative concentration) that one may traverse the entire range of existential possibility, from the gross to the most subtle. For details see *Maṇḍala Meaning and Method (op. cit.)*.
22. *pañcābhisaṁbodhi, mngon byang lnga.* These five 'clear realizations' are described later in the present text.
23. *catvāri prātihāryāṇi, cho 'phrul bzhi*: (1) blessings (*adhiṣṭhāna, byin rlabs*), (2) empowerment (*abhiṣekha, dbang bskur*), (3) miraculous activity (*karma, 'phrin las*), and (4) meditative absorption (*samādhi, ting nge 'dzin*).
24. *ṣodaśaśūnyatā, stong pa nyid bcu drug.* These are: (1) *adhyātmaśūnyatā*, internal emptiness, *nang stong pa nyid*; (2) *bahirdhāśūnyatā*, external emptiness, *phyi stong pa nyid*; (3) *adhyātmabahirdhāśūnyatā*, emptiness of both internal and external, *phyi nang gnyis ka stong pa nyid*; (4) *śūnyatāśūnyatā*, emptiness of emptiness, *stong pa nyid stong pa nyid*; (5) *mahāśūnyatā*, great emptiness, *chen po stong pa nyid*; (6) *paramārthaśūnyatā*, emptiness of ultimate meaning, *don dam pa stong pa nyid*; (7) *saṁskṛtaśūnyatā*, emptiness of conditioned phenomena, *'dus byas stong pa nyid*; (8) *asaṁskṛtaśūnyatā*, emptiness of unconditioned phenomena, *'dus ma byas*

stong pa nyid; (9) *atyantaśūnyatā*, emptiness of infinity, *mtha' las 'das pa stong pa nyid*; (10) *anavarāgraśūnyatā*, emptiness of that which has neither beginning nor end, *thog ma dang mtha' ma med pa stong pa nyid*; (11) *anavakāraśūnyatā*, emptiness of non-repudiation, *dor ba med pa stong pa nyid*; (12) *prakṛtiśūnyatā*, emptiness of own-nature, *rang bzhin stong pa nyid*; (13) *sarvadharmaśūnyatā*, emptiness of all phenomena, *chos thams cad stong pa nyid*; (14) *svalakṣaṇaśūnyatā*, emptiness of own characteristics, *rang gi mtshan nyid stong pa nyid*; (15) *anupalambhaśūnyatā*, emptiness of non-apprehension, *mi dmigs pa stong pa nyid*; and (16) *abhāvasvabhāvaśūnyatā*, emptiness of the natural condition of that which does not exist, *dngos po med pa'i ngo bo nyid stong pa nyid*.

25. Tib: Phags-pa'i lha, *circa* 170-270 AD, foremost disciple of Nāgārjuna who founded the Middle Way school of philosophy.
26. Tib: Sangs-rgyas ye-shes zhabs, *circa* 900 AD, foremost disciple of Haribhadra.
27. In tantric practice, the stages of death are invoked in meditation, resulting in a series of progressively more subtle consciousnesses. The first three of these consciousnesses are called the 'empty', the 'very empty' and the 'great empty'. The fourth and last is called the 'clear light' and is the most subtle and powerful consciousness with which to realize *śūnyatā*.
28. These are the five ascetics with whom the *bodhisattva* formerly practised the path of austerities along the banks of the river Nairañjanā.
29. The basic *sūtra* of the Wheel of the Law of the Four Noble Truths is the *Dharma Wheel Sūtra*.
30. The Perfection of Wisdom (*prajñāpāramitā*) *sūtras* are: the most extensive, the *One Hundred Thousand Verses* (*Prajñāpāramitā-aṣṭasāhasrikā-sūtra*); the moderately extensive, the *Twenty-five Thousand Verses* (*Prajñāpāramitā-pañcaviṁśati-sāhasrikā-sūtra*); the middling, the *Eighteen Thousand Verses* (*Prajñāpāramitā-daśasāhasrikā-sūtra*); the condensed middling, the *Ten Thousand Verses* (*Prajñāpāramitā-daśasāhasrikā-sūtra*); the condensed version of the extensive, the *Eight Thousand Verses* (*Prajñāpāramitā-sāhasrikā-sūtra*); and the condensed condensed, the *Abbreviated* (*Sañcayagāthā*). Then there are the many very short summaries, including the famous *Heart Sūtra (Hṛdaya-sūtra)* and the tantric *Perfection of Wisdom in a Single Letter*.
31. The *abhidharma* teachings related to the first promulgation of the Law analyse the human condition into conditioned (*saṁskṛta*) and unconditioned (*asaṁskṛta*) elements of existence. The former category begins with the five aggregates (*skandha*), the first of which is form (*rūpa*), as well as the 12 bases of consciousness (*āyatana*) and the 18 elements (*dhātu*). Thus the list 'from form to omniscient mind' includes all those elements taken to be 'realities' by followers of the early schools.
32. 'Āryaparamārthasamudgata-paripṛcchā', *Saṁdhinirmocana-sūtra* VII.

33. The *prāsaṅgika* and the *svātantrika* schools of philosophy are the two principal streams of the later Middle Way Schools (*mādhyamika*).
34. 8th century Indian *paṇḍit*, one of the first scholars to come to Tibet. He founded the *yogācārasvātantrika mādhyamika* school, introduced Buddhist ordination to Tibet and consecrated the first Tibetan monastery at bSam-yas.
35. Late 8th century, disciple of Śāntarakṣita.
36. 'Proponents of External Objects', a group of Hīnayāna schools that believe in the true existence of external phenomena.
37. 11th century, 'gate-keeper' of the eastern gate of Vikramaśila.
38. *dvādaśāṅga-dharmapravacana*: (1) *sūtra*, often teachings of substantial length; (2) verses of intermediate length (*geya*) are sūtras in mingled prose and verse; (3) prophetic teachings (*vyākaraṇa*) are explanations, usually given in response to questions asked of the Buddha; (4) verses (*gāthā*) are uttered in metre; (5) verses of uplift (*udāna*) are joyous utterances; (6) legends (*ityuktaka*) are stories beginning with "thus it was said"; (7) rebirth stories (*jātaka*) are stories of previous lives of the Buddha; (8) marvellous teachings (*adbhūtadharma*) are accounts of miraculous events; (9) expansive teachings (*vaipulya*) are collections of miscellaneous teachings; (10) introductory teachings (*nidāna*) are statements of topics; (11) parables (*avadāna*) are parables about monks and nuns, mostly about their previous lives; and (12) finalized teachings (*upadeśa*) are oral instructions.
39. An earlier classification of scriptures omitted the final three items from the list above.
40. *tripiṭaka*: (1) the basket of ethical conduct (*vinaya-piṭaka*); (2) the basket of aphorisms (*sūtra-piṭaka*), dealing with meditative stabilization; and (3) the basket of higher knowledge or metaphysics (*abhidharma-piṭaka*).
41. A city in which the Buddha had given many important teachings.
42. The barber of the *saṅgha*.
43. 490-570 AD. First main exponent of the Middle Way *svātantrika* school. It seems unlikely, however, that Bhāvaviveka was the author of *Blaze of Reasoning*. See Bibliography for details.
44. *circa* 700 AD.
45. aka Padmākaraghoṣa. Tāranātha (p.276) describes him as a Kashmiri *ācārya* contemporary with the eastern Pāla king Dharmapāla (*circa* 770-810).
46. Another name for Pāṭaliputra.
47. Sanskrit, Apabhraṁśa, Paiśācika and Prakrit.
48. Thus the Mahāsāṅghika sect is divided into five schools, the Sarvāstivādin into seven, the Sthavira sect consists of three, and the Saṁmitīya, also, consists of three schools. These are explained further by bSod-nams grags-pa, below.

49. In his *chos 'byung* (*History of Buddhism* ii.98) Bu-ston quotes this *sūtra* and explains its significance: "Oh great monarch, in thy dream thou hast seen how 18 men were pulling at a piece of cloth. This means that the teaching of the Buddha Śākyamuni will be split into 18 sects. But the cloth, that is (the Doctrine of) Salvation, will not be torn asunder." And Bu-ston adds that this passage proves that all (the canonical texts acknowledged by the 18 sects) represent the authentic word of the Buddha.
50. *circa* 300-370 AD.
51. The *abhidharmapiṭaka* of the Sarvāstivādin canon consists of seven works: the *Jñānaprasthāna* by Katyāyanīputra, *Prakaraṇapāda* by Vasumitra, *Vijñānakāya* by Devaśarman, *Dharmaskandha* by Śāriputra, *Prajñaptiśāstra* by Maudgalyāyana, *Dhātukāya* by Pūrṇa, and *Saṅgītiparyāya* by Mahākausṭhila. Only Maudgalyāyana's *Prajñaptiśāstra* is to be found in Tibetan translation but Vasubandhu's *Treasury* is believed to be a summarization of all these texts, written for the most part soon after the Buddha's passing into ultimate *nirvāṇa*.
52. Disciple of Saṅghadāsa who was contemporary with Vasubandhu.
53. These are the 'Six Collections of Reasonings' (*ṣaḍ-yuktiśāstra*). See Bibliography.
54. Founder of the Middle Way (*mādhyamika*) school. Modern scholarship places this author *circa* 1st-2nd century AD. Traditional sources, however, believe him to have flourished from *circa* 100 BC-460 AD due to his mastery of alchemy.
55. *circa* 600-650 AD.
56. 695-743 AD.
57. 4th century AD.
58. Some of the most important texts in later Mahāyāna Buddhism are attributed to Lord Maitreya (Maitreyanāthā), the coming Buddha. *Āryāsaṅga* is traditionally said to have visited the Tuṣita paradise and received these teachings directly from Maitreya, who is thus credited with their authorship. It is also possible, however, that the name Maitreyanāthā refers to Asaṅga himself (or another) 'Whose Lord is Maitreya'.
59. 7th century AD.
60. This grove, located in the city of Śrāvastī, was donated to the *saṅgha* by the wealthy merchant Sudatta (Anāthapiṇḍada) during the lifetime of the Buddha.
61. *circa* 1050 AD, disciple of Śrīgupta and teacher of Marpa.
62. Acceptance of a self-knowing consciousness implies that consciousness is truly existent. Thus the schools referred to here assert that consciousness, but not external phenomena, does exist from its own side.
63. aka Siṁhabhadra, late 8th century.

64. aka Buddhajñāpada, *circa* 900 AD, foremost disciple of Haribhadra.
65. For the 18 root infractions of the bodhisattva vows and the 46 auxiliary downfalls see the Appendix.
66. *ṣaṭpāramitā*: (1) *dāna*, generosity, (2) *śīla*, moral conduct, (3) *kṣānti*, patience, (4) *vīrya*, enthusiastic perseverance, (5) *dhyāna*, concentration, (6) *prajñā*, wisdom.
67. *catvāri saṁgrahavastu*: (1) *dāna*, generosity (in support of one's pupils), (2) *priyavādita*, speaking pleasantly, (3) *arthacaryā*, helping others (i.e. encouraging others to practise), (4) *samānārthatā*, consistency between words and deeds.
68. *mananāt trāṇanāc ca mantraḥ*, "Because it derives from 'intrinsic knowledge' and 'protection', it [is called] *mantra*." Kṛṣṇācārya, *Yogaratnamālā*. This exegetical etymology (*nirukti*) derives from the initial syllables of the words *manana* (intrinsic knowledge) and *trāṇa* (protecting). Other exegetes derive the first syllable from the word *manas*, mind.
69. 11th century AD, *upādhyāya* of the eastern gate of Vikramaśila.
70. 10th century AD.
71. 'In the manner of insects' indicates non-contaminated great bliss and emptiness; just as an insect is generated from wood and then eats the wood itself, so meditative stabilisation is generated from bliss [in dependence on desire] and is cultivated as emptiness [whereupon desire is consumed]. Vīryavajra, *Commentary on the Embrace of the Four Yoginīs Tantra.* Jeffrey Hopkins, *Tantra in Tibet*, p.161. In ancient India, insects such as termites were thought to be born from wood.
72. *tathāgata-śatākṣara-vidhi*. Meditation upon these 100 syllables purifies the defilements of body, speech and mind.
73. mKhas-grub rJe ascribes this work, which he considers spurious, to Dārikapa (*circa* 1040-1200, formerly King Nāgeśa in the land of Oḍiviśa, converted to Buddhism by the *mahāsiddha* Lūipa). F.Lessing & A.Wayman, *Introduction to the Buddhist Tantric Systems*, pp.108-109. Our source text appears to have a line missing here.
74. Late 11th century *yogin* from South India, disciple of Dharmakīrti, Saraha, Anaṅgavajra and Saroruha. Travelling to Tibet, he became the *guru* of rMa lo-tsā-ba and Ma-gcig lab-sgron.
75. *aṣṭābhisamaya*. These are the eight topics of the *Abhisamayālaṅkāra*. Tsepak Rigzin's *Tibetan-English Dictionary of Buddhist Terminology* lists them: (1) omniscient mind (*rnam mkhyen, sarvajñāna*); (2) knowledge of paths (*lam shes, mārgajñāna*); (3) knowledge of bases (*gzhi shes, vastujñāna*); (4) complete training of all aspects of the mind (*rnam rdzogs sbyor ba, sarvākaraprayoga*); (5) peak training (*rtse mo'i sbyor ba, mūrdhaprayoga*); (6) serial training (*mthar gyis sbyor ba, anupūrvaprayoga*); (7) instantaneous training (*skad cig ma'i sbyor ba, kṣaṇikaprayoga*); (8) Wisdom Truth Body (*ye shes chos sku, jñānadharmakāya*).

76. These are the *Extensive Sūtra of the Aspiring Prayers of the Exalted Vaiḍūrya Light of the Medicine Buddhas* and the *Especially Extensive Sūtra of the Aspiring Prayers of the Seven Tathāgatas.*
77. 11th century. mKhas-grup rJe states that this explanation is found in Ratnakīrti's *Bright Sun-rays.* Lessing & Wayman, *Introduction to the Buddhist Tantric Systems*, pp.108-109.
78. These are the *mahāpañcarakṣā* goddesses (five great deities of protection) so popular in Nepal.
79. No *maṇḍala* rite for the five goddesses is found in P or Toh. mKhas-grub rJe states: "Śāntipa composed three basic commentaries on them: the *sādhana* of Pratisarā (possibly Toh. 3125, [*Knowledge Ritual of She Who Leads Each One*] no author listed), the way of drawing the protective circle of Pratisarā [*Method of Drawing the Circle of She Who Leads Each One*] (Toh.3118), and a *sādhana* of the five goddesses [*Ritual of the Five Protectors*] (Toh. 3126, the *bsrung ba lnga'i cho ga = pañcarakṣā-vidhi*). Lessing & Wayman, *Introduction to the Buddhist Tantric Systems*, pp.112-113.
80. 10th century?
81. mKhas-grub rJe (*ibidem*, pp.112-113) states: "Jetari composed a rite of the *gzungs* (*grva*) (possibly [*Offering Ritual of the Five Protectors*] Toh.3128, the *pañcarakṣārcana-vidhi,* no author mentioned), a *sādhana* of Pratisarā, together with the method of drawing her protective circle [*Ritual of Drawing the Circle of She Who Leads Each One*] (Toh.3127, the *Mahāpratisarā-cakra-lekhana-vidhi*), *sādhanas* of the five goddesses (probably [*Sādhana of She Who Leads Each One, Sādhana of the Peacock Lady, Sādhana of the Lady of a Thousand Conquests, Sādhana of the Subsequent Holder of Secret Mantra,* and *Sādhana of the Cool Grove*] Toh.3119-3123 inclusive)."
82. Possibly: *Chapter of the Dhāraṇī of the Crown Protrusion Victor of All Tathāgatas and Related Topics* (Toh.594) and *Chapter of the Dhāraṇī of the Crown Protrusion Victor of All Tathāgatas—'Holding the Club of the Lord of Death'—and Related Topics,* which are merely two different translations of an identical original. Or, *Chapter of the Dhāraṇī of the Crown Protrusion Victor of All Tathāgatas.*
83. A *stūpa* dedicated to Uṣṇīṣavijayā.
84. *circa* 673 AD, contemporary of Candrakīrti. All 14 of his rituals mentioned here concerning the practice of Sitātapatrā are to be found in the section of the bsTan-'gyur from sDe-dge Pu 177b6-192b2 (Toh.3083-3104).
85. aka Padmavajrāṅkuśa, 9th century.
86. Sahajalalita, Sahajavajra or Sahajalalitavajra, *circa* 1050, was a disciple of Maitrīpa. By *General Compendium* is probably meant his *Compendium of Devotions,* whereas *Specific Compendium* probably refers to his *Explanation of the Dhāraṇī of Perfect Observance of Commitment and the*

Essence of All Tathāgatas, the Shining Stainless Light of the Crown Protrusion that Places All in the Door to Liberation.

87. These two names refer to a single text but are listed by bSod-nams grags-pa in Sanskrit and Tibetan as if referring to two separate works.
88. There is a text called the *One Hundred and Eight Names of* ... for each of eight bodhisattvas (Toh.634-641).
89. Two texts with the same title: *Mahāyāna Sūtra of the Ārya 'Limitless Life and Wisdom'* (Toh. 674 and 675).
90. Apparently the *Dhāraṇi of the Essence of the Ārya 'Limitless Life and Wisdom'.*
91. Probably either the *Detailed Ritual of the Āryabodhisattva Avalokiteśvara With a Thousand Arms and a Thousand Eyes* or the *Dhāraṇi of the Āryabodhisattva Avalokiteśvara With a Thousand Arms and a Thousand Eyes, the Perfected Vast Mind of Compassion Unbound by Conceptuality.*
92. Late 11th century. Disciple of Yogendratilaka (a disciple of Nāropa) and teacher of Jñānadhara.
93. Second half of the 9th century, disciple of Lalitavajra, Anaṅgavajra and Mañjuśrīmitra.
94. Contemporary with the Pāla king Devapāla, *circa* 810-50 AD.
95. There is also a *Post-subsequent Tantra of the Secret Mind of the Glorious Vajra Fierce One [Vajrapāṇi].*
96. Scholar of Vikramaśīla monastery, died 1125.
97. aka Kambalapāda, Kamaripa and Śrī Prabhata. *Mahāsiddha* active during the latter half of 9th century.
98. 7th century.
99. *circa* 900 AD, disciple of lDong-ngar-pa, who was himself a disciple of Virūpa.
100. Much controversy surrounds the name Indrabodhi, aka Indrabhūti. Possibly there were three persons by that name: (1) King of Oḍḍiyāna, *circa* 7th century; (2) King of Zahor in the upper Kangra Valley, early 8th century; and (3) a later King of Oḍḍiyāna, late 9th century, disciple of Kambalapāda. This last was probably the author of the many mother-tantra texts ascribed to Indrabodhi.
101. Pacifying (*śāntika*), enriching (*pauṣṭika*), overpowering (*vāśya*) and destroying (*māraṇa*); these are the four classes of magical accomplishment.
102. 11th century Kashmiri contemporary of Maitrīpa, Virūpa and Anaṅgavajra, teacher of Pha dam-pa sangs-rgyas, Jñānabhadra and Śrībhadra.
103. Atiśa Dīpaṅkaraśrījñāna, 980-1053.
104. Emmending the Tibetan text to *spyod rgyud* at this point.
105. The visualized assembly of the three roots (*guru, deva* and *ḍākinī*) of one's practice.

106. In the sDe-dge edition of the *bKa' 'gyur*, this 'continuation' is included in the *Compendium* itself. The *Compendium* runs from folio 1 to 142a; the continuation begins at 106a6.
107. This term is taken to refer to the Wisdom Truth Body (*jñāna-dharma-kāya*) and signifies that aspect of Buddhahood which results from the completed accumulation of wisdom.
108. Analysis of *yogatantra* literature demonstrates that *ādiyoganāmasamādhi* involves cultivation of the five *abhisamaya*, climaxing in the generation of oneself as the deity. *Maṇḍalarājāgrināmasamādhi* begins with the summoning of the *jñānasattva* and ends with the pleasing of the deity (*anurāgana*). *Karmarājāgrināmasamādhi* involves the spread of countless divine emanations of great compassion throughout the universe for the benefit of all sentient beings.
109. *circa* 1100 AD.
110. The hand symbol (*hastacihṇa*) of Vairocaṇa is the wheel (*dharmacakra*).
111. *Stages of the Path of a Conqueror and Pervaṣive Master, a Great Vajradhara: Revealing All Secret Topics.*
112. The *Lesser King of Tantras of Glorious Supreme Bliss* (root tantra of *heruka* Cakrasaṁvara).
113. These two deities are transposed in the Tibetan text.
114. Dates uncertain. See David Templeman, *Tāranātha's Life of Kṛṣṇācārya*, LTWA, 1989.
115. Bu-ston rin-chen-grub, 1290-1364.
116. *circa* 800 AD.
117. Tārānātha's *Causing Wondrous Belief*, a detailed history of the *Vajra Terrifier Tantra*, has been translated by Gareth Sparham as part of the Yamāntaka Cycle Translation Project, under the auspices of Tibet House, New Delhi. Bulcsu Siklos has translated the seven chapter tantra, the four chapter tantra and the Musk Shrew Chapter into English as part of the requirements for a doctoral dissertation at SOAS, University of London.
118. In the sNar-thang edition of the *bka' 'gyur* the seven chapters [called in the beginning of the work *Śrīvajramahābhairavanāmatantra*, Ca 389a-404a] are entitled *dkyil 'khor bstan pa ste rtog pa dang po, las thams cad grub pa'i rtog pa, sngags btu ba bstan pa'i ste rtog pa de gsum pa, sgom pa'i rtog pa bzhi, bris sku'i cho ga'i rtog pa de lnga pa, sbyin sregs kyi las kyi cho ga de drug pa, bsam gtan gyi las sgrub pa brtag pa'i rtog pa de bdun pa.* lHun-grub paṇḍita's *Jewel Treasure House of the Three Bodies* states (ff.5-6): "In the first of the seven chapters [just mentioned] (a) retreat and empowerment rituals are mentioned, in the second (b) rituals for mixing the root mantras are mentioned, in the third (c) the way in which one accomplishes, by way of a myriad of devices (*'khrul khor, yantra*), the peaceful [wrathful, expansive and overpowering] activities is discussed, in the fourth (d) it talks about the *sādhana* having reference to

the 49 deities and eight zombies (*vetāla*), in the fifth (e) rituals for the preparation of icons and texts are mentioned, in the sixth (f) it says how to accomplish activities by way of *homa* [ritual fire] offerings and in the seventh (g) it says how to accomplish the boundless activities by relying solely on concentrations (*dhyāna*). In the *Explanatory Tantra in Three Chapters,* devices are explained in detail. The *Musk-shrew Chapter* discusses the way to accomplish activities by relying on substances such as the skin of the animal [called] the musk shrew (*chucchundara*)."

119. In a footnote to Gos Lo-tsa-wa's *Blue Annals* (p.754), George Roerich identifies Śrī Dhānyakaṭaka with the great *caitya* of Amarāvatī in the Sattenapalle Tāluka of Guṇṭūr District, Madras.
120. Dates disputed, from 8th-11th century, disciple of Vajrabodhi.
121. The great translator Rva lo-tsā-wa rDo-rje grags-pa, mid-12th century, disciple of the Nepali master Mahākaruṇa. For an interesting anecdote from his biography see M.Boord, *The Cult of the Deity Vajrakila,* pp.120-121.
122. A certain 'sKyo-ston of Yung' is referred to in Roerich's *Blue Annals* (p.273) as a student of Śar-ba-pa (1070-1141).
123. Zhang lo-tsā-wa Phur-pa-skyabs, d.1237, ordained by Śākyaśrī, teacher of the Nepali translator Bhā-ro. See G.Roerich, *The Blue Annals,* pp.445-8.
124. According to Tārānātha's history of the Vajra Terrifier cycle, called *Wondrous Belief,* Mal-gyo lo-tsā-wa Blo-gros grags-pa requested the three cycles of the Black Destroyer of the Lord of Death and the Vajra Terrifier from the Nepali Ha-du dkar-po who, according to the *Blue Annals* (p.394), was himself a disciple of Devākaracandra (folio 78). gNyos lo-tsā-wa "translated the Dharma of the three *Kṛṣṇa* cycles [i.e. the two of the Black Destroyer of the Lord of Death and the *Seven Chapters*]." This was about 15 or 20 years after the work of Nag-tsho tshul-khrims rgyal-ba, a *lo tsā wa* who was a disciple of Jowo Atiśa Dīpaṅkaraśrījñāna (folio 77).
125. *circa* 1100, disciple of Abhayākaragupta.
126. A reference to the *Sūtra Requested by the Nāga King Unwarmed.*
127. In this practice, one visualizes oneself as the commitment being (*samayasattva*) in the form of the principal deity, with the wisdom being (*jñānasattva*) in one's heart and the concentration being (*samādhisattva*) in the form of a seed-syllable at the heart of the wisdom being.
128. Saroruha, Sakara, Padmavajra (the middle), mid-late 9th century, disciple of Anaṅgavajra, contemporary of Lva-pa. Here paṇ-chen bSod-nams grags-pa may be referring to either of two works listed in the *bsTan 'gyur* concerning Highest Yoga Tantra: the *Glorious Secret Attainment, Invocation of the Complete Meanings of Tantra* or the *Explanation of (Buddhaguhya's) Introduction to the Meanings of Tantra.*

129. Ḍombhiheruka, second half of 8th century, disciple of Virūpa. Here paṇ-chen bSod-nams grags-pa may be referring to the *Yogic Practice by Means of the Winds and Drops* or the *Oral Instructions on the Two Letters.*
130. 11th century AD.
131. Nāḍapāda, 1016-1100, northern gate-keeper of Vikrama-śila. Disciple of Tilopa, contemporary of Śāntipa and teacher of Marpa chos-kyi blo-gros.
132. Anaṅgavajra or Anaṅgapāda, middle of the 9th century. Teacher of Indrabodhi, Virūpa, Saroruha and Līlāvajra. His tantric practice focussed on the *Hevajra Tantra* and *Great Bliss Tantra.*
133. *circa* 900 AD. The eighth *tāntrika* teacher of Vikramaśila, disciple of Ḍombipa.
134. 8th century AD, disciple of Jayadeva, contemporary of Śāntideva, *guru* of Ḍombipa.
135. *Saḍaṅgayoga* : (1) withdrawal or isolation (*pratyāhāra*), (2) concentration (*dhyāna*), (3) control of the life force (*prāṇāyāma*), (4) retention (*dhāraṇā*), (5) recollection (*anusmṛti*), and (6) meditative stabilization (*samādhi*).
136. *Pañcakrama*: (1) vajra recitation (*vajrajāpa*), (2) purification of the mind (*cittaviśuddhi*), (3) self-empowerment (*svādhiṣṭhāna*), (4) clear realization (*abhisambodhi*), and (5) the stage of union (*yuganaddha*).
137. Contemporary of the Pāla emperor Devapāla, 810-883 AD. Disciple of Dārikapa and teacher of Dharmakīrti, Jālandhara and Kāṇhapa.
138. Born 1017, disciple of Maitrīpa.
139. *circa* 1200 AD. He is said by the followers of Rva lo-tsā-wa to have decided to go to Śambhala in search of the *Kālacakra-tantra* when, in a vision, he "obtained the doctrines from *ārya* Avalokiteśvara himself."
140. Upāsakabodhi, late 11th and early 12th century. *Paṇḍit* at Nālandā, teacher of Abhayākaragupta and Mañjuśrīkīrti.
141. Otherwise known as Bodhibhadra or Nalendrapāda. Studied with Nāropa under Mahākālacakrapāda.
142. *circa* 1100 AD. Studied along with Somanātha and Samantaśrībhadra under the master Piṇḍopa (Vāgīśvarakīrti), the southern gate-keeper of Vikramaśila.
143. Somanātha or Candranātha of Kashmir, *circa* 1100 AD. Student of Piṇḍopa and teacher of the Tibetan translators sGom-pa dKon-mchog bsrungs, sGro-ston gnam-la-brtsegs and Grub-chen yu-mo.
144. Early 12th century translator. Disciple of Bodhibhadra (Kālacakrapāda junior).
145. *circa* 1100 AD. Student of Piṇḍopa and teacher of Rva chos-rab.
146. The translator of 'Bro, 'Bro shes-rab grags-pa, 'Brog-mi, 993-1074. Disciple of Prajñā Indraruci. He and his contemporary Rva lo-tsā-wa were the two chief expounders of the Wheel of Time in Tibet.

147. Born in 'Phan-yul, early 12th century.
148. Mid-12th century, son of the translator Mar-pa do-pa.
149. Mid-12th century, son of Dharmeśvara.
150. Mid-12th century, student of Rva 'Bum seng-ge.
151. Early 12th century. Disciple of both Rva lo-tsā-wa and the Nepali Samantaśrībhadra.
152. Bu-ston rin-chen-grub, 1290-1364. Compiler of the Tibetan canon and one of the foremost scholars in Tibetan history.
153. Bla-ma Tsong-kha-pa, 1357-1419. Founder of the dGe-lugs school and dGa'-ldan monastery.
154. mKhas-grub dge-legs dpal bzang-po, 1385-1438, one of the chief disciples of Tsong-kha-pa.
155. Early 12th century.
156. Early 12th century translator in the lineage of Buddhajñāna. Teacher of dPal-ldan seng-ge, who was a teacher of Bu-ston rin-po-che.
157. This explanatory tantra of the *Secret Assembly* was not translated into Tibetan. For an account of the history of this text in the commentarial literature see A. Wayman, *Yoga of the Guhyasamāja Tantra*, pp.84-85.
158. Padmavajra or Saroruha, second half of the 9th century, teacher of Anaṅgavajra (Devacandra).
159. The *Blue Annals* (p.359) describes Visukalpa as "a king of the Southern country".
160. All seven texts are grouped together in the *bsTan 'gyur*.
161. This last text is not clearly indicated. Another which would fit into this category is the *Instructions on the Stages of Inconceivable Reality* (*Acintyādvayakramopadeśa*) by Kuddālapāda.
162. Date uncertain, *circa* 9th century.
163. Nāgabodhi or Nāgabuddhipāda, 9th century, disciple of Nāgārjuna and teacher of Virūpa.
164. This root text is not listed in the Peking or Tohoku catalogues.
165. The text referred to here is uncertain. Nāropa's *Condensed Ultimate Meaning, Explanation Showing the Abbreviated Empowerment*, concerning the *Concise Explanation of Initiation* (a tantra of the Wheel of Time), refers extensively to the *Subsequent Tantra* of the Secret Assembly.
166. Alaṅkakalaśa, Alaṅkara-upādhyāya or Prajñākaragupta of Vikramaśīla, *circa* 1200 AD. Contemporary with Kālacakra-pāda the elder.
167. Mid-9th century. Predecessor of Līlavajra as 'gate-keeper' of Vikramaśīla.
168. Muniśrībhadra or Munīndraśrībhadra, early 13th century.
169. There is no text by Vīryaśrīmitra (Tib: brTson-'grus dpal bshes-gnyen) listed in the catalogues, but there is a commentary by Vīryabhadra on the difficult points of the five stages: *Clear Meanings, Commentary on the Difficult Points of the Five Stages.*
170. *circa* 1200 AD. Tenth *upādhyāya* of Vikramaśīla.

171. 10th century disciple of Śāntipa and Vāgīśvarakīrti. Teacher of Tathāgatarakṣita and Padmākara.
172. *circa* 1050 AD.
173. First half of 11th century, contemporary of Atiśa Dīpaṅkaraśrījñāna. Student of Sahajalalita and teacher of 'Gos lo-tsā-wa.
174. The *Blue Annals* (pp.359-60) explains: "... the *ācārya* Nāgārjuna ... had many disciples, but the chief ones were the four: Śākyamitra, Āryadeva, Nāgabodhi, and Candrakīrti."
175. In the catalogues this work, the *Maṇḍala Ritual of the Secret Assembly*, is attributed to Dīpaṅkarabhadra (mid 10th century) This teacher followed Jñānapāda and was succeeded by Laṅkājayabhadra, who was in turn succeeded by Śrīdhara as 'gate-keeper' of Vikramaśīla.
176. In all probability, this is a reference to the *Extensive Oral Instructions, Completely Explaining the Questions of the Four Goddesses Tantra*, attributed in the catalogues to Smṛtijñānakīrti (9th century).
177. 1012-97. Student of Tilopa and teacher of Milarepa.
178. The *Blue Annals* (p.360) calls him Candrarāhula.
179. The *Blue Annals* (p.361) has "the great *upāsaka* of Ye-rang, or the Nepālese Mahākaruṇa (*sic.*)."
180. The *Blue Annals* (p.361) has Na-ba-kū-ṭi-pa.
181. 1349-1412.
182. For these 10 categories see F. Lessing & A. Wayman, *Introduction to the Buddhist Tantric Systems*, pp.272-3.
183. *circa* 1040-1200.
184. Water to sip, cooling water for the feet, cooling water for the face and bathing water.
185. *Pañcopacāra:* Flowers, incense, light, perfume and food.
186. *Saptarājyaratna:* (1) precious wheel (*cakra*), (2) precious jewel (*maṇi*), (3) precious queen (*strī*), (4) precious householder (*gṛhapati*), (5) precious elephant (*hastin*), (6) precious supreme horse (*aśva*), (7) precious general (*senāpati*).
187. See above, pp.52-53.
188. *Wisdom Wheel of Lightning Mahāyāna Sūtra, Tantra of the Accomplishment of Great Ethical Conduct, Lamp of the Inexhaustible Mine, Treasury of Secrets, Secret of All Tathāgatas.*
189. These are the delusory power of the personal aggregates (*skandhamārā*), the delusory power of defilement (*kleśamārā*), the delusory power of high status (*devaputramārā*) and the delusory power of death (*mṛtyumārā*).
190. For example, by severe ascetic practices.

Bibliography

P *Catalogue and Index of the Peking Edition of the Tibetan Tripiṭaka*
Suzuki Research Foundation, Tokyo, 1971

Toh. *Complete Catalogue of the Tibetan Buddhist Canons (bka' 'gyur and bstan 'gyur)*
Tohoku Imperial University, Sendai, 1934

CANONICAL TEXTS (BKA'-'GYUR)

Sūtras and Tantras

Abbreviated Perfection of Wisdom
shes rab kyi pha rol tu phyin pa bsdus pa tshigs su bcad pa
sañcayagāthā
P735, vol.21; Toh.13; sDe-dge Ka 1b1-286a6

Accomplishment of Goodness Tantra
legs par grub par byed pa'i rgyud chen po las sgrub pa'i thabs rim par phye ba
susiddhikaramahātantrasādhanopāyikapaṭala
P431, vol.9; Toh.807; sDe-dge Wa 168a1-222b7

Analyzing the Stages of the Subsequent Concentration Tantra
bsam gtan gyi phyi ma rim par phye ba
dhyānottarapaṭalakrama
P430, vol.9; Toh.808; sDe-dge Wa 223a1-225b7

Arising of Nectar Dhāraṇī
bdud rtsi 'byung ba zhes bya ba'i gzungs
amṛtabhavanāmadhāraṇī
P354, vol.7; Toh.645; sDe-dge Ba 129a3-129b7

Black Destroyer of the Lord of Death
(The cycle of these teachings includes:)

a) *Root Tantra of the Black Destroyer of the Lord of Death*
de bzhin gshegs pa thams cad kyi sku gsung thugs gshin rje gshed nag po zhes bya ba'i rgyud
sarvatathāgatakāyavākcittakṛṣṇayamārināmatantra
P103, vol.4; Toh.467; sDe-dge Ja 134b1-151b4

b) *(Explanatory) Tantra of the Black Destroyer of the Lord of Death in Three Chapters*
dpal gshin rje'i gshed nag po'i rgyud kyi rgyal po rtog pa gsum pa zhes bya ba
śrīkṛṣṇayamāritantrarājatrikalpanāma
P107, vol.4; Toh.469; sDe-dge Ja 164a1-167b5

(Note: Although this is listed as a Kṛṣṇayamāri-tantra, it is also a tantra of the Vajra Terrifier.)

Chapter of Secret Victory Over the Three Worlds
'jig rten gsum las rnam par rgyal ba rtog pa'i rgyal po chen po
trailokyavijayamahākalparāja
(The most abridged form of this tantra consists of 1,000 ślokas in 21 chapters)
P115, vol.5; Toh.482; sDe-dge Ta 10a1-58a7

Chapter of the Dhāraṇī of the Crown Protrusion Victor of All Tathāgatas
de bzhin gshegs pa thams cad kyi gtsug tor rnam par rgyal ba zhes bya ba'i gzungs rtog pa
sarvatathāgatoṣṇīṣavijayanāmadhāraṇīkalpa
P200, vol.7; Toh.598; sDe-dge Pha 248a3-250a5

Chapter of the Dhāraṇī of the Crown Protrusion Victor of All Tathāgatas—
   'Holding the Club of the Lord of Death' and Related Topics
de bzhin gshegs pa thams cad kyi gtsug tor rnam par rgyal ba zhes bya ba'i gzungs rtog pa dang bcas pa
sarvatathāgatoṣṇīṣavijayanāmadhāraṇīkalpasahita
P197, vol.7; Toh.595; sDe-dge Pha 237b4-242a6

Chapter of the Dhāraṇī of the Crown Protrusion Victor of All Tathāgatas and
   Related Topics .
de bzhin gshegs pa thams cad kyi gtsug tor rnam par rgyal ba zhes bya ba'i gzungs rtog pa dang bcas pa
sarvatathāgatoṣṇīṣavijayanāmadhāraṇīkalpasahita
P199, vol.7; Toh.594; sDe-dge Pha 230a1-237b4

Chapter of the Dhāraṇī of the Crown Protrusion Victor of All Tathāgatas and
   Related Topics
de bzhin gshegs pa thams cad kyi gtsug tor rnam par rgyal ba zhes bya ba'i gzungs rtog pa dang bcas pa
āryasarvadurgatipariśodhanyuṣṇīṣavijayanāmadhāraṇī-kalpasahita
P198, vol.7; Toh.597; sDe-dge Pha 242a6-243b1

Chapter of the King of Magnificence, the Complete Purification of All the
   Completed Foe-destroying Tathāgatas Gone Beyond Sorrow ('Purification
   Tantra')
de bzhin gshegs pa dgra bcom pa yang dag par rdzogs pa'i sangs rgyas ngan song thams cad yongs su sbyong ba gzi brjid kyi rgyal po'i rtog pa zhes bya ba ('sbyong rgyud')
sarvadurgatipariśodhanatejorājasya tathāgatasya arhato samyaksam-buddhasya kalpanāma
P116, vol.5; Toh.483; sDe-dge Ta 58b1-96a3

Chapter of the Questions of the Very Pure Ārya on the Ultimate Truth of the Revealed View of the Sūtras
mdo sde dgongs 'grel gyi don dam yang dag 'phags zhus kyi le'u
(This is the seventh chapter, don dam yang dag 'phags, of the *Sūtra Unravelling the Thought*)

Chapter of the Tantra Arisen from the Radiant Lady of Illusion
sgyu ma'i 'od zer can 'byung ba'i rgyud las 'byung ba'i rtog pa'i rgyal po zhes bya ba
māyāmārīcijātatantrād uddhṛtakalparājānāma ('mārīcikalpa')
P183, vol.7; Toh.565; sDe-dge Pha 158b2-165b5

Close Placement of Mindfulness on the True Dharma
'phags pa dam pa'i chos dran pa nye bar bzhag pa
saddharmasmṛtyupasthāna
P953, Vols.37-38; Toh.287; sDe-dge Ya 82a1-318a7, Ra 1b1-307a5, La 1b1-229b7 and Sha 1b1-229b7

Commitment of the Nāga Vajra Lips
rdo rje mchu zhes bya ba klu'i dam tsig go
vajratuṇḍanāmanāgasamaya
P411, vol.9 and P589, vol.11; Toh.759 (=Toh.964); sDe-dge Wa 27b4-50a3

Compendium of the Reality of All Tathāgatas
de bzhin gshegs pa thams cad kyi de kho na nyid bsdus pa zhes bya ba theg pa chen po'i mdo ('de nyid bsdus pa')
sarvatathāgatatattvasaṁgrahanāmamahāyānasūtra ('tattvasaṁgraha')
P112, vol. 4; Toh.479; sDe-dge Nya 1b1-142a7

Compendium of the Vajra Wisdom Tantra
(Explanatory tantra of the Secret Assembly)
ye shes rdo rje kun las btus pa zhes bya pa'i rgyud
vajrajñānasamuccayanāmatantra
P84, vol.3; Toh.447; sDe-dge Ca 282a1-286a6

Complete Union Tantra
yang dag par sbyor ba zhes bya ba'i rgyud chen po
saṁpuṭanāmamahātantra
P26, vol. 2; Toh.381; sDe-dge Ga 73b1-158b7

Concise Explanation of Empowerments
(a tantra of the Wheel of Time cycle)
dbang mdor bstan pa
sekoddeśa
P3, vol.1; Toh.361; sDe-dge Ka 14a1-21a6

Conduct of the Yoginī
rnal 'byor ma'i kun tu spyod pa ('kun spyod')

yoginīsañcārya
P23, vol.2; Toh.375; sDe-dge Ga 34a1-44b5

Conquest of the Great Trichiliocosm Sūtra
stong chen mo rab tu 'joms pa zhes bya ba'i mdo
mahāsahasrapramardanasūtra
P177, vol.7; Toh.558; sDe-dge Pha 87b1-117a5

Continuation of the Subsequent Tantra of the Secret Mind of the Glorious Vajra Fierce One [Vajrapāṇi]
dpal rdo rje gtum po thugs gsang ba'i rgyud phyi ma'i phyi ma
śrīvajracaṇḍacittaguhyatantrottarottara
P95, vol.4; Toh.460; sDe-dge Ja 36b4-39b7

Cool Garden Sūtra
bsil ba'i tsal chen po'i mdo
mahāśitavanasūtra
P180, vol.7; Toh.562; sDe-dge Pha 138b6-150b1

Descent into Laṅkā Sūtra
'phags pa lang kar gshegs pa rin po che'i mdo las sangs rgyas thams cad kyi gsung gi snying po zhes bya ba'i le'u
laṅkāvtārasūtra
P775; Toh.107

Detailed Rite of Amoghapāśa
'phags pa don yod pa'i zhags pa'i cho ga zhib mo'i rgyal po
āryāmoghapāśakalparāja
P365, vol.8; Toh.686; sDe-dge Ma 1b1-316a6 and sDe-dge Tsa 1b1-57b7

Detailed Rite of the Noble Bodhisattva Avalokiteśvara With a Thousand Arms and a Thousand Eyes
byang chub sems dpa' 'phags pa spyan ras gzigs dbang phyug lag pa stong dang mig stong dang ldan pa'i cho ga zhib mo
Toh.690; sDe-dge Tsa 66a1-94a7

Dhāraṇī of Hayagrīva Avalokiteśvara
('Abbreviated Hayagriva Tantra')
'phags pa spyan ras gzigs dbang phyug ha ya grī ba'i gzungs
āryāvalokiteśvarahayagrīvadhāraṇī
P531, vol.11; Toh.733; sDe-dge Tsa 225a3-225b6

Dhāraṇī of Relying on Many Sons
'phags pa bu mang po rton pa zhes bya ba'i gzungs
āryabahuputrapratisaraṇanāmadhāraṇī
P215, vol.7 and P601, vol.11; Toh.615 (=Toh.976); sDe-dge Ba 52a5-52b5

Dhāraṇī of the Noble Bodhisattva Avalokiteśvara With a Thousand Arms and a Thousand Eyes, the Perfected Vast Mind of Compassion Unbound by Conceptuality
'phags pa byang chub sems dpa' spyan ras gzigs dbang phyug phyag stong spyan stong dang ldan pa thogs pa mi mnga' ba'i thugs rje chen po'i sems rgya cher yongs su rdzogs pa zhes bya ba'i gzungs
āryāvalokiteśvarasahasrabhujanetrāsaṅgamahākāruṇika-cittaparipūrṇanāmadhāraṇī
P369, vol.8; Toh.691 (=Toh.897); sDe-dge Tsa 94a1-129b6

Dhāraṇī of the Complete Vajra Conqueror
rdo rje rnam par 'joms pa zhes bya ba'i gzungs
vajravidāraṇanāmadhāraṇī
P406, vol.8 and P574, vol.11; Toh.750 (=Toh.949); sDe-dge Dza 265b3-266b7
(This is the first chapter of the *Tantra of the Complete Vajra Conqueror*, the only part to be translated into Tibetan.)

Dhāraṇī of the Completely Enlightening Invincible Vajra
('Dhāraṇī of the Blazing Flames')
'phags pa rdo rje mi 'pham pa me ltar rab tu rmongs byed ces bya ba'i gzungs
āryavajrājitānalapramohanīnāmadhāraṇī
P408, vol.8 and P579, vol.11; Toh.752 (=Toh.954); sDe-dge Wa 1b1-4b4

Dhāraṇī of the Continuity of Wealth ('Kubera Tantra')
'phags pa nor gyi rgyun zhes bya ba'i gzungs
āryavasudhārānāmadhāraṇī
P341, vol.7 and P632, vol.11; Toh.662 (=Toh.1007); sDe-dge Ba 186a5-190a3

Dhāraṇī of the Crown Protrusion Victor Who Completely Purifies All Those in Lower Births
'phags pa ngan 'gro thams cad yongs su sbyong ba gtsug tor rnam par rgyal ba zhes bya ba'i gzungs
āryasarvadurgatipariśodhanyuṣṇīṣavijayanāmadhāraṇī
P198, vol.7; Toh.597 (=Toh.984); sDe-dge Pha 243b1-248a3

Dhāraṇī of the Essence of the Noble 'Limitless Life and Wisdom'
('Immortal Drum-roll of Amitāyus')
'phags pa tshe dang ye shes dpag tu med pa'i snying po zhes bya ba'i gzungs
('tshe dpag med 'chi med rnga sgra'i gzungs')
āryāparimitāyurjñānahṛdayanāmadhāraṇī
P363, vol.7 and P475, vol.11; Toh.676 (=Toh.850); sDe-dge Ba 220b5-222b1

Dhāraṇī of the Fourth Application of the Hearth and Nectar
'phags pa bdud rtsi thab sbyor gyi snying po bzhi pa zhes bya ba'i gzungs
āryakuṇḍalyamṛtahṛdayacaturthanāmadhāraṇī
P419, vol.9 and P582, vol.11; Toh.755; sDe-dge Wa 6a6-7b4

Dhāraṇī of the Goddess of Invocation
'phags pa lha mo bskul byed ma zhes bya ba'i gzungs
āryacundīdevīnāmadhāraṇī
P188, vol.7 and P614, vol.11; Toh.613 (=Toh.989); sDe-dge Ba 46b5-47a7

Dhāraṇī of the Leaf-clad Noble Hermit Lady
'phags pa ri khrod lo ma gyon ma zhes bya ba'i gzungs
āryaparṇaśavarīnāmadhāraṇī
P186, vol.7 and P620, vol.11; Toh.736 (=Toh.995); sDe-dge Tsa 228b1-229a3

Dhāraṇī of the Radiant Noble Lady
'phags ma 'od zer can zhes bya ba'i gzungs
āryamārīcīnāmadhāraṇī
P182, vol.7; Toh.564 (=Toh.988); sDe-dge Pha 156b1-158b2

Dhāraṇī of the Stainless Crown Protrusion
kun nas sgor 'jug pa'i 'od zer gtsug tor dri ma med par snang ba de bzhin gshegs pa thams cad kyi snying po dang dam tshig la rnam par lta ba zhes bya ba'i gzungs
samantamukhapraveśaraśmivimaloṣṇīṣaprabhāsasarva-tathāgatahṛdayasamayavilokitanāmadhāraṇī
P608, vol.11; Toh.599 (=Toh.983); sDe-dge Pha 250a5-259b7

Dhāraṇī Purifying All Obscurations of Karma
('Vajra Akṣobhya Tantra')
'phags pa las kyi sgrib pa thams cad rnam par sbyong ba zhes bya ba'i gzungs
āryasarvakarmvaraṇaviśodhaninārnadhāraṇī
P146, vol.6 and P634, vol.11; Toh.743; sDe-dge Tsa 236a3-236b7

Dharma Wheel Sūtra
chos kyi 'khor lo'i mdo
dharmacakrasūtra
P1003, vol.39; Toh.337 (=Toh.31); sDe-dge Sa 275a6-277a4

Discrimination of Ethical Discipline [Sūtra]
'dul brnam par 'byed pa
vinayavibhaṅga
P1032, vol.42-43; Toh.3; sDe-dge Ca 21a1-292a7

Drop of the Great Seal
dpal phyag rgya chen po'i thig le zhes bya ba rnal 'byor ma chen mo'i rgyud kyi rgyal po'i mnga' bdag
śrīmahāmudrātilakanāmamahāyoginītantrarājādhipati
P12, vol.1; Toh.420; sDe-dge Nga 66a1-90b7

Drop of the Secret Moon
dpal zla gsang thig le shes bya ba rgyud kyi rgyal po chen po
śrīcandraguhyatilakanāmamahātantrarāja
P111, vol.4; Toh.477; sDe-dge Ja 247b4-303a7

Drop of Wisdom, Great King of Yoginī Tantras Called the Supreme Wonder
dpal ye shes thig le rnal 'byor ma'i rgyud kyi rgyal po chen po mchog tu rmad du byung ba zhes bya ba
śrijñānatilakayoginītantrarājaparamamahādhbutanāma
P14, vol.2; Toh.422; sDe-dge Nga 96b6-136b4

Embrace of the Four Yoginīs Tantra
('Divine Embrace')
rnal 'byor ma bzhi'i kha sbyor gyi rgyud ('kha sbyor')
caturyoginīsampuṭatantranāma
P24, vol.2; Toh.376; sDe-dge Ga 44b6-52b5

Empowerment of Vajrapāṇi Tantra
'phags pa lag na rdo rje dbang bskur ba'i rgyud chen po
āryavajrapāṇyabhiṣekatantra
P130, vol.6; Toh.496; sDe-dge Da 1b1-156b7

Especially Extensive Sūtra of the Aspiring Prayers of the Seven Tathāgatas
'phags pa de bzhin gshegs pa bdun gyi sngon gyi smon lam gyi khyad par rgyas pa zhes bya ba theg pa chen po'i mdo
āryasaptatathāgatapūrvapraṇidhānaviśeṣavistaranāma-mahāyānasūtra
P135, vol.6; Toh.503; sDe-dge Da) 248b1-273b7

Essence of the Tantra of the Glorious Wheel of Time
dpal dus kyi 'khor lo zhes bya ba'i rgyud kyi snying po
śrīkālacakragarbhanāmatantra
P6, vol.1; Toh.364; sDe-dge Ka 144b1-146a7

Essence of the Tathāgata Sūtra
'phags pa de bzhin gshegs pa'i snying po zhes bya ba theg pa chen po'i mdo
āryatathāgatagarbhanāmamahāyānasūtra
P924, vol.36; Toh.258; sDe-dge Za 245b2-259b4

Explication of the Highest Tantra
mngon par brjod pa'i rgyud bla ma zhes bya ba ('mngon brjod')

abhidānottaratantranāma
P17, vol.2; Toh.369; sDe-dge Ka 247a1-370a7

Expression of the Ultimate Names of the Wisdom-being Mañjuśrī
'jam dpal ye shes sems dpa'i don dam pa'i mtsan yang dag par brjod pa
mañjuśrīśrījñānasattvasya paramārthanāmasaṅgīti
('mañjuśrīnāmasaṅgīti')
P2, vol.1; Toh.360; sDe-dge Ka 1b1-13b7

Extensive Sūtra of the Aspiring Prayers of the Exalted Vaidurya Light of the Medicine Buddhas
'phags pa bcom ldan 'das sman gyi bla baidurya'i 'od kyi sngon gyi smon lam gyi khyad par rgyas pa zhes bya ba theg pa chen po'i mdo
āryabhagavato bhaiṣajyaguruvaiḍūryaprabhasya pūrva-praṇidhānaviśeṣavistarasūtra
P136, vol.6; Toh.504; sDe-dge Da 274a1-283b7

General Secret Tantra
dkyil 'khor thams cad kyi spyi'i cho ga gsang ba'i rgyud
sarvamaṇḍalasāmānyavidhiguhyatantra
P429, vol.9; Toh.806; sDe-dge Wa 141a-167b7

Glorious Fierce One, [Explanatory] Tantra of the Secret Mind of the Glorious Vajra Fierce One [Vajrapāṇi]
dpal rdo rje gtum po thugs gsang ba'i rgyud dpal gtuṃ po
śrīvajracaṇḍacittaguhyatantra
P93, vol.4; Toh.458; sDe-dge Ja 15a5-30a7

Golden Light (small, medium and large recensions: gser 'od che 'bring chung):

1) *Mahāyāna Sūtra of Complete Victory of the Supreme Sacred Golden Light* (in 31 chapters: 'large')
'phags pa gser 'od dam pa mchog tu rnam par rgyal ba'i mdo sde'i rgyal po theg pa chen po'i mdo
āryasuvarṇaprahāsottamasūtrendrarājanāma-mahāyānasūtra
P174, vols.6-7; Toh.555; sDe-dge Pa 19a1-151a7

2) *Mahāyāna Sūtra of Complete Victory of the Supreme Sacred Golden Light* (in 29 chapters: 'medium')
'phags pa gser 'od dam pa mchog tu rnam par rgyal ba'i mdo sde'i rgyal po theg pa chen po'i mdo
āryasuvarṇaprahāsottamasūtrendrarājanāma-mahāyānasūtra
P175, vol.7; Toh.556; sDe-dge Pa 151b1-273a7

3) *Mahāyāna Sūtra of Complete Victory of the Supreme Sacred Golden Light* (in 22 chapters: 'small')
'phags pa gser 'od dam pa mchog tu rnam par rgyal ba'i mdo sde'i rgyal po theg pa chen po'i mdo
āryasuvarṇaprahāsottamasūtrendrarājanāma-mahāyānasūtra
P176, vol.7; Toh.557; sDe-dge Pha 1b1-62a7

Great Chapter, the Secret Assembly, the Great Secret of the Body, Speech and Mind of All Tathāgatas ('Root Tantra of The Secret Assembly')
de bzhin gshegs pa thams cad kyi sku gsung thugs kyi gsang chen gsang ba 'dus pa zhes bya ba brtag pa'i chen po ('dpal gsang ba 'dus pa zhes bya ba rgyud kyi rgyal po chen po')
sarvatathāgatakāyavākcittarahasya guhyasamājanāma-mahākalparāja ('śrīguhyasamājamahātantrarājanāma')
P81, vol.3; Toh.442; sDe-dge Ca 90a1-148a6

Great King of Tantras, Subduing the Elemental Forces
'byung po 'dul ba zhes bya ba'i rgyud kyi rgyal po chen po
bhūtaḍāmaramahātantrarājanāma
P404, vol.8; Toh.747; sDe-dge Dza 238a1-263a7

Great Powerful One Mahāyāna Sūtra
'phags pa stobs po che zhes bya ba theg pa chen po'i mdo
āryamahābalanāmamahāyānasūtra
P416, vol.9 and P572, vol.11; Toh.757 (=Toh.947); sDe-dge Wa 8a7-19a5

Great Ultimate Nirvāṇa Sūtra
'phags pa yongs su mya ngan las 'das pa chen po'i mdo
āryamahāparinirvāṇanāmamahāyānasūtra
P787-9, vol.30-1; Toh.120, 121; sDe-dge Tha 1b1-151a4 and Tha 151a4-152b7

Heap of Jewels Sūtra
'phags pa rin po che'i mtha' zhes bya ba theg pa chen po'i mdo ('dkon mchog kyi mdo')
āryaratnakoṭināmamahāyānasūtra
P786, vol.30; Toh.118; sDe-dge Ja 290b1-298a7

Heart of Wisdom Sūtra
bcom ldan 'das ma shes rab kyi pha rol tu phyin pa'i snying po
bhagavatīprajñāpāramitāhṛdaya
P160, vol.6; Toh.531 (=Toh.21); sDe-dge Na 94b1-95b3

Hevajra Tantra
('Root Tantra of Hevajra', 'The Two Examinations')
kye'i rdo rje zhes bya ba rgyud kyi rgyal po and kye'i rdo rje mkha' 'gro ma dra ba'i sdom pa'i rgyud kyi rgyal po

P & Toh.: hevajratantrarājanāma and P: śrīhevajraḍākinījālasaṁvaramahātantrarāja, Toh.: (no Sanskrit title)
('hevajratantra', 'brtag gnyis')
P10-11, vol.1,; Toh. 417-418; sDe-dge Nga 1b1-13b5, Nga 13b5-30a3

Exaltation of Heruka
dpal khrag 'thung mngon par 'byung ba ('he ru ka mngon 'byung')
śrīherukābhyudayanāma
P21, vol.2; Toh.374; sDe-dge Ga 1b1-33b7

History Chapter [of the Vajra Terrifier]
gtam rgyud kyi rtog pa
ākhyānakalpa
P108, vol.4; Toh.471; sDe-dge Ja 173b3-174a2

Homage to Tārā, Twenty-one Verses of Praise to She Who Helps ('Twenty-one Homages to Tārā')
P: bcom ldan 'das ma sgrol ma la yang dag par rdzogs pa'i sangs rgyas bstod pa gsungs pa, Toh.: sgrol ma la phyag 'tsal nyi su rtsa gcig gis bstod pa phan yon dang bcas pa
P: ekaviṁśatistotram, Toh.: namastāre ekaviṁśatistotra-guṇahitasahita
P77, vol.3; Toh.438; sDe-dge Ca 42b3-43b6

Hundred [Verses on] Karma
las brgya pa
karmaśataka
P1007, vol.39-40; Toh.340; sDe-dge Ha 1b1-309a7 and sDe-dge A 1b1-128b7

Hundred Verses of Stories of Realization
gong po la sogs pa'i rtogs pa brjod pa brgya pa
('rtogs brjod brgya pa')
pūrṇapramukhāvadānaśataka ('avadānaśataka')
P1012, vol.40; Toh.343; sDe-dge Am 1b1-286b7

Introduction to the Signs of Definite and Indefinite Progress Sūtra
nges pa dang mi nges par 'gro ba'i phyag rgya la 'jug pa
niyatāniyatagatimudrāvatāra
P868, vol.34; Toh.202; sDe-dge Tsa 63a5-78a4

King of Meditative Stabilizations Sūtra
'phags pa chos thams cad kyi rang bzhin mnyam pa nyid rnam par spros pa ting nge 'dzin gyi rgyal po zhes bya ba theg pa chen po'i mdo ('ting nges 'dzin gyi rgyal po'i mdo')
āryasarvadharmasvabhāvasamatāvipañcitasamādhirājanāmamahāyānasūtra ('samādhirājasūtra')
P795, vol.31-32; Toh.127; sDe-dge Da 1b1-170b7

King of Tantras, Exaltation of Vajravārāhī, the Wisdom of the Non-dual Immeasurable Mind of All Ḍākinīs ('Exaltation of Vajravārāhī')
mkha' 'gro ma thams cad kyi thugs gnyis su med pa bsam gyis mi khyab pa'i ye shes rdo rje phag mo mngon par 'byung ba'i rgyud kyi rgyal po ('phag mo mngon 'byung')
ḍākinīsarvacittādvayācintyajñānavajravārāhyabhibhāvatantra-rājanāma
P60, vol.3; Toh.378; sDe-dge Ga 60b1-71a3

Lady of Supreme Attainment
'phags pa de bzhin gshegs pa'i gtsug tor nas byung ba'i gdugs dkar po can gzhan gyis mi thub pa phyir zlog pa chen mo mchog tu grub pa zhes bya ba'i gzungs ('mchog grub ma')
āryatathāgatoṣṇīṣasitātapatrāparājitāmahāpratyaṅgirāmahā-(vidyārājñī)paramasiddhināmadhāraṇī
P203, vol.7; Toh.591; sDe-dge Pha 212b7-219a7
(A second translation of the original *Praise of Her Who is Unconquerable by Others.*)

Lamp of Suchness, Great Yoginī Tantra
dpal de kho na nyid kyi sgron ma zhes bya ba'i rnal 'byor chen mo'i rgyud kyi rgyal po
śrītattvapradīpanāmamahāyoginītantrarāja
P15, vol.2; Toh.423; sDe-dge Nga 136b5-142b7

Lesser King of Tantras of Glorious Supreme Bliss
('Root Tantra of Heruka Cakrasaṁvara')
rgyud kyi rgyal po dpal bde mchog nyung ngu zhes bya ba
tantrarājaśrīlaghuśambaranāma
P16, vol.2; Toh.368; sDe-dge Ka 213b1-246b7

(Greater) Lion's Roar of Avalokiteśvara Dhāraṇī
'phags pa spyan ras gzigs dbang phyug seng ge'i sgra'i gzungs zhes bya ba
āryāvalokiteśvarasiṁhanādanāmadhāraṇī
P386, vol.8; Toh.703; sDe-dge Tsa 165b5-171a5

(Lesser) Lion's Roar of Avalokiteśvara Dhāraṇī
seng ge'i sgra'i gzungs
P387, vol.8 and P3977, vol.80; Toh.704; sDe-dge Tsa 171a5-171b1

Lion's Roar Tantra
seng ge sgra'i rgyud ces bya ba
siṁhanādatantranāma
P385, vol.8; Toh.702; sDe-dge Tsa 164b4-165b5

Lotus Net, Root Tantra of Avalokiteśvara
'phags pa spyan ras gzigs dbang phyug gi rtsa ba'i rgyud kyi rgyal po padma dra ba zhes bya ba
āryāvalokiteśvarapadmajālamūlatantrarājanāma
P364, vol.7; Toh.681; sDe-dge Ba 224b1-278a7

Mahāyāna Sūtra of the Noble 'Limitless Life and Wisdom'
'phags pa tshe dang ye shes dpag tu med pa zhes bya ba theg pa chen po'i mdo
āryāparimitāyurjñānanāmamahāyānasūtra
P362, vol.7 and P474, vol.11; Toh.674 (=Toh.849); sDe-dge Ba 211b2-216a7

Mahāyāna Sūtra of the Noble 'Limitless Life and Wisdom'
'phags pa tshe dang ye shes dpag tu med pa zhes bya ba theg pa chen po'i mdo
āryāparimitāyurjñānanāmamahāyānasūtra
P362, vol.7 and P474, vol.11; Toh.675; sDe-dge Ba 216a7-220b5

Ocean of Ḍākinīs
dpal mkha' 'gro rgya mtsho rnal 'byor ma'i rgyud kyi rgyal po chen po zhes bya ba
('bde mchog mkha' 'gro rgya mtsho'i rgyud')
śrīḍākārṇavamahāyoginītantrarājanāma ('ḍākārṇava')
P19, vol.2; Toh.372; sDe-dge Ga 219a2-220a7

One Hundred and Eight Names of Avalokiteśvara With Their Mantras
'phags pa spyan ras gzigs dbang phyug gi mtshan brgya rtsa rgyad pa gzungs sngags dang bcas pa
āryāvalokiteśvarāṣṭottaraśatakanāmadhāraṇīmantrasahita
P320, vol.7 and P499, vol.11; Toh.634 (=Toh.874); sDe-dge Ba 105a3-107a7

One Hundred and Eight Names of Khagarbha With Their Mantras
'phags pa nam mkha'i snying po'i mtshan brgya rtsa rgyad pa gzungs sngags dang bcas pa
āryakhagarbhāṣṭottaraśatakanāmadhāraṇīmantrasahita
P322, vol.7 and P501, vol.11; Toh.636 (=Toh.876); sDe-dge Ba 109a5-112a4

One Hundred and Eight Names of Kṣitigarbha With Their Mantras
'phags pa sa'i snying po'i mtshan brgya rtsa rgyad pa gzungs sngags dang bcas pa
āryakṣitigarbhāṣṭottaraśatakanāmadhāraṇīmantrasahita
P327, vol.7 and P506, vol.11; Toh.641 (=Toh.881); sDe-dge Ba 124a5-126a5

One Hundred and Eight Names of Maitreya With Their Mantras
'phags pa byams pa'i mtshan brgya rtsa rgyad pa gzungs sngags dang bcas pa
āryamaitreyāṣṭottaraśatakanāmadhāraṇīmantrasahita

P321, vol.7 and P500, vol.11; Toh.635 (=Toh.875); sDe-dge Ba 107b1-109a5

One Hundred and Eight Names of Samantabhadra With Their Mantras
'phags pa kun tu bzang po'i mtshan brgya rtsa rgyad pa gzungs sngags dang bcas pa
āryasamantabhadrāṣṭottaraśatakanāmadhāraṇīmantrasahita
P323, vol.7 and P502, vol.11; Toh.637 (=Toh.877); sDe-dge Ba 112a4-116a2

One Hundred and Eight Names of Sarvanīvaraṇaviṣkambhin With Their Mantras
'phags pa sgrib pa thams cad rnam par sel ba'i mtshan brgya rtsa rgyad pa gzungs sngags dang bcas pa
āryasarvanīvaraṇaviṣkambhinaṣṭottaraśatakanāmadhāraṇī-mantrasahita
P326, vol.7 and P505, vol.11; Toh.640 (=Toh.880); sDe-dge Ba 122a2-124a4

One Hundred and Eight Names of the Youthful Mañjuśrī With Their Mantras
'phags pa 'jam dpal gzhon nur 'gyur pa'i mtshan brgya rtsa rgyad pa gzungs sngags dang bcas pa
āryamañjuśrīkumārabhūtāṣṭottaraśatakanāmadhāraṇī-mantrasahita
P325, vol.7 and P504, vol.11; Toh.639 (=Toh.879); sDe-dge Ba 118b5-122a1

One Hundred and Eight Names of Vajrapāṇi With Their Mantras
'phags pa lag na rdo rje'i mtshan brgya rtsa rgyad pa gzungs sngags dang bcas pa
āryavajrapāṇyaṣṭottaraśatakanāmadhāraṇīmantrasahita
P324, vol.7 and P503, vol.11; Toh.638 (=Toh.878); sDe-dge Ba 116a2-118b5

Ornament of the Vajra Essence Tantra
dpal rdo rje snying po rgyan gyi rgyud
śrīvajrahṛdayālaṅkāratantranāma
P86, vol.3; Toh.451; sDe-dge Cha 36a1-58b3

Peacock Lady Sūtra
rig snags kyi rgyal mo rma bya chen mo ('rma bya chen mo'i mdo')
mahāmāyūrīvidyārājñī ('mahāmāyūrīsūtra')
P178, vol.7; Toh.559; sDe-dge Pha 87b1-117a5

Perfect Enlightenment of Great Vairocana Sūtra
rnam par snang mdzad chen po mngon par rdzogs par byang chub par rnam par sprul ba byin gyis rlob pa shin tu rgyas pa mdo sde'i dbang po rgyal po zhes bya ba'i chos kyi rnam grangs ('spyod rgyud rnam snang mngon byang')
mahāvairocanābhisambodhivikurvitādhiṣṭhānavaipulyasūtra-indrarājanāmadharmaparyāya
P126, vol.5; Toh.494; sDe-dge Tha 151b2-260a7

Perfection of Wisdom Sūtra in Eight Thousand Verses
shes rab kyi pha rol tu phyin pa brgyad stong pa'i mdo
prajñāpāramitāṣṭāsāhasrikāsūtra
P734, vol.21; Toh.12; sDe-dge Ka 1b1-286a6

Perfection of Wisdom Sūtra in Eighteen Thousand Verses
shes rab kyi pha rol tu phyin pa bcu brgyad stong pa'i mdo
prajñāpāramitāṣṭādaśasāhasrikāsūtra
P732, vol.19-20; Toh.10; sDe-dge Ka 1b1-300a7, Kha 1b1-304a7 and Ga 1b1-206a7

Perfection of Wisdom Sūtra in One Hundred Thousand Verses ('Mother Sūtra')
shes rab kyi pha rol tu phyin pa 'bum ba'i mdo ('yum mdo')
prajñāpāramitāśatasāhasrikāsūtra
P730, vols. 12-18; Toh.8; sDe-dge Ka-Na

Perfection of Wisdom Sūtra in Ten Thousand Verses
shes rab kyi pha rol tu phyin pa bcu stong pa'i mdo
prajñāpāramitādaśasāhasrikāsūtra
P733, vol.20-21; Toh.11; sDe-dge Ka 1b1-300a7

Perfection of Wisdom Sūtra in Twenty-five Thousand Verses
shes rab kyi pha rol tu phyin pa nyi shu lnga stong pa'i mdo
prajñāpāramitāpañcaviṁśatisāhasrikāsūtra
P731, vol.18-19; Toh.9; sDe-dge Ka 1b1-382a4, Kha 1b1-393a6 and Ga 1b1-381a5

Presentation of the Three Commitments, King of Tantras
dam tshig gsum bkod pa'i rgyal po zhes bya ba'i rgyud
trisamayavyūharājanāmatantra
P134, vol.6; Toh.502; sDe-dge Da 181a2-247a7

Praise of She Who is Unconquerable by Others
'phags pa de bzhin gshegs pa thams cad kyi gtsug tor nas byung ba gdugs dkar po can zhes bya ba gzhan gyis mi thub ma phyin zlog pa'i rig sngags kyi rgyal mo chen mo
āryasarvatathāgatoṣṇīṣasitātapatrānāmāparājitāpratyaṅgirāmahāvidyārājñī
P202, vol.7; Toh.590; sDe-dge Pha 205a1-212b6

Prophetic Dream Sūtra
'phags pa rmi lam bstan pa zhes bya ba theg pa chen po'i mdo
āryasvapnanirdeśanāmamahāyānasūtra
P760 (4), vol.22; Toh.48; sDe-dge Ka 203b1-237b7

Questions of Subāhu Sūtra
'phags pa lag bzangs kyi zhus pa zhes bya ba theg pa chen po'i mdo
āryasubāhuparipṛcchānāmamahāyānasūtra

P760 (26), vol.24; Toh.70; sDe-dge Ca 154a1-180b7

Questions of Subāhu Tantra
'phags pa dpung bzang gis zhus pa zhes bya ba'i rgyud
āryasubāhuparipṛcchānāmatantra
P428, vol.9; Toh.805; sDe-dge Wa 118a1-140b7

Questions of the Noble King Udayana Sūtra
'phags pa bat sa'i rgyal po 'char byed kyis zhus pa zhes bya'i le'u
āryodayanavatsarājaparipṛcchānāmaparivarta
P760(29), vol.24; Toh.73; sDe-dge Ca 204b1-215b7

Questions of the Four Goddesses
lha mo bzhis zhus pa
caturdevīparipṛcchā
P85, vol.3; Toh.446; sDe-dge Ca 277b3-281b7

Questions of the God Indra
(Explanatory Tantra of the Secret Assembly)
lha'i dbang pos zhus pa
devendraparipṛcchā
(Not translated into Tibetan)

Questions of the Nāga King Unwarmed Sūtra
'phags pa klu'i rgyal po ma dros pas zhus pa zhes bya ba theg pa chen po'i mdo
āryānavataptanāgarājaparipṛcchānāmamahāyānasūtra
P823, vol.33; Toh.156; sDe-dge Pha 206a1-253b7

Questions of Vīradatta Sūtra
'phags pa khyim bdag dpas byin gyis zhus pa zhes bya ba theg pa chen po'i mdo
āryavīradattagṛhapatiparipṛcchānāmamahāyānasūtra
P760(28), vol.24; Toh.72; sDe-dge Ca 194a1-204b1

Revelation of the Intention
dgongs pa lung bstan pa zhes bya ba rgyud
sandhivyākaraṇanāmatantra
P83, vol.3; Toh.444; sDe-dge Ca 158a1-207b7

Rite of the Chapter of the Noble Amoghapāśa
'phags pa don yod zhags pa'i rtog pa'i rgyal po'i cho ga zhes bya ba
āryāmoghapāśakalparājavidhināma
P365, vol.8; Toh.689; sDe-dge Tsa 62a3-66a1

Root Tantra of Mañjuśrī
'phags pa 'jam dpal gyi rtsa ba'i rgyud
āryamañjuśrīmūlatantra (°mūlakalpa)

P162, vol.6; Toh.543; sDe-dge Na 105a1-351a6

Root Tantra of the Secret Assembly
de bzhin gshegs pa thams cad kyi sku gsung thugs kyi gsang chen gsang ba 'dus pa zhes bya ba brtag pa'i chen po ('dpal gsang ba 'dus pa zhes bya ba rgyud kyi rgyal po chen po')
sarvatathāgatakāyavākcittarahasyātirahasya guhyasamājanāma mahāguhyakalparāja ('śrīguhyasamājamahātantrarājanāma')
P81, vol.3; Toh.442; sDe-dge Ca 90a1-148a6

Root Tantra of Vajrapāṇi
P: 'phags pa lag na rdo rje gos sngon pa can rdo rje sa 'og ces bya ba'i rgyud
Toh.: 'phags pa rdo rje sa 'og gi rgyud kyi rgyal po zhes bya ba
P: āryavajrapāṇinīlāmbaradharavajrapātālanāmatantra
Toh.: āryavajrapātālanāmatantrarājapaṇḍita
P129, vol.6; Toh.744; sDe-dge Tsa 237a1-266a7

Secret Tantra Rite of Complete Wrathful Victory
khro bo rnam par rgyal ba'i rtog pa gsang ba'i rgyud
krodhavijayakalpaguhyatantra
P291, vol.7; Toh.604; sDe-dge Pha 269a3-287a7

Seven Hundred Stanzas of the Radiant Noble Lady of Illusion
'phags ma 'od zer can gyi dkyil 'khor gyi cho ga 'od zer can 'byung ba'i rgyud stong phrag bcu gnyis pa las 'byung ba'i rtog pa'i snying pa bdun brgya pa zhes bya ba
('sgyu ma rjes su byed pa'i rtog pa')
āryamārīcimaṇḍalavidhimārīcijātadvādaśasahasrād uddhṛta-kalpahṛdayasaptaśatanāma ('māyāmārīcisaptaśatanāma')
P184, vol.7; Toh.566; sDe-dge Pha 165b5-186a3

Source of Commitment Tantra
(Explanatory Tantra of Heruka Cakrasaṁvara)
dpal bde mchog 'byung ba zhes bya ba'i rgyud kyi rgyal po chen po ('sdom pa 'byung ba'i rgyud kyi rgyal po chen po'), ('sdom 'byung')
śrīmahāsaṁvarodayatantrarājanāma
P20, vol.2; Toh.373; sDe-dge Kha 1b1-125a7

Subsequent Holder of Secret Mantra Sūtra
gsang sngags chen po rjes su 'dzin pa'i mdo
mahāmantrānudhāriṇīsūtra
P181, vol.7; Toh.563; sDe-dge Pha 150b2-156a6

Subsequent Tantra of The Secret Assembly
['dus pa'i] rgyud phyi ma
[guhyasamāja] uttaratantra

P61, vol.3; Toh.443; sDe-dge Ca 148a6-157b7

Subsequent Tantra of the Secret Mind of the Glorious Vajra Fierce One [Vajrapāṇi]
dpal rdo rje gtum po thugs gsang ba'i rgyud phyi ma
śrīvajracaṇḍacittaguhyatantrottara
P94, vol.4; Toh.459; sDe-dge Ja 30b1-36b3

Subsequent Tantra, the Essence of the Tantra of the Glorious Wheel of Time
dpal dus kyi 'khor lo'i rgyud phyi ma rgyud kyi snying po zhes bya ba
śrīkālacakratantrottaratantrahṛdayanāma
P5, vol.1; Toh.363; sDe-dge Ka 129a1-144a7

Supreme Glory Tantra
dpal mchog dang po zhes bya ba theg pa chen po'i rtog pa'i rgyal po
śrīparamādyanāmamahāyānakalparāja
P119, vol.5; Toh.487; sDe-dge Ta 150b1-173a4

Sūtra of She Who Leads Each One
'phags pa rig pa'i rgyal mo so sor 'brang ba chen mo ('so sor 'brang ma'i mdo')
āryamahāpratisarāvidyārājñī ('pratisarāsūtra')
P179, vol.7; Toh.561; sDe-dge Pha 117b4-138b5

Sūtra of the Noble Glorious Great Mother
('The Great Glorious Mother Tantra')
'phags pa dpal chen mo'i mdo ('dpal chen mo'i rgyud')
āryamahālakṣmīsūtra
P399, vol.8 and P630, vol.11; Toh.740 (=Toh.1005); sDe-dge Tsa 234b2-235a3

Sūtra Unravelling the Thought
'phags pa gongs pa nges par 'grel ba'i mdo ('dgongs 'grel ril po')
sandhinirmocanasūtra
P774, vol.29; Toh.106; sDe-dge Ca 1b1-55b7
Tantra of the Red Destroyer of the Lord of Death
P: dpal gshin rje dmar po zhes bya ba rgyud kyi rgyal po
Toh: dpal ldan gshin rje gshed dmar po'i rgyud kyi rgyal po zhes bya ba
P: śrīraktayamāritantrarājanāma
Toh: śrīmadraktayamāritantrarājanāma
P109, vol.4; Toh.475; sDe-dge Ja 215a1-244b7)

Teachings of the Great Compassion of the Tathāgata Sūtra
('Questions of Indra Dhāraṇī')

'phags pa de bzhin bshegs pa'i snying rje chen po nges par bstan pa zhes bya ba theg pa chen po'i mdo
tathāgatamahākaruṇānirdeśasūtra ('dhāraṇīśvararājaparipṛcchā')
P814, vol.32; Toh.147; sDe-dge Pa 142a1-242b7

Tantra of the Solitary Hero Mañjuśrī
(*'Sādhana of the Solitary Hero Mañjuśrī'*)
dpa' bo gcig bu grub pa zhes bya ba'i rgyud kyi rgyal po chen po
mañjuśrīsiddhaikavīratantra
P163, vol.6; Toh.544; sDe-dge Pa 1b1-13a6

Tārā, Mother of All Tathāgatas, Arising of Various Actions Tantra
de bzhin gshegs pa thams cad kyi yum sgrol ma las sna tsogs 'byung ba zhes bya ba'i rgyud
sarvatathāgatamātṛtārāviśvakarmabhavatantranāma
P390, vol.8; Toh.726; sDe-dge Tsa 202a1-217a2

Vajra Garland, the Explanatory Tantra of the Secret Assembly
rnal 'byor chen po'i rgyud dpal rdo rje phreng ba mngon par brjod pa rgyud thams cad kyi snying po gsang ba rnam par phye zhes bya ba ('bshad rgyud rdo rje 'phreng ba')
śrīvajramālābhidhānamahāyogatantrasarvatantrahṛdaya-rahasyavibhaṅga ('vajramālā')
P82, vol.3; Toh.445; sDe-dge Ca 208a1-277b3

Vajra Peak Yoga Tantra (Explanatory Tantra of the Yoga Tantras)
gsang ba rnal 'byor chen po'i rgyud rdo rje rtse mo ('rdo rje rtse mo')
vajraśekharamahāguhyayogatantra
P113, vol. 5; Toh.480; sDe-dge Nya 142b1-274a5

Vajra Tent Tantra
mkha' 'gro ma rdo rje gur zhes bya ba'i rgyud kyi rgyal po chen po'i brtag pa ('rdo rje gur')
āryaḍākinīvajrapañjaramahātantrarājakalpa ('vajrapañjaratantra')
P11, vol. 1; Toh.419; sDe-dge Nga 30a4-65b7

Vajra Terrifier (Vajrabhairava, rDo-rje 'jigs-byed)
(The cycle of texts for this deity includes:)
a) *Root Tantra of the Vajra Terrifier* ('Seven Chapters')
dpal rdo rje 'jigs byed chen po'i rgyud ces bya ba
śrīvajramahābhairavanāmatantra
P105, vol.4; Toh.468; sDe-dge Ja 151b4-164a1

b) *Ritual Procedure Tantra of the Vajra Terrifier*
dpal rdo rje 'jigs byed kyi rtog pa'i rgyud kyi rgyal po
śrīvajrabhairavakalpatantrarāja

P106, vol.4; Toh.470; sDe-dge Ja 167b5-173b3

c) *(Explanatory) Tantra of the Vajra Terrifier* ('Three Chapters')
dpal rdo rje 'jigs byed kyi rgyud kyi rgyal po rtog pa gsum pa
śrīkṛṣṇayamāritantrarājatrikalpanāma
P107, vol.4; Toh.469; sDe-dge Ja 164a1-167b5
(Note: Although this is listed as a tantra of the Black Destroyer of the Lord of Death, its subject matter involves the practice of the Vajra Terrifier.)

d) *Musk-shrew Chapter [of the Vajra Terrifier]*
te'u lo pa'i cho ga zhes bya ba
chucchundarakalpanāma
P2849, vol.67; Toh.472; sDe-dge Ja 174a2-174b7

e) *History Chapter [of the Vajra Terrifier]*
gtam rgyud kyi rtog pa
ākhyānakalpa
P108, vol.4; Toh.471; sDe-dge Ja 173b3-174a2

Vajraḍāka Tantra
rdo rje mkha' 'gro gsang ba'i rgyud kyi rgyal po
śrīvajraḍākaguhyatantrarāja
P44, vol. 3; Toh.399; sDe-dge Ga 230a2-231b3

Very Extensive Garland of Buddhas Sūtra (*'Garland Sūtra'*)
sangs rgyas phal po che zhes bya ba shin tu rgyas pa chen po'i mdo ('phal chen mdo')
buddhāvataṁsakanāmamahāvaipulyasūtra ('avataṁsakasūtra')
P761, vols. 25-26; Toh.44; sDe-dge Ka 1b1-393a5, Kha 1b1-396a6, Ga 1b1-396a7, A 1b1-363a6

Web of Illusion, Great King of Tantras
rgyud kyi rgyal po chen po sgyu 'phrul dra ba zhes bya ba ('sgyu 'phrul dra ba'i rgyud') ('rnam snang sgyu dra')
māyājālamahātantrarājanāma
P102, vol.4; Toh.466; sDe-dge Ja 94b1-134a7
(Note: This text belongs to the Highest Yoga class of tantra.)

Wheel of Time, King of Tantras, Issued from the Supreme Original Buddha
(Root Tantra of the Wheel of Time)
mchog gi dang po'i sangs rgyas las byung ba rgyud kyi rgyal po dpal dus kyi 'khor lo
paramādibuddhoddhṛtaśrīkālacakranāmatantrarāja
P4, vol. 1; Toh.362; sDe-dge Ka 22b1-128b7

Wisdom Wheel of Lightning Mahāyāna Sūtra, Tantra of the Accomplishment of Great Ethical Conduct, Lamp of the Inexhaustible Mine, Treasury of Secrets, Secret of All Tathāgatas ('Treasury of Secrets')
de bzhin gshegs pa thams cad kyi gsang ba, gsang ba'i mdzod chen po mi zad pa gter gyi sgron ma, brtul zhugs chen po bsgrub pa'i rgyud, ye shes rnam pa glog gi 'khor lo zhes bya ba theg pa chen po'i mdo ('gsang ba'i mdzod')
sarvatathāgataguhyamahāguhyakośākṣayanidhadīpamahā-pratapasādhanatantrajñānāścaryadyuticakranāmamahāyāna-sūtra ('guhyakośa')
P453, vol.9; Toh.830; sDe-dge Ka 290b1-358a7

CANONICAL TEXTS (BSTAN-'GYUR)

Works by Indian and Tibetan Authors
Listed alphabetically by author

Abhayākaragupta(pāda)
Moonlight, Commentary on the Import of the Five Stages (Commentary on the completion stage of the Secret Assembly)
rim pa lnga pa'i dgongs 'grel zla ba'i 'od zer zhes bya ba
pañcakramamatiṭikācandraprabhānāma
P2700, vol.62; Toh.1831; sDe-dge Ci 180b3-203a4

Vajra Garland of Maṇḍala Rituals
dkyil 'khor gyi cho ga rdo rje phreng ba zhes bya ba ('rdo rje phreng ba')
vajrāvalināmamaṇḍalavidhi (*maṇḍalopāyikā)
P3961, vol.80; Toh.3140; sDe-dge Phu 1b1-94b4

Advayavajra: Nyi-su-med-pa'i rdo-rje
Establishing the Four Seals
phyag rgya bzhi gtan la dbab pa
caturmudrāniścaya
P3069, vol.68; Toh.2225; sDe-dge Wi 77a3-79b2

Ten Verses on Suchness
de kho na nyid bcu pa zhes bya ba
tattvadaśakanāma
P3080, vol.68; Toh.2236; sDe-dge Wi 112b7-113a6

Akṣobhyavajra: Mi-bskyod rdo-rje
Commentary on the Difficult Points of the Tantra of the Glorious Vajra Terrifier
dpal rdo rje 'jigs byed kyi rgyud kyi dka' 'grel
śrīvajrabhairavatantraṭikā
P2834, vol.67; Toh.1970; sDe-dge Mi 110b1-120b2

Alaṅkārakalaśa

Commentary on the Profound Meaning, Very Extensive Commentary on the Great Yoga Tantra Vajra Garland

rnal 'byor chen po'i rgyud dpal rdo rje phreng ba'i rgya cher 'grel pa zab mo'i don gyi 'grel pa zhes bya ba

śrīvajramālāmahāyogatantraṭikāgambhīrārthadīpikānāma

P2660, vol.61; Toh.1795; sDe-dge Gi 1b1-220a7

Ten Principles of Suchness

de kho na nyid bcu pa

daśatattva

P2759, vol.66; Toh.1895; sDe-dge Pi 234a1-253b7

Ānandagarbha: Kun-dga' snying-po

Commentary on the Difficult Points of the Secret Assembly Tantra

dpal gsang ba 'dus pa'i dka' 'grel

śrīguhyasamājapañjikā

P2780, vol.66; Toh.1917; sDe-dge Bi 1b1-81a

Extensive Commentary on the Supreme Glory Tantra

dpal mchog dang po'i rgya cher bshad pa

śrīparamādivivaraṇa

P3335, vol.72-73; Toh.2512; sDe-dge Si 49b2-242a7

Illumination of the Compendium of the Reality of All Tathāgatas

de bzhin gshegs pa thams cad kyi de kho na nyid bsdus pa theg pas chen po mngon par rtogs pa zhes bya ba'i rgyud kyi bshad pa de kho na nyid snang bar byed pa ('de nyid snang ba')

sarvatathāgatatattvasaṁgrahamahānabhisamayanāmatantra-vyākhyatattvālokākari ('tattvālokā')

P3333, Vols. 71-2; Toh.2510; sDe-dge Shi 1b1-317a7

Source of the Vajra

rdo rje dbyings kyi dkyil 'khor chen po'i cho ga rdo rje thams cad 'byung ba zhes bya ba ('dkyil chog rdo rje'i 'byung ba')

vajradhtāumahāmaṇḍalavidhisarvavajrodayanāma ('vajrodaya')

P3339, vol.74; Toh.2516; sDe-dge Ku 1b1-50a4

Very Extensive Commentary on the Secret Assembly Tantra

rgyud kyi rgyal po chen po dpal gsang ba 'dus pa'i rgya cher 'grel pa

guhyasamājamahātantrarājaṭikā

P4787, vol.84-85; Toh.1917; sDe-dge Bi 1b1-81a7

Anaṅgavajra

The Attainment of Method and Wisdom

prajñopāyaviniścayasiddhi

thabs dang shes rab rnam par gtan la dbab pa'i grub pa

Toh.2218

Anonymous

Great Ocean of Specific Explanation (*'Great Exposition'*)
bye brag bshad mtso mdzod chen mo
abhidharmamahāvibhāṣāśāstra
This text, which condenses the meaning of the *Seven Collections on Higher Knowedge*, and whose meaning is further condensed in Vasubandhu's *Treasury of Higher Knowledge*, is the principal text employed by the Vaibhāśika school of Theravādin Buddhism. It was not translated into Tibetan, but has been translated into Chinese: 60 vols., Taisho No.1546 (older version); 200 vols., Taisho No.1545 (newer version).

Āryadeva: 'Phags-pa lha

Commentary Explaining *Elucidating the Lamp*
sgron ma gsal ba zhes bya ba'i 'grel bshad
pradīpodyotananāmaṭikā
P2659, vol.60; Toh.1794; sDe-dge Khi 155a6-205a7

Compendium of the Vajra Wisdom
(Commentary on the *Compendium of Vajra Wisdom Tantra*)
P: ye shes rdo rje kun las btus pa zhes bya ba
Toh.: ye shes snying po kun las btus pa zhes bya ba
jñānasārasamuccayanāma
P5251, vol.95; Toh.3851; sDe-dge Tsa 26b2-28a3

Discriminating the Stages of Self Blessing
(Commentary on the completion stage of the Secret Assembly)
bdag byin gyis brlab pa'i rim pa rnam par dbye ba
svādhiṣṭhānakramaprabheda
P2670, vol.62; Toh.1805; sDe-dge Ngi 112a3-114b1

Lamp Compendium of Practice
spyod pa bsdus pa'i sgron ma
caryāmelāpakapradīpa
P2668, vol.61; Toh.1803; sDe-dge Ngi 57a2-106b7

Oral Instructions on the Stages of Realizing Enlightenment
mngon par byang chub pa'i rim pa'i man ngag
abhibodhikramopadeśa
P2671, vol.62; Toh.1806; sDe-dge Ngi 114b2-117a2

Ritual of Cremating a Corpse (Secret Assembly cremation ritual)
ro bsreg pa'i cho ga
śmaśānavidhi
P2672, vol.62; Toh.1807; sDe-dge Ngi 117a2-118b1

Gone to the End, Completion Stage of the Glorious Secret Assembly
dpal gsang ba 'dus pa'i rdzogs rim mthar phyin pa
śrīguhyāsamājaniṣpannakramāntaka

P2673, vol.62; Toh.1808; sDe-dge Ngi 118b1-121a6

(Ārya) Asaṅga: ('Phags-pa) Thogs-med
Five Treatises on the Levels of Yogic Practice (sa sde lnga)

1) *Bases of the Grounds*
sa'i dngos bzhi
bhūmivastu
P5536-5538, vol.109-110; Toh.4035-4037; sDe-dge Tsi 1b1-283a7, sDe-dge Dzi 1b1-195a7 and sDe-dge Wi 1b1-213a7
The *Bases of the Grounds* includes:
   a) *Grounds of the Bodhisattvas*
   rnal 'byor spyod pa'i sa las byang chub sems pa'i sa
   yogacaryābhūmau bodhisattvabhūmi
   P5538, vol.110; Toh.4037; sDe-dge Wi 1b1-213a7
   b) *Grounds of the Hearers*
   rnal 'byor spyod pa'i sa las nyan sa
   yogacaryābhumau śrāvakabhūmi
   P5537, vol.110; Toh.4036; sDe-dge Dzi 1b1-195a7
   c) *Grounds of Yogic Practice*
   rnal 'byor spyod pa'i sa ('sa mang pos')
   yogacaryābhūmi ('bahubhūmika')
   P5536, vol.109; Toh.4035; sDe-dge Tsi 1b1-283a7

2) *Compendium of Ascertainments*
rnal 'byor spyod pa'i sa rnam par gtan la dbab pa bsdus ba
yogacaryābhūmau nirṇayasaṁgraha ('viniścayasaṁgraha')
P5539, vol.110-111; Toh,4038; sDe-dge Zhi 1b1-289a7 and sDe-dge Zi 1b1-127a4

3) *Compendium of Bases*
P: rnal 'byor spyod pa'i sa rnam par gtan la dbab pa bsdus ba Toh.: rnal 'byor spyod pa'i sa las gzhi bsdu pa
yogacaryābhūmivastusaṁgraha
P5540-5541, vol.111; Toh.4039-4040; sDe-dge Zi 127a4-335a7 and sDe-dge 'i 1b1-22a7

4) *Compendium of Enumerations*
rnam grangs bsdu ba
paryāyasaṁgraha
P5542, vol.111; Toh.4041; sDe-dge 'i 22b1-47b7

5) *Compendium of Explanations*
rnam par bshad pa bsdu ba
vivaraṇasaṁgraha
P5543, vol.111; Toh.4042; sDe-dge 'i 47b7-68b7

Sādhana of Maitreya
'phags pa byams pa'i sgrub thabs
āryamaitreyasādhana
P4471, vol.81; Toh.3648; sDe-dge Mu 260b5-261b2

The Two Anthologies (sdom rnam pa gnyis, the two vivekas) These include:
1) *Compendium of Higher Knowledge*
chos mngon pa kun las btus pa
abhidharmasamuccaya
P5550, vol.112; Toh.4049; sDe-dge Ri 1b1-77a7 and 44b1-120a7
2) *Compendium of the Great Vehicle*
theg pa chen po['i mtshan nyid] kun las btus pa zhes bya ba
mahāyānasaṁgraha
P5301, vol.102; Toh.4048; sDe-dge Ri 1b1-43a7

Atiśa Dīpaṅkaraśrījñāna
Ritual of the Dhāraṇī of Stainless Crown Protrusion
gtsug tor dri med kyi gzungs cho ga
P3901, vol.79; Toh.3082; sDe-dge Pu 177a6-177b6

Bhavyakīrti: Legs-ldan-grags
Commentary on the Difficult Points of the Five Stages
rim pa lnga pa'i dka' 'grel zhes bya ba
pañcakramapañjikānāma
P2696, vol.62; Toh.1838; sDe-dge Chi 1b1-7b7

Explanatory Commentary, Illuminating the Thought of the Elucidating Lamp
sgron ma gsal bar byed pa'i dgongs pa rab gsal zhes bya ba bshad pa'i ṭikā
pradīpodyotanābhisandhiprakāśikānāmavyākhyāṭīkā
P2658, vols.60-61; Toh.1793; sDe-dge Ki 1b1-292a7 and Khi 1b1-155a5

Bhāvaviveka, Bhavya: Legs-ldan-'byed
Heart of the Middle Way, Root Verses
bdu ma'i snying po
madhyamakahṛdayakārikā
P34a7ff.; sNar-thang 31a5ff.; sDe-dge 31a7ff.

Blaze of Reasoning, a Commentary on the Heart of the Middle Way
dbu ma'i snying po'i 'grel pa rtog ge 'bar ba
madhyamakahṛdayavṛttitarkajvālā
P5256, vol.96; Toh.3856; sDe-dge Dza 40b7-329b4
Note: Although this text is traditionally described as an auto-commentary to the *Heart of the Middle Way*, on the grounds of both style and content such attribution is untenable.

Explanation of the Condensed Difficult Points of the Elucidating Lamp
sgron ma gsal bar byed pa'i [tsig gi] dka' ba btus pa'i 'grel pa zhes bya ba
pradīpodyotanaviṣamapañjikānāma
P2657, vol.60; Toh.1792; sDe-dge A 201b4-212a7

Wheel of Proclaiming the Distinctions of the Classes of Scripture
sde pa tha dad par 'byed pa dang rnam par bshad pa ('sde pa tha dad bklag pai 'khor lo')
nikāyabhedavibhaṅgavyākhyāna
P5640, vol.127; Toh.4139; sDe-dge Su 147a3-154b2

Buddhaguhya: Sangs-rgyas gsang-ba

Extensive Commentary Gradually Unfolding the Subsequent Concentration Tantra
bsam gtan phyi ma rim par phye ba rgya cher bshad pa
dhyānottarapaṭalaṭīkā
P3495, vol.78; Toh.2670; sDe-dge Thu 1b1-38a3

Introduction to the Meaning of Highest Tantra
[bla med kyi] rgyud don la 'jug pa
tantrārthāvatāra
P3324, vol.70; Toh.2501; sDe-dge 'i 1b1-91b6

Buddhajñānapāda: Sangs-rgyas ye-shes-zhabs

Completely Good Sādhana (*sādhana* of the Secret Assembly)
kun tu bzang po zhes bya ba'i sgrub pa'i thabs
samantabhadranāmasādhana
P2718, vol.65; Toh.1855; sDe-dge Di 28b6-36a5

Engaging in the Means of Self-achievement
bdag sgrub pa la 'jug pa
ātmasādhanāvatāra
P2723, vol.65; Toh.1860; sDe-dge Di 52a7-62a7

Liberating Drop
grol ba'i thig le zhes bya ba
muktitilakanāma
P2722, vol.65; Toh.1859; sDe-dge Di 47a1-52a7

Revelation
zhal lung
mukhāgama
P2717, vol.65; Toh.1854; sDe-dge Di 17b3-28b6

Revelation; Meditation on the Suchness of the Two Stages ('The Great Exposition')
rim pa gnyis pa'i de kho na nyid sgom pa zhes bya ba'i zhal gyi lung
dvikramatattvabhāvanānāmamukhādhyāpana (°mukhāgama)

P2716, vol.65; Toh.1853 ; sDe-dge Di 1b1-17b2

Candragomin: Tsan-dra-pa
Sādhana of Tārā Who Gives Refuge from the Eight Fears
'phags ma sgrol ma 'jigs pa brgyad las skyob pa zhes bya ba'i sgrub thabs
āryatārāṣṭabhayatrātanāmasādhana
P4494, vol.81; Toh.3672; sDe-dge Mu 284b5-286a7
Sādhana of the Noble Lady with White Parasol Called She Who is Unconquerable by Others
'phags ma gdugs dkar mo can gzhan gyis mi thub ma zhes bya ba'i sgrub thabs
āryasitātapatrāparājitānāmasādhana
P3903, vol.80; Toh.3083 (=Toh.592); sDe-dge Pu 177b6-178a7
Bali Ritual of the Noble Lady with White Parasol Called She Who is Unconquerable by Others
'phags ma gzhan gyis mi thub pa gdugs dkar mo can gyi gtor ma'i cho ga zhes bya ba
āryasitātapatrāparājitābalividhināma
P3904, vol.80; Toh.3084; sDe-dge Pu 178a7-184b4
Wheel of Protection
bsrung ba'i 'khor lo
rakṣācakra
P3906, vol.80; Toh.3086; sDe-dge Pu 185b6-186a4
Offering Ritual
gtor ma'i cho ga
balividhi
P3915, vol.80; Toh.3095; sDe-dge Pu 188b7-189a5
Fire Offering
sbyin sreg
homa
P3920, vol.80; Toh.3101; sde deg Pu 191b1-191b2
(Note: the rituals composed by Candragomin contained in the section of the bsTan-'gyur from sDe-dge Pu 177b6-192b2 [Toh.3083-3104] are all concerned with Sitātapatrā.)

Candrakīrti: Zla-ba grags-pa
Commentary on the Ornament for Clear Realization of the Secret Assembly
gsang ba 'dus pa'i mngon par rtogs pa'i rgyan gyi 'grel pa
guhyasamājābhisamayālaṅkāravṛtti
P2681, vol.62; Toh.1817; sDe-dge Ngi 210b1-232b6

Extensive Commentary, the Elucidating Lamp (*'Clear Lamp Compendium of the Five Stages'*)
sgron ma gsal bar byed pa zhes bya ba'i rgya cher bshad pa ('rim lnga bsdus pa'i sgron ma gsal ba') ('sgron gsal')
pradīpoddyotananāmaṭikā
P2650, vol.60; Toh.1785; sDe-dge Ha 1b1-201b2

Seventy Stanzas of Going for Refuge to the Three Jewels
gsum la skyabs su 'gro ba bdun cu pa
triśaraṇa[gamana]saptati
P5478, vol.103; Toh.4564; sDe-dge jo bo'i chos chung 202a1-204b1

Dārikapa, Dārikapāda: Da-ri-pa

Instruction on Reality
de kho na nyid kyi man ngag
tattvopadeśa
Toh.1632

Sādhana of the Heart of Wisdom
shes rab kyi pha rol tu phyin pa'i snying po'i sgrub thabs zhes bya ba
prajñāpāramitāhṛdayasādhananāma
P3465, vol.77; Toh.2641; sDe-dge Ju 245b3-246b2

Dharmakīrti: Chos-grags

Seven Logical Treatises: mKhas-grub rje (*Introduction to the Buddhist Tantric Systems*, p.73) says that the three chief treatises are comparable to a trunk (i.e. main part of body). The extensive one is the *Pramāṇavārttika[kārikā]*; the intermediate one is the *Pramāṇaviniścaya*; the abbreviated one is the *Nyāyabindu-[prakaraṇa]*. The seven are:

1) *Analysis of Relations*
'brel ba brtag pa
sambandhaparīkṣā
P5713, vol.130; Toh.4214; sDe-dge Ce 255a2-256a2

2) *Ascertainment of Prime Cognition*
tshad ma rnam par nges pa
pramāṇaviniścaya
P5710, vol.130; Toh.4211; sDe-dge Ce 152b1-230a7

3) *Commentary on (Dignāga's) Compendium on Prime Cognition*
tshad ma rnam 'grel gyi tshig le'ur byas pa
pramāṇavārtikakārikā
P5709, vol.130; Toh.4210; sDe-dge Ce 94b1-151a7

4) *Drop of Reasoning*
rigs pa'i thigs pa zhes bya ba'i rab tu byed pa
nyāyabinduprakaraṇa
P5711, vol.130; Toh.4212; sDe-dge Ce 231b1-238a6

5) *Drop of Reasons*
gtan tshigs kyi thigs pa zhes bya ba'i rab tu byed pa
hetubindunāmaprakaraṇa
P5712, vol.130; Toh.4213; sDe-dge Ce 238a7-255a1

6) *Principles of Debate*
tshod pa'i rigs pa
vādanyāya
P5715, vol.130; Toh.4218; sDe-dge Che 326b4-355b5

7) *Proof of Others' Continuums*
rgyud gzhan grub pa zhes bya ba'i rab tu byed pa
santānāntarasiddhināmaprakaraṇa
P5716, vol.130; Toh.4219; sDe-dge Che 355b5-359a7

Dīpaṅkarabhadra: Mar-me-mdzad bzang-po
Maṇḍala Ritual of the Glorious Secret Assembly (*'Maṇḍala Ritual in 450 Verses'*)
dpal gsang ba 'dus pa'i dkyil 'khor gyi cho ga zhes bya ba ('dkyil 'khor gyi cho ga shlo ka bzhi brgya lnga bcu pa')
śrīguhyasamājamaṇḍalavidhināma
P2728, vol.65; Toh.1865; sDe-dge Di 69a4-87a3

Ḍombīpa, Ḍombīpāda, Ḍombī Heruka
Ten Principles of Suchness
de kho na nyid bcu pa
daśatattva
P2358, vol.56; Toh.1229; sDe-dge Nya 37a1-41a7

Attainment of the Innate
lhan cig skyes grub
sahajasiddhi
Toh.2260

Yogic Practice by Means of the Winds and Drops
rtsa rlung gi sgo nas rnal 'byor gyi spyod pa zhes bya ba
nāḍibindudvārayogacaryānāma
P3231, vol.69; Toh.2389; sDe-dge Zi 21a3-21a7

Durjayacandra: Mi-thub zla-ba
Commentary on the Difficult Points of the Hevajra Tantra (*'Kumutri'*)
kau mu dī zhes bya ba'i dka' 'grel
kaumudīnāmapañjikā
P2315, vol.53; Toh.1185; sDe-dge Ga 1b1-58b4

*Ekādaśasvara: sGra-dbyangs bcu-gcig
Secret Nectar of Oral Instructions, Stages of the Path of Vajradhara (Secret Assembly ritual text)
rdo rje 'chang chen po'i lam gyi rim pa'i man ngag bdud rtsi gsang ba

mahāvajradharapathakramopadeśāmṛtaguhya
P2687, vol.62; Toh. 1823; sDe-dge Ngi 267b1-278a5

Ghaṇṭāpāda: Dril-bu-pa
Five Stages of the Glorious Cakrasaṁvara
dpal 'khor lo sdom pa'i rim pa lnga
śrīcakrasaṁvarapañcakrama
P2150, vol.51; Toh.1433; sDe-dge Wa 224b5-227a1
Commentary on the Five Stages of the Glorious Cakrasaṁvara
dpal 'khor lo sdom pa'i rim pa lnga pa'i 'grel pa
śrīcakrasaṁvarapañcakramavṛtti
P2152, vol.51; Toh.1435; sDe-dge Wa 227b3-233a4

Indrabodhi, Indrabhūti
Complete Explanation of the Condensed Tantra of Heruka Cakrasaṁvara
dpal 'khor lo sdom pa'i rgyud kyi rgyal po bde mchog bsdus pa zhes bya ba'i rnam par bshad pa
śrīcakrasaṁvaratantrarājasambarasamuccayanāmavṛtti
Toh.1413; sDe-dge Tsa 1b1-119b7
The Attainment of Wisdom
ye shes grub pa
jñānasiddhi
Toh.2219

*Jagbhadra: 'Gro-bzang snying-po
Sādhana of the Destroyer of the Lord of Death
gshin rje gshed kyi sgrub pa'i thabs
yamārisādhana
P2824, vol.67; Toh.1961; sDe-dge Mi 98b3-99b3

Jinadatta: rGyal-ba-byin
Commentary on the Difficult Points of the Secret Assembly Tantra
dpal gsang ba 'dus pa'i rgyud kyi dka' 'grel zhes bya ba
śrīguhyasamājatantrapañjikānāma
P2710, vol.63; Toh.1847; sDe-dge Nyi 145a7-318a7

Jetari: Dze-ta-ri-pa
Offering Ritual of the Five Protectors
bsrung ba lnga'i mchod pa'i cho ga
pañcarakṣārcanavidhi
P3947, vol.80; Toh.3128; sDe-dge Pu 230a2-234b3
Ritual of Drawing the Circle of She Who Leads Each One
so sor 'brang ma chen mo'i 'khor lo bri ba'i cho ga
mahāpratisarācakralekhanavidhi
P3948, vol.80; Toh.3127; sDe-dge Pu 228b6-230a2

Sādhanas of the Five Goddesses:
1) *Sādhana of She Who Leads Each One*
so sor 'brang ma'i sgrub thabs
pratisarāsādhana
P3940, vol.80; Toh.3119; sDe-dge Pu 219a2-219b1

2) *Sādhana of the Peacock Lady* (no author listed)
'phags ma rma bya chen mo'i sgrub thabs
āryamahāmāyūrīsādhana
P3941, vol.80; Toh.3120; sDe-dge Pu 219b1-219b5

3) *Sādhana of the Lady of a Thousand Conquests* (no author listed)
stong chen mo rab tu 'joms ma'i sgrub thabs
mahāsahasrapramardanīsādhana
P3942, vol.80; Toh.3121; sDe-dge Pu 219b5-219b7

4) *Sādhana of the Subsequent Holder of Secret Mantra* (no author listed)
'phags ma gsang sngags chen mo rjes su 'dzin ma'i sgrub thabs
āryamahāmantrānudhāraṇīsādhana
P3943, vol.80; Toh.3122; sDe-dge Pu 219b7-220a2

5) *Sādhana of the Cool Grove* (no author listed)
bsil ba'i tshal chen mo'i sgrub thabs
śītavatīsādhana
P3944, vol.80; Toh.3123; sDe-dge Pu 220a2-220a6

Kāruṇyaśrī: Thugs-rje dpal
Commentary on the Difficult Points, Elucidating the Elucidating Lamp
sgron ma gsal bar byed pa'i gsal byed ces bya ba'i dka' 'grel
pradīpodyotanodyotanāmapañjikā
P2655, vol.60; Toh.1790; sDe-dge A 10b1-170a7

mKhas-grub rje, mKhas-grub dge-legs dpal bzang-po
Introduction to the Buddhist Tantric Systems (Extensive Overview of the Classes of Tantra)
rgyud spyi'i rnam par gzhag pa rgyas par brjod
Toh.5489

Kṛṣṇācārya, Kṛṣṇapāda, Kāṇha: Nag-po-pa
Discrimination of the Four Stages
rim pa bzhi'i rnam par 'byed pa zhes bya ba
kramacatuṣṭayavibhaṅganāma
P2169, vol.51; Toh.1452; sDe-dge Wa 358b7-367b3

Four Stages
rim pa bzhi pa
kramacatuṣṭaya
P2168, vol.51; Toh.1451; sDe-dge Wa 355b7-358b7

Kṛṣṇasamayavajra: Nag-po dam-tshig rdo-rje

Commentary on the Difficult Points of the Five Stages (commentary on the Secret Assembly completion stage)
rim pa lnga'i dka' 'grel
pañcakramapañjikā
P2698, vol.62; Toh.1841; sDe-dge Chi 157b1-187a7

Maṇḍala Ritual of the Glorious Secret Assembly
dpal gsang ba 'dus pa'i dkyil 'khor gyi cho ga
śrīguhyasamājamaṇḍalavidhi
P2683, vol.62; Toh.1819; sDe-dge Ngi 247b1-258b1

Offering Ritual of Vajrasattva (text associated with Secret Assembly practice)
[dpal] rdo rje sems dpa' mchod pa'i cho ga
vajrasattvapūjāvidhi
P2684, vol.62; Toh.1820; sDe-dge Ngi 258b1-261a7

Kumāra: gZhon-nu

Mirror of the Essential Condensed Explanation of the Elucidating Lamp
sgron ma gsal ba mdor bshad pa'i sa bcad snying gi me long zhes bya ba
pradīpadīpaṭippaṇīhṛdayādarśanāma
P2656, vol.60; Toh.1791; sDe-dge A 170b1-201b4

Kumāracandra (°vajra): gZhon-nu zla-ba (°rdo-rje)

Commentary on the Difficult Points of the Vajra Terrifier Tantra
rdo rje 'jigs byed kyi rgyud kyi dka' 'grel
vajrabhairavatantrapañjikā
P2837, vol.67; Toh.1973; sDe-dge Mi 132b6-135b6

Lalitavajra, Līlāvajra: sGeg-pa rdo-rje

Sādhana of the Forty-nine Deities of Vajrabhairava
dpal rdo 'jigs byed kyi [zhe dgu ma'i] sgrub thabs
śrīvajrabhairavasādhana
Toh.1998; sDe-dge Mi 196b3-201b3

Commentary on the Vajrasattva Sādhana (text associated with Secret Assembly practice)
rdo rje sems dpa'i sgrub thabs kyi 'grel pa
vajrasattvasādhananibandha
P2679, vol.62; Toh.1815; sDe-dge Ngi 204b6-209a3

Explanation of the Guru's Oral Instructions on the Introduction to the Secret Assembly Tantra
gsang ba 'dus pa'i rgyud kyi gleng gzhi bla ma'i man ngag gi bshad pa
guhyasamājatantranidānagurūpadeśabhāṣya
P2773, vol.66; Toh.1910; sDe-dge Phi 89b1-97b5

Excellent View of the Meaning of the Names of Secret Mantra, Commentary on the Expression of the Names [of Mañjuśrī]
'phags pa mtshan yang dag par brjod pa'i rgya cher 'grel pa mtshan gsang ngags kyi don du rnam par lta ba zhes bya ba
(Sanskrit title not recorded)
P3356, vol.74; Toh.2533; sDe-dge Khu 27b1-115b3

Lūyīpāda: Lu'i-pa
Realization of the Glorious Bhagavan
dpal bcom ldan 'das mngon par rtogs pa zhes bya ba ('rdzogs rim sangs rgyas 'char pa')
śrībhagavadabhisamayanāma
P2207, vol.52; Toh.1427; sDe-dge Wa 186b3-193a1

Maitreyanātha: Byams-pa'i mgon-po
Discrimination of Phenomena and Suchness
chos dang chos nyid rnam par 'byed pa
dharmadharmatāvibhaṅga
P5523, vol.108, Toh.4022 (=Toh.4023); sDe-dge Phi 46b1-49a6

Discrimination of the Middle and the Extremes
dbus dang mtha' rnam par 'byed pa
madhyāntavibhaṅga
P5522, vol.108; Toh.4021; sDe-dge Phi 40b1-45a6

Analysis of the Jewel Matrix, Great Vehicle Treatise on the Later Scriptures
theg pa chen pa rgyud bla ma'i bstan bcos ('rgyud bla ma')
ratnagotravibhāga mahāyānottaratantraśāstra ('uttaratantra')
P5525, vol.108; Toh.4024; sDe-dge Phi 54b1-73a7

Ornament for Clear Realization
mngon par rtogs pa'i rgyan
abhisamayālaṅkāra
P5184, vol.88; Toh.3786; sDe-dge Ka 1b1-13a7

Ornament of the Mahāyāna Sūtras
theg pa chen po'i mdo sde'i rgyan gyi tsig le'ur byas pa
mahāyānasūtrālaṅkāra
P5521, vol.108; Toh.4020; sDe-dge Phi 1b1-39a4

Mañjughoṣa: 'Jam-dbyangs
Sādhana of the Vajra Terrifier with One Face and Two Hands
rdo rje 'jigs byed zhal gcig phyag gnyis pa'i sgrub pa'i thabs
vajrabhairavaikānanadvibhujasādhananāma
P2839, vol.67; Toh.1976; sDe-dge Mi 147b5-150a2

Mañjuśrīkīrti: 'Jam-dpal-grags
Extensive Commentary on the Expression of the Names of Ārya Mañjuśrī

'phags pa 'jam dpal gyi mtshan yang dag par brjod pa'i rgya cher bshad pa
āryamañjuśrīnāmasaṅgītiṭikā
P3357, vol.74; Toh.2534; sDe-dge Khu 115b3-301a7

Muniśrībhadra: Thub-pa dpal-bzang
Captivating the Minds of Yogins, Condensed Explanation of the Meanings of the Five Stages (commentary on the Secret Assembly completion stage)
rim pa lnga'i don mdor bshad pa rnal 'byor pa'i yid kyi 'phrog ces bya ba
pañcakramārthayogimanoharaṭippaṇināma
P2691, vol.62; Toh.1813; sDe-dge Ngi 148b4-195b6

Nāgabodhi: Klu'i byang-chub
Clarifying the Meanings of the Five Stages
rim pa lnga'i don gsal bar byed pa zhes bya ba
pañcakramārthabhāskaraṇanāma
P2702, vol.62; Toh.1833; sDe-dge Ci 207b2-237a7

Jewel Rosary, Explanation of the Five Stages
rim pa lnga pa'i bshad pa nor bu'i phreng ba zhes bya ba
(Sanskrit title not recorded)
P2697, vol.62; Toh.1840; sDe-dge Chi 14a6-157a7

Treatise of Oral Instructions on the Inner Condensed Five Stages
rim pa khongs su bsdu ba'i man ngag ces bya ba'i rab tu byed pa
kramāntarbhāvanopadeśanāmaprakaraṇa
P2677, vol.62; Toh.1812; sDe-dge Ngi 147a1-148b4

Nāgārjuna: Klu-sgrub
Abbreviated Sādhana (Commentary on the Secret Assembly Tantra)
sgrub pa'i thams mdor byas pa ('mdor byas')
piṇḍīkṛtasādhana
P2661, vol.61; Toh.1796; sDe-dge Ngi 1b1-11a2

Commentary on the Secret Assembly Tantra
dpal gsang ba 'dus pa'i rgyud kyi rgyud 'grel zhes bya ba
śrīguhyasamājatantrasya tantraṭīkānāma
P2648, vol.59; Toh.1784; sDe-dge Sa 1b1-324a7

Compendium of Sūtras
mdo kun las btus pa
sūtrasamuccaya
P5530, vol.102; Toh.3934; sDe-dge Ki 148b1-215a5

Extensive Commentary on the Eighteenth Chapter [of the Secret Assembly Tantra]
le'u bco brgyad pa'i rgya cher 'grel pa

aṣṭādaśapaṭalavistaravyākhyā
P2649, vol.60; not in Toh.

Integration of the Sūtras and the Method of Meditating on the Generation Stage of the Great Yoga of the Glorious Secret Assembly
rnal 'byor chen po'i rgyud dpal gsang ba 'dus pa'i skyed pa'i rim pa bsgom pa'i thabs mdo dang bsres pa zhes bya ba
śrīguhyasamājamahāyogatantrotpādakramasādhanasūtra-melāpakanāma
P2662, vol.61; Toh.1797; sDe-dge Ngi 11a2-15b1

Maṇḍala Ritual of the Glorious Secret Assembly
dpal gsang ba 'dus pa'i dkyil 'khor gyi cho ga zhes bya ba
śrīguhyasamājamaṇḍalavidhināma
P2663, vol.61; Toh.1798; sDe-dge Ngi 15b1-35a7

Sādhana of Thousand-armed Avalokiteśvara
'phags pa spyan ras gzigs dbang phyug phyag stong pa'i sgrub thabs
āryasahasrabhujāvalokiteśvarasādhana
P3555, vol.79; Toh.2736; sDe-dge Nu 114b2-123b7

Six Collections of Reasonings (rigs tshogs drug, ṣaḍyuktiśāstra):

1) *Precious Garland*
rgyal po la gtam bya ba rin po che'i phreng ba
rājaparikathāratnāvali ('ratnāvalī')
P5658, vol.129; Toh.4158; sDe-dge Ge 107a1-126a4

2) *Refutation of Objections*
rtshod pa bzlog pa'i tshig le'ur byas pa
vigrahavyāvartanikārikā
P5528, vol.95; Toh.3828; sDe-dge Tsa 27a1-29a7

3) *Seventy Stanzas on Emptiness*
stong pa nyid bdun cu pa'i tshig le'ur byas pa
śūnyatāsaptatikārikā
P5227, vol.95; Toh.3827; sDe-dge Tsa 24a6-27a1

4) *Sixty Stanzas of Reasoning*
rigs pa drug cu pa'i tshig le'ur byas pa
yuktiṣaṣṭikārikā
P5525, vol.95; Toh.3825; sDe-dge Tsa 20b1-22b6

5) *Treatise Called 'The Finely Woven'*
zhib mo rnam par 'thag pa zhes bya ba'i mdo
vaidalyasūtranāma
P5526, vol.95; Toh.3826; sDe-dge Tsa 22b6-24a6

6) *Treatise on the Middle Way / Fundamental Treatise on the Middle Way, Called 'Wisdom'*
dbu ma rtsa ba'i tshig le'ur byas pa shes rab ces bya ba
prajñānāmamūlamadhyamakakārikā / madhyamakaśāstra

P5524, vol.95; Toh.3824; sDe-dge Tsa 1b1-19a6

Treatise on the Four Empowerments
dbang bzhi pa'i rab tu 'byed pa
sekacatuḥprakaraṇa
P2664, vol.61; Toh.1799; sDe-dge Ngi 35a7-38a5

Twenty Maṇḍala Rituals of the Glorious Secret Assembly
dpal gsang ba 'dus pa'i dkyil 'khor gyi cho ga nyi shu pa zhes bya ba
śrīguhyasamājamaṇḍalaviṁśatividhināma
P2675, vol.62; Toh.1810; sDe-dge Ngi 131a5-145b3

Nāropa, Nāḍapāda

Clear Compendium on the Five Stages
rim pa lnga bsdus pa gsal ba
pañcakramasaṁgrahaprakāśa
P4790, vol.85; Toh.2333; sDe-dge Zhi 276a7-278a7

Condensed Ultimate Meaning, Explanation Showing the Abbreviated Empowerment
dbang mdor bstan pa'i 'grel bshad don dam pa bsdus pa zhes bya ba
paramārthasaṁgrahanāmasekoddeśaṭikā
P2068, vol.47; Toh.1351; sDe-dge Na 220b1-289a7

Jewel Light
rin po che'i 'od ces bya ba
ratnaprabhānāma
P2472, vol.57; Toh.1342; sDe-dge Ta 350b5-358a4

Single Vajra Word of the Oral Lineage
snyan brgyud rdo rje'i tshig rkang zhes bya ba
karṇatantravajrapadanāma
[Not in P] Toh.2338; sDe-dge Zhi 302b6-304b4

Padmākaraghoṣa: Pad-ma 'byung-dbyangs

Questions for the Novice Monk's Year
dge tshul gyi dang po'i lo dri ba ('dge tshul gyi lo dri ba nams')
śrāmaṇeravarśāgrapṛcchā
P5634, vol.127; Toh.4132; sDe-dge Su 64a5-66a1

Padmāṅkuśa: Pad-ma'i lcags-kyu

Maṇḍala Ritual of the Lady of the White Parasol, She Who is Unconquerable by Others
'phags ma de bzhin gshegs pa thams cad kyi gtsug tor nas byung ba'i gdugs dkar mo can gzhan gyis mi thub ma zhes bya ba'i dkyil 'khor gyi cho ga zhes bya ba
āryatathāgatoṣṇīṣasitātapatrāparājitānāmamaṇḍalavidhināma
P3932, vol.80; Toh.3106; sDe-dge Pu 194a6-200b1

Ritual of Making Plaque-images of the Lady of the White Parasol
'phags ma gdugs dkar mo can gyi tsha tsha'i cho ga zhes bya ba
āryasitātapatrāsācchavidhināma
P3933 vol.80; Toh.3107; sDe-dge Pu 200b1-203b7

Padmavajra, Mahāsukha: Pad-ma rdo-rje, bDe-ba chen-po
Secret Attainment, Invoking the Definitive Meaning of All Tantras
rgyud ma lus pa'i don nges par skul bar byed pa ('gsang ba'i grub')
sakalatantrasambhavasañcodani śrīguhyasiddhināma
P3061, vol.68; Toh.2217; sDe-dge Wi 1b1-28b4

Puṇḍarika: Pad-ma dkar-po
Approaching the Ultimate Meaning
dpal don dam pa'i bsnyen pa
śrīparamārthasevā
P2065, vol.47; Toh.1348; sDe-dge Na 1b1-20a3

Stainless Light (commentary on the Lesser Wheel of Time Tantra)
bsdus pa'i rgyud kyi rgyal po dus kyi 'khor lo'i 'grel bshad rtsa ba'i rgyud kyi rjes su 'jug pa stong phrag bcu gnyis pa dri ma med pa'i 'od ces bya ba ('grel chen dri med 'od')
vimlaprabhānāmamūlatantrānusāriṇidvādaśasāhasrikālaghukālacakratantrarājaṭikā ('vimalaprabhā')
P2064, vol.46; Toh.845; sDe-dge Shri 1b1-469a7

Rāhulaśrīkalyāṇamitra: sGra-gcan-'dzin dpal bshes-gnyen
Clear Placement in Union, Practice of Empowerment
zung du 'jug pa gsal ba zhes bya ba'i dbang gi bya ba
yuganaddhaprakāśanāmasekaprakriyā
P2682, vol.62; Toh.1818; sDe-dge Ngi 232b6-247a7

Ratnākaraśānti: dKon-mchog 'byung-gnas zhi-ba
Handful of Flowers, Explanation of the Secret Assembly Tantra
gsang ba 'dus pa'i bshad sbyar snyim pa'i me tog
kusumāñjaliguhyasamājanibandhanāma
P2714, vol.64; Toh.1851; sDe-dge Thi 202b1-325a7

Knowledge Ritual of She Who Leads Each One
'phags ma so sor 'brang ma chen mo'i rig pa'i cho ga zhes bya ba
āryamahāpratisarāvidyāvidhināma
P3946, vol.80; Toh.3125; sDe-dge Pu 224b4-225b6

Jewel Light Ornament, Commentary on [Nāgārjuna's] Compendium of Sūtras
mdo kun las bdus pa'i bshad pa rin po che snang ba'i rgyan zhes bya ba
sūtrasamuccayabhāṣyaratnālokālaṅkāranāma
P5331, vol.102; Toh.3935; sDe-dge Ki 215a5-334a3

Method of Drawing the Protective Circle of She Who Leads Each One
so sor 'brang ma'i bsrung ba'i 'khor lo bri ba'i thabs
pratisarārakṣācakralekhopāya
P3939, vol.80; Toh.3118; sDe-dge Pu 217b6-219a2

Precious Garland, Commentary on the Abbreviated Sādhana
mdor bsdus pa'i sgrub thabs kyi 'grel pa rin chen phreng ba zhes ba
piṇḍīkṛtasādhanavṛttiratnāvalīnāma
P2690, vol.62; Toh.1826; sDe-dge Ci 1b1-95a6

Ritual of the Five Protectors
bsrung ba lnga'i cho ga
pañcarakṣāvidhi
P3947, vol.80; Toh.3126; sDe-dge Pu 225b6-228b6

Supreme Essence, Commentary on the Difficult Points of the Eight Thousand Verse Perfection of Wisdom
'phags pa shes rab kyi pha rol tu phyin pa brgyad stong pa'i dka' 'grel snying po mchog ces bya ba
āryāṣṭasāhasrikāprajñāpāramitāpañjikā sārottamānāma
P5200, vol.92; Toh.3803; sDe-dge Tha 1b1-230a7

Ratnakīrti: dKon-mchog grags-pa

Maṇḍala Rite for all Dhāraṇī
gzungs thams cad kyi dkyil 'khor gyi cho ga
sarvadhāraṇīmaṇḍalavidhi
P3957, vol.80; Toh.3136; sDe-dge Pu 307a7-316a5

Sahajalalita: lHan-skyes rol-pa

Explanation of the Dhāraṇī of Perfect Observance of Commitment and the Essence of All Tathāgatas, the Shining Stainless Light of the Crown Protrusion that Places All in the Door [to Liberation] ('Specific Compendium')
kun nas sgor 'jug pa'i 'od zer gtsug tor dri ma med par snang ba de bzhin gshegs pa thams cad kyi snying po dang dam tshig la rnam par blta ba zhes bya ba'i gzungs kyi rnam par bshad pa ('so so'i bsdus pa')
samantamukhapraveśaraśmivimaloṣṇīṣaprabhāsa-sarvatathāgatahṛdayasamayavilokitanāma dhāraṇīvṛtti
P3512, vol.78; Toh.2688 (=Toh.599); sDe-dge Thu 269a3-320b2

Compendium of Devotions ('General Compendium')
gnas pa bsdus pa ('spyi'i bsdus pa')
sthitisamuccaya
P3071, vol.68; Toh.2227; sDe-dge Wi 92a6-99b5

Ritual of Impressing Plaques [with Images of the Five Buddhas]
tsha tsha [lnga] gdab pa'i cho ga
sañcakanirvapaṇavidhi

P3667 vol.79; Toh.3080; sDe-dge Pu 176a3-176b4

Saraha
Song of the Unborn Vajra Mind Treasure
thugs kyi mdzod skye med rdo rje'i glu
cittakoṣājavajragīti
P3117, vol.69; Toh.2271; sDe-dge Zhi 115b4-117a2

Saroruha: mTsho-skyes
Lotus Bearer, Commentary on the Difficult Points of the Hevajra Tantra
kye'i rdo rje'i rgyud lyi dka' 'grel padma can zhes bya ba
hevajratantrapañjikāpadmininām a
P2311, vol.53; Toh.1181; sDe-dge Ka 126b1-173a7

Explanation of (Buddhaguhya's) Introduction to the Meanings of Tantra
rgyud kyi don la 'jug pa'i 'grel bshad
tantrārthāvatāravyākhyāna
P3325, vol.70; Toh.2502; sDe-dge 'i 91b6-351a7

Seven Collections on Higher Knowledge:
1) *Devaśarman (Set of Perceptions)* (vijñānakāya)
2) *Katyāyanaputra* (*Entrance into Knowledge*) (jñānaprasthāna)
3) *Mahākauṣṭhila* (*Well-sung Terminology*) (saṅgītiparyāya)
4) *Maudgalyāyana* (*Treatise of Classification*) (prajñaptiśāstra)
5) *Pūrṇa* (*Set of Elements*) (dhātukāya)
6) *Śāriputra* (*Aggregate of Phenomena*) (dharmaskandha)
7) *Vasumitra* (*Organized Presentation*) (prakaraṇapāda)
Note: Only a portion of the *Treatise of Classification*, namely the *Lokaprajñāpti* (*'jig rten gzhag pa*, P5587, vol.115, Toh.4086; sDe-dge I 1b1-93a7), and presumably also including the *Kāraṇaprajñāpti* (*rgyu gdags pa*, P5588, vol.115, Toh.4087; sDe-dge I 93a7-172b4) and the *Karmaprajñāpti* (*las gdags pa*, P5589, vol.115, Toh.4088; sDe-dge I 172b4-229a7), has been translated into Tibetan.

Śākyamitra: Shā-kya bshes-gnyen
Explanation for the Oral Instructions on Entering the Yoga of the Great Seal (instructions on the completion stage of the Secret Assembly)
phyag rgya chen po'i rnal 'byor la 'jug pa'i man ngag tu bshad pa
mahāmudrāyogāvatārapiṇḍārtha
P4594, vol.81; Toh.3776; sDe-dge Tsu 195a5-204a7

Extensive Explanation, Lamp Compendium of Practice (Secret Assembly completion stage commentary)
spyod pa bsdus pa'i sgron ma zhes bya ba'i rgya cher bshad pa
caryāsamuccayapradīpanāmaṭīkā
P2703, vol.62; Toh.1834; sDe-dge Ci 237b1-280b2

Ornament of Kosala, Commentary on the Compendium of the Reality [of All Tathāgatas]
de kho na nyid bsdus pa'i rgya cher bshad pa ko sa la'i rgyan
kosalālaṅkāratattvasaṁgrahaṭīkā
P3326, vol.70-71; Toh.2503; sDe-dge Yi 1b1-245a7

Śāntideva: Zhi-ba-lha
Compendium of Training
bslab pa kun las btus pa'i tshig le'ur byas pa
śikṣāsamuccayakārikā
P5336, vol.102; Toh.3939 (=Toh.4549); sDe-dge Khi 1b1-3a2

Engaging in the Bodhisattva's Deeds
byang chub sems pa'i spyod pa 'jug pa
bodhicaryāvatāra
P5272, vol.99, Toh.3871; sDe-dge La 1b1-40a7

Śraddhākaravarma
Explanation to Completely Clarify the Seven Ornaments, Arisen from the Compendium of the Vajra Wisdom Tantra
ye shes rdo rje kun las btus pa'i rgyud las 'byung ba'i rgyan bdun rnam par 'grol ba
P2654, vol.60; Toh.1789; sDe-dge A 8b6-10a7

Very Extensive Explanation of the Vajra Recitation (commentary on the Vajrasattva *sādhana* in conjunction with the practice of the Secret Assembly)
rdo rje bzlas pa'i rgya cher bshad pa
vajrajapaṭīkā
P2653, vol.60; Toh.1788; sDe-dge A 1b1-8b6

Śrīdhara: dPal-'dzin
Sādhana of the Black Destroyer of the Lord of Death
gshin rje gshed nag po'i sgrub thabs zhes bya ba
kṛṣṇayamārisādhananāma
P2786, vol.67; Toh.1923; sDe-dge Mi 1b1-8b4

Sādhana of the Red Destroyer of the Lord of Death
dpal gshin rje gshed dmar po'i sgrub thabs
Śrīraktayamārisādhana
P2882, vol.67; Toh.2023; sDe-dge Tsi 88a5-95a1

Co-emergent Light, Commentary on the Difficult Points of the Black Destroyer of the Lord of Death
dpal gshin rje gshed kyi rgyud kyi dka' 'grel lhan cig skyes pa'i snang ba
Śrīyamāritantrapañjikāsahajālokanāma
P2781, vol.66; Toh.1918; sDe-dge Bi 81b1-123b7

(bhikṣuṇī) Śrīlakṣmi: (dge-slong-ma) dPal-mo
Clarifying the Meanings of the Five Stages (Secret Assembly completion stage commentary)
rim pa lnga'i don gsal bar byed pa zhes bya ba
pañcakramavṛttārthavirocananāma
P2702, vol.62; Toh.1842; sDe-dge Chi 187b1-277a7
Sādhana of the Exalted Eleven-faced Avalokiteśvara
rje btsun 'phags pa spyan ras gzigs dbang phyug zhal bcu gcig pa'i sgrub thabs
bhaṭṭārakāryaikādaśamukhāvalokiteśvarasādhana
P3357, vol.79; Toh.2737; sDe-dge Nu 123b7-125b2

Smṛtijñānanakīrti: Dran-pa ye-shes grags
Extensive Oral Instructions, Completely Explaining the Questions of the Four Goddesses [Tantra]
lha mo bzhis yongs su zhus pa'i rnam par bshad pa man ngag rgyas pa zhes bya ba
caturdevatāparipṛcchāvyākhyānopadeśapauṣṭikanāma
P2778, vol.66; Toh.1915; sDe-dge Phi 217b3-249b7

Śūraṅgamavarmavajra
Commentary on the Lady with a White Parasol, Arisen from the Crown Protrusion of All Tathāgatas (commentary on the practice of Sitātapatrā)
de bzhin gshegs pa thams cad kyi gtsug tor nas byung ba gdugs dkar mo can zhes bya ba'i 'grel pa
sarvatathāgatoṣṇiṣodbhūtasitātapatrānāmavṛtti
P3513, vol.78; Toh.2689 (=Toh.590); sDe-dge Thu 320b2-330a7 (cf. Toh.590)
Ritual of the Lady with a White Parasol, Arisen from the Crown Protrusion
gtsug tor nas byung ba'i gdugs dkar mo can gyi cho ga zhes bya ba
uṣṇiṣodbhūtasitātapatrāvidhināma
P3927, vol.80; Toh.3108; sDe-dge Pu 204a1-205a1

Sūryagupta: Nyi-ma sbas-pa
Condensed Sūtra of the Sādhana of the Venerable Ārya Tārā, With the Branches of the Twenty-one Activities
rje btsun 'phags ma sgrol ma'i sgrub thabs nyi shu rtsa gcig pa'i las kyi yan lag dang bcas pa mdor bsdus pa zhes bya ba
P2558, vol.59; Toh.1686; sDe-dge Sha 10a7-24b6
Perfected Crown Jewel, Twenty-one Praises to the Goddess Tārā
lha mo sgrol ma nyi shu rtsa gcig la bstod pa rnam dag gtsug gi nor bu zhes bya ba
devitāraikaviṁśatistotraviśuddhacūḍāmaṇināma
P2561, vol.59; Toh.1689; sDe-dge Sha 35a1-35b2

Sādhana of the Twenty-one Praises to the Bhagavatī Tārā
bcom ldan 'das ma [lha mo] sgrol ma la bstod pa nyi shu rtsa gcig pa'i sgrub thabs
bhagavatītārādevyekaviṁśatistotrasādhana
P2560, vol.59; Toh.1688; sDe-dge Sha 25b6-35a1

Sādhana of the Twenty-one Praises to the Goddess Tārā
lha mo sgrol ma'i bstod pa nyi shu rtsa gcig pa'i sgrub thabs zhes bya ba
tārādevīstotraikaviṁśatikasādhananāma
P2557, vol.59; Toh.1685; sDe-dge Sha 6b5-10a7

Sequential Oral Instructions on the Tārā Sādhana
sgrol ma'i sgrub thabs man ngag gi rim pa
tārāsādhanopadeśakrama
P2559, vol.59; Toh.1687; sDe-dge Sha 24b7-25b6

Tārānātha: Kun-dga' snying-po (1575-1634)

[Causing] Wondrous Belief: Elaborate History of the Yamāntaka-tantra Cycle
rgyud rgyal gshin rje gshed skor gyi chos 'byung rgyas pa yid ches ngo mtsar (Composed in 1631)

Collected Works of Jo-nang rje-btsun Tārānātha, vol.X (Tha). Leh, 1984. Reproduced from prints from the rTag-brtan phun-tshogs-gling blocks preserved in Stog Palace in Ladakh.
Also: Tashi Jong, India: Khamtrul Rinpoche, 1970.

Tathāgatarakṣita: De-gshegs-'tsho

Explanation of the Vajrasattva Sādhana (text associated with Secret Assembly practice)
rdo rje sems dpa'i sgrub pa'i thabs kyi bshad pa
P: vajrasattvasādhanabhāṣya, Toh.: vajrasattvasādhanavyākhyā
P2704, vol.62; Toh.1835; sDe-dge Ci 280b2-285b4

Tīkṣṇavajra: rDo-rje rnon-po

Fire Offering Ritual of the Lady with a White Parasol, Arisen from the Crown Protrusion
gtsug tor nas byung ba'i gdugs dkar mo can gyi sbyin sreg gi cho ga zhes bya ba
uṣṇīṣasitātapatrāhomavidhi
P3926 vol.80; Toh.3105; sDe-dge Pu 192b2-194a6

Tsong-kha-pa

Annotated Commentary, Discriminating in Accordance with the Words and Meanings of [Candrakīrti's] Elucidating Lamp; the Very Extensive Explanation on the King of All the Tantras, the Glorious Secret Assembly
rgyud thams cad kyi rgyal po dpal gsang ba 'dus pa'i rgya cher bshad pa sgron gsal ba'i tshig don ji bzhin 'byed pa'i 'can gyi yang 'grel

Toh.5282; Nga 1-476

Stages of the Path of a Conqueror and Pervasive Master, a Great Vajradhara: Revealing All Secret Topics ('Great Exposition of Secret Mantra')
rgyal ba khyab bdag rdo rje 'chang chen po'i lam gyi rim pa gsang ba kun gyi gnad rnam par phye ba ('ngags rim chen mo')
P6210, vol.161; Toh. 5281

Vairocanarakṣita: rNam-par snang-mdzad 'tsho
Elucidating Maṇḍala Ritual of the Vajra Terrifier
dpal rdo rje 'jigs byed kyi dkyil 'khor gyi cho ga gsal ba
Śrīvajrabhairavavajramaṇḍalaprakāśavidhināma
P2869, vol.67 [not in Toh.]

Vajra Light, Sādhana of the Vajra Terrifier
dpal rdo rje 'jigs byed kyi sgrub pa'i thabs rdo rje 'od
Śrīvajrabhairavavajraprabhākarasādhana
P2868, vol.67; Toh.2013; sDe-dge Mi 221a2-246a7

Vajrahāsa: rDo-rje bshad-pa
Complete Explanation of the King of Tantras, the Glorious Secret Assembly
rgyud kyi rgyal po dpal gsang ba 'dus pa'i rnam par bshad pa
tantrarājaśrīguhyasamājaṭikā
P2772, vol.66; Toh.1909; sDe-dge Phi 38a7-89a7

Vajrapāṇi: Lag-na rdo-rje
Vajra Word
rdo rje'i tshig ces bya ba
vajrapadanāma
P3100; vol.68; Toh.2255; sDe-dge Wi 177b1-180b3

Six Stages of Meditation
bsgom rim drug pa zhes bya ba
bhāvanākramaṣaṭkanāma
P3148, vol.69; Toh.2299; sDe-dge Zhi 228a5-228b5

Sequential Oral Instructions of the Lineage Masters
bla ma brgyud pa'i rim pa'i man ngag ces bya ba
guruparamparakramopadeśanāma
P4539, vol.81; Toh.3716; sDe-dge Tsu 164b2-183a5

Vajrāsana: rDo-rje gdan-pa
Instructions on the Lady with a White Parasol, Arisen from the Crown Protrusion of All Tathāgatas, She Who is Unconquerable by Others
'phags pa de bzhin gshegs pa'i gtsug tor nas byung ba'i gdugs dkar mo can gzhan gyis mi thub pa zhes bya ba'i nye bar bshad pa
āryatathāgatoṣṇiṣasitātapatrāparājitanāmopadeśa
P3929, vol:80; Toh.3110; sDe-dge Pu 205a6-206a1

Varabodhi: Byang-chub-mchog

Condensed Means of Realising the Accomplishment of Goodness; Abbreviated sādhana for the Susiddhi-tantra

legs par grub par byed pa'i sgrub pa'i thabs bsdus pa ('legs grub kyi mngon rtogs')

P3890, vol.79; Toh.3066; sDe-dge Pu 120b4-131b3

Varmavajra: rDo-rje go-cha

Maṇḍala Ritual of the Vajra Conqueror

rdo rje rnam par 'joms pa'i dkyil 'khor gyi cho ga zhes bya ba

vajravidāranamamaṇḍalavidhināma

P4852, vol.86; Toh.2907; sDe-dge Nu 297b3-305a2

Vasubandhu

Auto-commentary on the Treasury of Higher Knowledge

chos mngon pa'i mdzod kyi bshad pa

abhidharmakoṣabhāṣya

P5591, vol.115; Toh.4090; sDe-dge Ku 26b1-258a7

The Eight Collections of Logic:

1) *Commentary on [Maitreya's] Ornament of the Mahāyāna Sūtras*
mdo sde'i rgyan gyi bshad pa
sūtrālaṅkāravyākhyā
P5527, vol.108; Toh.4026; sDe-dge Phi 129b1-260a7

2) *Commentary on [Maitreya's] Discrimination of Phenomena and Suchness*
chos dang chos nyid rnam par 'byed pa'i 'grel pa
dharmadharmatāvibhaṅgavṛtti
P5529, vol.108; Toh.4028; sDe-dge Bi 27b1-38b6

3) *Commentary on [Maitreya's] Discrimination of the Middle and the Extremes*
dbus dang mtha' rnam par 'byed pa'i 'grel pa
madhyāntavibhaṅgaṭikā
P5528, vol.108; Toh.4027; sDe-dge Bi 1b1-27a7

4) *Principles of Reasoning*
rnam par bshad pa'i rigs pa
vyākhyāyukti
P5562, vol.113; Toh.4061; sDe-dge Shi 29a2-134b2

5) *Presentation of the Establishment of Karma*
las grub pa'i rab tu byed pa
karmasiddhiprakaraṇa
P5563, vol.114; Toh.4062; sDe-dge Shi 134b2-145a6

6) *Presentation of the Five Aggregates*
phung po lnga'i rab tu byed pa

pañcaskandhaprakaraṇa
P5560, vol.113; Toh.4059; sDe-dge Shi 11b4-17a7

7) *Twenty Verse Commentary*
nyi shu pa'i tshig le'ur byas pa
viṁśakākārikā
P5557, vol.113; Toh.4056; sDe-dge Shi 3a4-4a2

8) *Thirty Verse Commentary*
sum cu pa'i tshig le'ur byas pa
triṁśikākārikā
P5556, vol.113; Toh.4055; sDe-dge Shi 1b1-3a3

Treasury of Higher Knowledge
chos mngon pa'i mdzod kyi tshig le'ur byas pa
abhidharmakoṣakārikā
P5590, vol.115; Toh.4089; sDe-dge Ku 1b1-25a7

Vibhūticandra, Vitapāda
Commentary on the Difficult Points of the Abbreviated Sādhana
sgrub thabs mdor byas kyi dka' 'grel
piṇḍikṛtasādhanapañjikā
P2701, vol.62; Toh.1832; sDe-dge Ci 203a4-207b2

Vimalakīrti: Dri-med grags-pa
Ten Principles of Suchness
de kho na nyid bcu pa
daśatattva
P2455, vol.57; Toh.1323; sDe-dge Ta 261b2-265b4

Vīryabhadra: brTson-'grus bzang-po
Clear Meanings; Commentary on the Difficult Points of the Five Stages
rim pa lnga pa'i dka' 'grel don gsal ba zhes bya ba
pañcakramapaṇjikāprabhāsārthanāma
P2699, vol.62; Toh.1830; sDe-dge Ci 142b7-180b3

Vīryavajra: dPa'-bo rdo-rje
Commentary on the Complete Union Tantra
rgyud thams cad kyi gleng gzhi dang gsang chen dpal kun tu kha sbyor zhes bya ba'i rgyud kyi rgyal po'i rgya cher bshad pa rin chen phreng ba zhes bya ba
sarvatantrasya nidāna mahāguhyaśrīsaṁpuṭanāma-tantrarājaṭikā ratnamālā
P2329, vol.55; Toh.1199; sDe-dge Ja 111a2-154b1

Viśākhadeva
Flower Garland of Ethics (*'Commentary on Ethics'*)
'dul ba'i tshig le'ur byas pa ('me tog phreng ba'i rgyud')
vinayapuṣpamālānāma ('vinayakārikā')

P5625, vol.127; Toh.4123; sDe-dge Shu 1b1-63a6

Viśvamitra: sNa-tshogs bshes-gnyen
Drop from the Ocean of Oral Instructions on the Glorious Secret Assembly Tantra
dpal gsang ba 'dus pa'i rgyud kyi man ngag gi rgya mtsho thigs pa
P2707, vol.63; Toh.1844; sDe-dge Ji 53b7-161b1

MODERN STUDIES

Anacker, Stephen. *Seven Works of Vasubandhu: The Buddhist Doctor of Philosophy.*Delhi, 1986.

Batchelor, Stephen (trans.). *Guide to the Bodhisattva's Way of Life*. LTWA, 1992.

Bays, Gwendolyn. *The Voice of the Buddha: The Beauty of Compassion (Lalitavistara-sūtra).* (Translated from the French, 2 vols.) Berkley, 1983.

Benard, Elizabeth Anne. *Chinnamastā: The Aweful Buddhist and Hindu Tantric Goddess*. Delhi, 1994.

Bendall, Cecil & W.H.D. Rouse. *Śikṣāsamuccaya: A Compendium of Buddhist Doctrine*. London, 1922.

Beyer, Stephan. *The Cult of Tārā; Magic and Ritual in Tibet*. Berkeley, 1978.

Bharati, Agehananda. *The Tantric Tradition*. London, 1965.

Bhattacharya, K. *The Dialectical Method of Nāgārjuna*. Delhi, 1978.

Birnbaum, Raoul. *The Healing Buddha*. Boulder, 1979.

Boord, Martin. *The Cult of the Deity Vajrakīla*. Tring, 1993.

——. *Maṇḍala Meaning and Method*. London, 1996.

Boord, Martin & Somdev Vasudeva. *Tantric Studies*. Delhi, 1996.

Briggs, George W. *Goraknāth and the Kānphaṭa Yogis*. Oxford, 1938.

Bryant, Barry. *The Wheel of Time Sand Mandala*, Harper San Francisco, 1992.

Chandra, Lokesh. *Buddhist Iconography of Tibet*. (A New Tibeto-Mongol Pantheon Vols.I-XX. Revised edition in 2 vols. with index.) Kyoto, 1986.

Chattopadhyaya, Alaka with Lama Chimpa. *Tāranātha's History of Buddhism in India.* Simla, 1970.

Cleary, Thomas. *The Flower Ornament Scripture: Avataṁsaka-sūtra*. (3 vols.) Shambhala, Boston & London, 1984-1987.

Conze, Edward. *The Large Sūtra on Perfect Wisdom*. Berkeley, Los Angeles, & London, 1975.

——. *Abhisamayālaṅkāra*. Serie Orientale Roma VI, Rome, 1954.

——. *The Perfection of Wisdom in Eight Thousand Lines and its Verse Summary*. Bolinas, California, 1975.

——. *Prajñāpāramitā Literature*. Tokyo, 1975.

——. *The Short Prajñāpāramitā Texts*. London, 1973.

Conze, Edward et al (eds.). *Buddhist Texts Through the Ages*. Oxford, 1954.

Cowell, E.B. *The Jātaka or Stories of the Buddha's Former Lives.* London, 1981.

Cozort, Daniel. *Highest Yoga Tantra.* New York, 1986.

Dahman-Dallapiccola, A.L. (ed.). *The Stūpa: Its Religious, Historical and Architectural Significance.* Wiesbaden, 1980.

Dawa-Samdup, Kazi. *Śrī Cakrasaṁvara-tantra.* Calcutta, 1919.

Dayal, Har. *The Bodhisattva Doctrine in Buddhist Sanskrit Literature.* Delhi, 1978.

Dhargyey, Geshe Ngawang. *Kalacakra Tantra: A Commentary on the Kālacakra-tantra.* (Translated by Allan Wallace) LTWA, 1985.

——. *Tibetan Tradition of Mental Development.* LTWA, 1992.

DHĪḤ, *Journal of Rare Buddhist Texts Research Project.* Bi-annual publication of CIHTS, Sarnath. (in Sanskrit)

Dowman, Keith. *Masters of Mahāmudrā.* SUNY, New York, 1985.

Dutt, Nalinaksa. *Buddhist Sects in India.* Calcutta, 1970.

Elder, George R. *The Sampuṭa-tantra: Edition and Translation (chapters I-IV).* (Ph.D thesis) Columbia University, 1978.

Emmerick, R.E. *The Sūtra of Golden Light.* London, 1970.

English, Elizabeth. *Vajrayoginī.* (Ph.D thesis) Oxford University, forthcoming.

Ensink, Jacob. *The Question of Rāṣṭrapāla.* Zwolle, 1952.

Farrow, G.W. & I.Menon. *The Concealed Essence of the Hevajra Tantra.* Delhi, 1992.

Fremantle, Francesca. *A Critical Study of the Guhyasamāja-tantra.* (Ph.D. thesis) SOAS, London, 1971.

Friedman, D.L. *Sthiramati's Madhyāntavibhāgaṭīkā: Analysis of the Middle Path and the Extremes.* Utrecht, 1937.

Goodman, Stephen D. & Ronald M. Davidson (eds.) *Tibetan Buddhism: Reason and Revelation.* SUNY, New York, 1992.

Guenther, Herbert. *Buddhist Philosophy in Theory and Practice.* Berkeley, 1971.

——. *The Life and Teachings of Nāropa.* Oxford, 1963.

——. *The Royal Song of Saraha.* Seattle & London, 1969.

——. *The Jewel Ornament of Liberation by sGam-po-pa.* London, 1959.

——. *Ecstatic Spontaneity: Saraha's Three Cycles of Dohā.* Berkeley, 1993.

Gyatso, Geshe Kelsang. *Guide to Dakini Land: A Commentary to the Highest Yoga Tantra Practice of Vajrayogini.* London, 1991.

Gyatso, Tenzin (Dalai Lama XIV). *The Kalachakra Tantra* (Edited by Jeffrey Hopkins) London, 1985.

Hirakawa, Akira (translated by Paul Groner). *A History of Indian Buddhism.* Hawai, 1990.

Hodge, Stephen. *The Mahāvairocana-tantra,.with commentary by Buddhaguhya, translated from the Tibetan.* London, forthcoming.

Holmes, Katia and Ken Tsultrim Gyamtso. *The Changeless Nature.* Dumfriesshire, Scotland: Karma Drubgyud Darjay Ling, n.d. [1983].
Hookham, S.K. *The Buddha Within.* SUNY, New York, 1991.
Hopkins, Jeffrey. *Tantra in Tibet. The Great Exposition of Secret Mantra by Tsong-kha-pa, part 1.* London, 1975.
——. *The Yoga of Tibet. The Great Exposition of Secret Mantra by Tsong-kha-pa, parts 2 & 3.* London, 1975.
——. *Death, Intermediate State and Rebirth, by Lati Rinbochay.* London, 1979.
Hopkins, Jeffrey with Lati Rinpoche. *The Precious Garland and the Song of the Four Mindfulnesses.* New York: Harper & Row, 1975.
Iida, Shōtarō. *Reason and Emptiness* (includes a translation of *Blaze of Reasoning,* Ch. III, 1-136.) Tokyo: Hokuseido, 1982.
Inada, Kenneth. *Nāgārjuna: A Translation of his Mūlamadhyamakakārikā.* Tokyo: Hokuseido Press, 1970.
Jones, J.J. *The Mahāvastu.* (3 vols) London, 1949.
de Jong, J.W. "A New History of Tantric Literature in India." (English précis of the Japanese work; *Mikkyo kyoten seiritsushi-ron,* by Yukei Matsunaga, Kyoto, 1980.) *Acta Indologica* VI (1984) 91-113.
Kalff, Martin M. *Selected Chapters from the Abhidhānottara-tantra: The Union of Male and Female Deities.* (Ph.D thesis) Columbia University, 1979.
Kalupahana, David J. *Mūlamadhyamakakārikā of Nāgārjuna: The Philosophy of the Middle Way.* SUNY, New York, 1986.
Katz, Nathan. *Buddhist Images of Human Perfection.* Delhi, 1982.
Kern, H. & B. Nanjio. *Saddharmapuṇḍarika.* St. Petersburg, 1908.
Kloppenberg, R. *The Paccekabuddha: A Buddhist Ascetic.* Leiden, 1974.
Komito, David Ross et al. *Nāgārjuna's Seventy Stanzas: a Buddhist Psychology of Emptiness.* Ithaca, New York, 1987.
Kvaerne, Per. *An Anthology of Buddhist Tantric Songs; a study of the Caryāgīti.* (Revised edition.) Bangkok, 1986.
——. "On the Concept of Sahaja in Indian Buddhist Tantric Literature." *Temenos* XI (1975) 88-135.
Lamotte, Étienne. *The Teaching of Vimalakīrti:* London, 1976.
——. *History of Indian Buddhism.* (Translated from the French by Sara Boin.) Louvain, 1988.
——. *Saṁdhinirocana-sūtra: l'explication des mystéres.* Louvain: Université de Louvain, 1935.
Lancaster, Lewis R. (ed.). *Studies in Honour of Edward Conze: Prajñāpāramitā and Related Systems.* Berkeley, 1977.
Lessing, Ferdinand D. & Alex Wayman. *Mkhas-grub-rje's Introduction to the Buddhist Tantric Systems.* The Hague, 1968.
Lindtner, Christian. *Nāgārjuniāna.* Delhi, 1982.
Lopez, Donald S. (ed.). *Buddhist Hermeneutics.* Honolulu, 1988.

Matsunaga, Yukei. "A Doubt to Authority of the Guhyasamāja-ākhyāna-Tantras." *Journal of Indian and Buddhist Studies* XII:2 (1964) 16-25. (See also; J.W. de Jong, 1984.)
Mishra, Ramprasad. *Sahajayāna: A Study of Tantric Buddhism*. Calcutta, 1991.
Müller, Max. *Amitābhavyūha*. London, 1982.
Müller, Max & B. Nanjio. *Sukhāvativyūha*. Oxford, 1883.
Nanjio, Bunyiu. *A Catalogue of the Chinese Translation of the Buddhist Tripiṭaka*. Oxford, 1883.
Newman, John Ronald. *The Outer Wheel of Time: Vajrayāna Buddhist Cosmology in the Kālacakra-tantra*. (Ph.D thesis) University of Wisconsin, Madison, 1987.
Obermiller, E. *Sublime Science of the Great Vehicle to Salvation*. Acta Orientalia, 9 (1931), pp. 81-306.
——. *Analysis of the Abhisamayālaṅkāra*. Cacutta, 1943.
——. *History of Buddhism (Chos-'byung) by Bu-ston*. (2 vols.) Leipzig, 1931-1932.
Powers, John. *Two Commentaries on the Sandhinirmocana-sūtra by Asaṅga and Jñānagarbha*. New York, 1992.
Pruden, Leo. *Vasubandhu's Abhidharmakośabhāṣyam*. (Translated from the French of Louis de la Vallée Poussin.) (4 vols.) Berkeley, 1988-1990.
Pye, Michael. *Skilful Means: A Concept in Mahāyāna Buddhism*. London, 1978.
Régamey, Konstantin. *The Bhadramāyākāravyākarṇa*. Warsaw, 1938.
——. *Philosophy in the Samādhirāja-sūtra*. Warsaw, 1938.
Rhie, Marylin M. & Robert A.F. Thurman. *Wisdom and Compassion, the Sacred Art of Tibet*. New York, 1991.
Richardson, Hugh. *Ceremonies of the Lhasa Year*. Serindia, London, 1993.
Ricca, Franco & Erberto Lo Bue. *The Great Stūpa of Gyantse*. Serindia, London, 1993.
Rinpoche, Chokyi Nyima. *The Union of Mahāmudrā and Dzogchen*. Hong Kong, 1989.
Roerich, George. *The Blue Annals, compiled by 'Gos Lotsawa*. Calcutta, 1949.
Schmithausen, Lambert. *Ālayavijñāna: On the Origin and Development of a Central Concept of Yogācāra Philosophy*. (2 vols.) Tokyo, 1987.
Seyfort-Ruegg, David. *The Life of Bu-ston rin-po-che*. Rome, 1966.
——. *The Literature of the Madhyamaka School of Philosophy in India*. Wiesbaden, 1981.
——. *Buddha-nature, Mind and the Problem of Gradualism in a Comparative Perspective: On the Transmission and Reception of Buddhism in India and Tibet*. SOAS, London, 1989.
Shaw, Miranda. *Passionate Enlightenment: Women in Tantric Buddhism*. Princeton, 1994.
Sikløs, Bulcsu. *The Vajrabhairava Tantra*. Tring, 1995.

Skorupski, Tadeusz. *The Sarvadurgatipariśodhana-tantra; Elimination of all Evil Destinies*. Delhi, 1983.

Snellgrove, David L. *The Hevajra Tantra*. (2 vols.) London, 1959.

——. *Indo-Tibetan Buddhism*. London, 1987.

Snodgrass, Adrian. *The Matrix and Diamond World Maṇḍalas in Shingon Buddhism*. (2 vols.) Delhi, 1989.

Sopa, Geshe Lhundub with Roger Jackson & John Newman. *The Wheel of Time: The Kālacakra in Context*. Madison, 1985.

Sopa, Geshe Lhundub with Jeffrey Hopkins. *Cutting Through Appearances: Theory and Practice in Tibetan Buddhism*. New York, 1989.

Sparham, Gareth (et al). Yamāntaka Cycle Translation Project (ongoing). Under the auspices of Tibet House, New Delhi.

Stablein, William G. *The Mahākāla-tantra: A Theory of Ritual Blessings and Tantric Medicine*. (Ph.D thesis) Columbia University, 1976.

Stcherbatsky, Theodor. *Madhyānta-Vibhaṅga*. Calcutta, 1971.

——. *Buddhist Logic*. New York: Dover Publications, 1962.

Streng, Frederick J. *Emptiness: A Study in Religious Meaning*. Nashville and New York: Abingdon, 1967.

Suzuki, Daisetz T. *The Laṅkāvatāra-sūtra*. London, 1978.

Takasaki, Jikido. *A Study on the Ratnagotravibhāga (Uttaratantra): Being aTreatise on the Tathāgatagarbha Theory of Mahāyāna Buddhism*. Serie Orientale Roma XXXIII. Rome, 1966.

Templeman, David. *The Origin of the Tārā Tantra by Jo-nang Tāranātha*. LTWA, 1981.

——. *The Seven Instruction Lineages of Jo-nang Tāranātha*. LTWA, 1983.

——. *Tāranātha's Life of Kṛṣṇācārya/Kāṇha*. LTWA, 1989.

Thondup, Tulku. *Buddhist Civilisation in Tibet*. RKP, 1987.

——. *Buddha Mind; an anthology of Longchen Rabjam's writings on Dzogpa Chenpo*. Snow Lion Publications, New York, 1989.

——. *Enlightened Living: Teachings of Tibetan Buddhist Masters*.Shambhala, Boston & London, 1990.

——. *Enlightened Journey: Buddhist Practice as Daily Life*. Shambhala, Boston & London, 1995.

Todaro, Dale Allen. *An Annotated Translation of The Tatattvasaṁgraha (part I)*. (Ph.D thesis) Columbia University, 1985.

Tsuda, Shiníchi. "Classification of Tantras in dPal-brtsegs's lTa-ba'i rim-pa bzhad-pa and its Problems." JIBS XIII:1 (1965) 42-47.

——. *The Saṁvarodaya-tantra (Selected chapters)*. Tokyo, 1974.

Tucci, Giuseppe. *Minor Buddhist Texts*. (3 vols.) Rome, 1956-1971.

——. *The Religions of Tibet*. London, 1980.

——. *Indo-Tibetica*. (English translation). (4 vols., 7 parts). Delhi, 1988-1991.

Ui, Hakuju Toh (et al). *A Complete Catalogue of the Tibetan Buddhist Canons (bKa'-'gyur & bsTan-'gyur)*. Sendai, 1934.

van Gulik, R.H. *Hayagrīva; The Mantrayānic Aspect of Horse Cult in China and Japan.* Leiden, 1935.

Vitali, Roberto. *Early Temples of Central Tibet.* Serindia, London, 1993.

Vostrikov, A.I. *Tibetan Historical Literature.* (Translated by H.C.Gupta.) Calcutta, 1970.

Warder, A.K. *Indian Buddhism.* (reprint) Delhi, 1980.

Wayman, Alex. "Studies in Yama and Māra." IIJ III.2 (1959) 44-73, 112-131.

——. *The Buddhist Tantras; Light on Indo-Tibetan Esotericism.* New York, 1973.

——. *Yoga of the Guhyasamāja-tantra; the Arcane Lore of Forty Verses.* Delhi, 1977.

——. *Buddhist Insight.* Essays, edited with an introduction by George Elder. Delhi, 1984.

——. "The Sarvarahasya-tantra." *Acta Indologica* VI (1984) 521-569.

——. "Imperatives in the Buddhist Tantra Mantras." *Berliner Indologische Studien,* Band 1. Reinbek, 1985.

——. *Chanting The Names of Mañjuśrī: The Mañjuśrīnāmasaṅgīti.* Boston & London, 1985.

Wayman, Alex & R. Tajima. *The Enlightenment of Vairocana.* Delhi, 1992.

Wayman, Alex & H. Wayman. *The Lion's Roar of Queen Śrīmālā.* New York, 1974.

Williams, Paul. *Mahāyāna Buddhism.* London, 1989.

Willis, Janice Dean. *On Knowing Reality: The Tattvārtha Chapter of Asaṅga's Bodhisattvabhūmi.* Delhi, 1979.

Willson, Martin. *In Praise of Tārā.* London, 1986.

Yamada, Isshi. *Karuṇāpuṇḍarīka*. (2 vols.) London, 1968.

Yamamoto, Chikyo. *Mahāvairocana-sūtra* (translated from the Chinese). Delhi, 1990.

Yamamoto, K. *The Mahāyāna Mahāparinirvāṇa-Sūtra.* (3 vols.) Ube City: Karinbunko, 1974.